Pennsylvania Politics
and Policy

Edited by J. Wesley Leckrone
and Michelle J. Atherton

Pennsylvania Politics and Policy

A *COMMONWEALTH* READER

VOLUME 1

TEMPLE UNIVERSITY PRESS
Philadelphia • *Rome* • *Tokyo*

TEMPLE UNIVERSITY PRESS
Philadelphia, Pennsylvania 19122
www.temple.edu/tempress

Library of Congress Cataloging-in-Publication Data

Names: Leckrone, J. Wesley, 1969– editor. | Atherton, Michelle J., 1974– editor.
Title: Pennsylvania politics and policy : a commonwealth reader / edited by
    J. Wesley Leckrone and Michelle J. Atherton.
Description: Philadelphia : Temple University Press, 2018. | Includes bibliographical
    references.
Identifiers: LCCN 2017053427 (print) | LCCN 2017059176 (ebook) | ISBN 9781439916711
    (E-book) | ISBN 9781439916704 (paperback)
Subjects: LCSH: Pennsylvania—Politics and government. | Public administration—
    Pennsylvania. | BISAC: POLITICAL SCIENCE / Government / State & Provincial. |
    BUSINESS & ECONOMICS / Urban & Regional. | BUSINESS & ECONOMICS /
    Government & Business.
Classification: LCC JK3641 (ebook) | LCC JK3641 .P46 2018 (print) | DDC 320.9748—dc23
LC record available at https://lccn.loc.gov/2017053427

∞ The paper used in this publication meets the requirements of the American National
Standard for Information Sciences—Permanence of Paper for Printed Library Materials,
ANSI Z39.48-1992

Printed in the United States of America

9 8 7 6 5 4 3 2 1

Contents

Preface

The activities of state governments have always been important to the functioning of the American federal system. However, recent partisan gridlock in Washington, D.C., has placed states at the forefront of policy making as the national government maintains the status quo. This reader has been designed to show the activities of one state, Pennsylvania, on important contemporary issues. The best articles from recent issues of *Commonwealth: A Journal of Pennsylvania Politics and Policy* have been updated and provided with additional content to further explore their topics. Education, health care, the effects of an aging population, and tax policy are among the important issues that are explored in this book. The intent is to help Pennsylvania citizens understand not just the content of policies but also the processes and politics that go into the passage of laws and their implementation.

Overview of the Journal

Commonwealth is a peer-reviewed, online-only journal that publishes original research on political and policy topics of importance to Pennsylvania and contiguous states. It provides political scientists and experts in related disciplines such as law, economics, history, and public policy with a periodical to advance scholarship in their fields. The journal is also intended to inform political actors and governmental policy makers about the political, structural, and historical contexts for decision making and options for improving public policy outcomes on a wide variety of topics. Issues cover general-interest pieces, applied research, practitioners' or experts' analysis, research notes, essays, and book reviews.

Commonwealth is a joint publication of the Pennsylvania Political Science Association and Temple University Press with the assistance of the

Pennsylvania Policy Forum and Temple University's Institute for Public Affairs.

Organization of the Book

Each chapter is headlined by an article from an earlier edition of *Commonwealth*. A number of the articles have been updated to reflect policy changes through mid-2017. These are followed by additional content designed to help citizens and students more fully explore the topics raised in the articles. After each article is a series of discussion questions prepared to promote critical thinking about the policy issues raised by the authors. The questions are followed by a *"Commonwealth* Forum" providing pro-con perspectives on an issue that is related to the topic of the article. Finally, several sources of additional information are provided to continue the exploration of issues raised in the forums. Since Chapter 3 is itself a *Commonwealth* Forum, there is no separate pro-con section. The additional content was researched and written by the editors of this volume, not the authors of the articles.

Acknowledgments

We thank the editorial board of *Commonwealth*, particularly Tom Baldino (Wilkes University), Christopher Borick (Muhlenberg College), Paula Holoviak (Kutztown University), and Joseph McLaughlin (Temple University). Special thanks are dedicated to Joseph McLaughlin and Christopher Borick for serving as the guest editors of the "Education" and "Energy and Environment" special issues. Several articles from these issues are republished in this book. The Pennsylvania Political Science Association has generously provided financial support for *Commonwealth* that has made the content of this book possible.

Neither this book nor the publication of the journal would be possible without support from Temple University Press. In particular, we thank Mary Rose Muccie and Aaron Javsicas of Temple University Press for helping us reconceptualize the journal and for supporting the publication of this edited volume. Nikki Miller, Joan Vidal, Kate Nichols, and Dave Wilson have helped guide us through the editorial and production process with great patience. Ann-Marie Anderson and Gary Kramer have done a good job of marketing our journal and this book. Thanks also go to the journal's project manager and compositor, Kirsten Dennison, and our copy editor, Barbara Crawford. Finally, thanks go out to undergraduate research assistants Nicole Crossey, Ben Klein, and Catherine Long of Widener University, who have researched and fact-checked information for the journal.

Pennsylvania Politics
and Policy

Chapter 1
The Legislative Process

The Rules of the Game

The Constitution and the Lawmaking Process

MICHAEL R. DIMINO, SR.

This selection is from a speech delivered at a symposium sponsored by the Pennsylvania Policy Forum titled "The Constitutional Foundations of the Lawmaking Process." The symposium was attended by more than two-thirds of the Pennsylvania General Assembly. The Pennsylvania Policy Forum is a consortium of faculty members and academic and policy institute leaders from Pennsylvania colleges and universities who share an interest in generating ideas, analyses, and symposiums that might prove useful to citizens, elected officials, and civic leaders in addressing major issues confronting the Commonwealth and its local governments.

Thank you all for coming. I am here to introduce you to four provisions of the Pennsylvania Constitution that govern the lawmaking process: first, the requirement that bills concern only a single subject, which is reflected in the bill's title; second, the prohibition on amending a bill so as to alter its original purpose; third, the requirement that revenue bills originate in the House of Representatives; and fourth, the power of each house of the General Assembly to determine the rules of its proceedings.

As to each constitutional provision, I discuss the constitutional text and explain the reason for the provision's inclusion in the constitution. I then discuss the extent to which each limitation on the lawmaking process is, or should be, enforceable in the courts.

Single Subject

Article III, §3 of the Pennsylvania Constitution specifies that "no bill shall be passed containing more than one subject, which shall be clearly expressed in its title, except a general appropriation bill or a bill codifying or compiling the law or a part thereof."

The point of the provision is to make it more difficult for factions to enact unpopular or wasteful laws. It should therefore come as no surprise that the section was added to the constitution during a period in which the public was particularly distrustful of the legislature. As the Pennsylvania Supreme Court has noted, the Constitutional Convention of 1872–1873, which produced the limitations on the legislative process contained in Article III, "was convened to reform corrupt legislative behavior," which was thought to involve both logrolling and an undue solicitude for the interests of powerful industries (Pennsylvanians against Gambling Expansion Fund, Inc. v. Commonwealth 2005, 394).

Without a single-subject limitation, coalitions of legislators might band together to enact laws that contain multiple provisions, none of which would be popular enough to pass on their own. As a result of this logrolling, those legislators (and the factions they represent) would receive their pet projects, but the general interest of the Commonwealth would be harmed.

The single-subject provision makes such logrolling more difficult, as a legislator who wishes to trade his support for one measure in exchange for a colleague's vote on another measure will have to vote for a separate bill that could then be attacked as contrary to his or her constituents' interests. The single-subject rule also gives both legislators and the public improved notice about the content of a bill, because it prevents a legislator from burying a measure in a bill that is believed to focus on a different issue. The Pennsylvania Supreme Court has recognized that the single-subject rule promotes "open, deliberative, and accountable government" by giving "fair notice to the public and to legislators" of the substance of bills (City of Philadelphia v. Commonwealth 2003, 586). This notice function is so important that the

Figure 1.1
Governor Wolf and legislators celebrate the signing of an animal rights law.
(Source: Pennsylvania Office of the Governor.)

Pennsylvania Supreme Court has referred to "reasonable notice" as "the keystone of Article III, Section 3" (Pennsylvanians against Gambling Expansion Fund 2005, 395). Additionally, the single-subject rule preserves the effectiveness of the governor's veto power, in that the rule prevents the legislature from forcing the governor to choose between signing and vetoing a bill that contains some measures of which he approves and others of which he disapproves (Williams 1987, 100).

Similarly, the requirement that the bill's title reflect its subject makes it more difficult to pass an unpopular measure while escaping public attention. This section became part of the Pennsylvania Constitution in 1864, but the movement of states to require bill titles stems from the notorious Yazoo land scandal, in which the Georgia legislature engaged in a corrupt sale of extensive public land to favored companies at prices far below their value (Eskridge, Frickey, and Garrett 2007, 359–360). The title of the bill ordering the sale did not disclose the bill's true purpose; rather, it claimed that the bill was "an act supplementary to an act for appropriating part of the unlocated territory of this state, for the payment of the late state troops, and for other purposes therein mentioned, and declaring the right of this state to the unappropriated territory thereof, for the protection and support of the frontiers of this state, and for other purposes."

We can all recognize the potential harms that can result from legislative logrolling. Logrolling has a positive aspect as well, however, and so one might characterize the single-subject rule as producing negative—or at least split—consequences. Imagine a situation in which certain interest groups (perhaps identified by occupation, race, community of residence, or something else) have an intense desire for a certain type of law, but they lack the numbers to enact it. Logrolling allows them to trade away their votes on matters less important to them so that they might obtain the law they consider more significant. Preventing logrolling thus protects the generalized public interest at the expense of the specialized interests. Whether this is a good or bad consequence depends on one's political philosophy.

Consider also a potential distinction between two different types of measures helped by being combined with others as part of a single bill. In one situation, a bill combines measures, none of which would have the votes to pass individually. In another situation, a bill combines one unpopular measure—a rider—with another measure that does have the votes to pass on its own. Some commentators have argued that the use of a rider should be considered worse than logrolling because logrolling requires more legislative bargaining, resulting in benefits for more legislators. The legislators who benefit from riders, by contrast, need not lose anything in the bargain. Regardless of whether it might be possible to maintain such a distinction, the constitution outlaws both, preferring that each legislative measure succeed or fail on its own, rather than be permitted to ride the coattails of a more popular measure or combine forces so as to obtain the votes needed for passage.

It is easy to see the purposes behind the single-subject rule, and we might be able to achieve consensus about the desirability of those purposes. The difficulty, however, is in the application of the rule to specific cases. The essential problem is in defining what the constitution means by "subject." Any two measures can be characterized as involving the same subject, if that subject is general enough. Think, for example, of all the different kinds of laws that could be passed relating to the "subject" of "crime." Conversely, any two measures could be characterized as relating to different subjects if what we mean by "subject" is defined narrowly enough. A law regulating the grade-school requirements in both science and math, for example, might be thought to regulate two subjects. As early as 1895, the Pennsylvania Supreme Court recognized that the vagueness of the term "subject" could create problems for judicial enforcement of the single-subject rule. As the court noted, "No two subjects are so wide apart that they may not be brought into a common focus, if the point of view be carried back far enough"; yet "few bills are so elementary in character that they may not be subdivided under several heads" (Payne v. School District of Coudersport Borough 1895, 1074). As an attempt to avoid the horns of this dilemma, the Pennsylvania Supreme Court has created and applied a deferential "germaneness" test: "'Where the provisions added during the legislative process assist in carrying out a bill's main objective or are otherwise "germane" to the bill's subject as reflected in its title,' the requirements of Article III, Section 3 [the single-subject rule] are met" (Pennsylvanians against Gambling Expansion Fund 2005, 395, quoting City of Philadelphia 2003, 587).

Of course, this germaneness test does very little, if anything, to lessen the problem that the bill's subject may be considered at any level of generality, and therefore the germaneness test is infinitely manipulable. Without a judicially manageable standard for determining what a bill's subject is, one might suspect that the courts would treat Article III, §3 as unenforceable in the courts.[1] The Pennsylvania Supreme Court, however, has concluded that it is up to the courts—as well as to the General Assembly itself—to ensure that laws comply with the single-subject rule.

Original Purpose

The second constitutional provision I wish to address is Article III, §1's direction that "no bill shall be so altered or amended, on its passage through either House, as to change its original purpose." Similar to the way the single-subject rule is designed to prevent special interests from short-circuiting the standard legislative process, the requirement that a bill not deviate from its original purpose is designed to prevent a legislative bait and switch.

As with the single-subject rule, the problem with the original-purpose requirement is the vagueness of the term "purpose." A sufficiently broad purpose (imagine, for example, the purpose of "promoting the general welfare"[2]) can encompass the entire range of legislation. Conversely, the slightest amendment to a bill could be characterized as altering the original purpose; after all, if the amendment were entirely consonant with the original bill, there would be no need for the amendment.

The courts have recognized this quandary, but have done little to address what is at bottom an insoluble dilemma. Pennsylvania courts require that the bill's original purpose must be considered in "reasonably broad terms," but, of course, that provides us no answer at all (Pennsylvanians against Gambling Expansion Fund 2005, 409). The courts recognize that some discretion must be afforded the General Assembly in crafting and amending bills, but they are unwilling to abandon a supervisory role that would allow them to rein in the clearest violations. In *Marcavage v. Rendell* (2008), for example, the Pennsylvania Supreme Court held that the General Assembly violated the original-purpose clause when a bill designed to criminalize crop destruction became instead an expansion of the offense of ethnic intimidation. The court was unmoved by the argument that both the original and final versions of the bill involved crime.

Until 1986, and for most practical purposes until 2005, Pennsylvania case law had followed the "enrolled bill doctrine," which prevented courts from looking beyond the enrolled bill itself—the version of the bill certified by the presiding officers of both chambers and filed with the Secretary of the Commonwealth (Kilgore v. Magee 1877). Such an approach all but eliminated judicial review of the original-purpose requirement, as the whole point of the requirement was to ensure that the purpose of the enrolled bill be the same as the purpose of the bill when it was introduced. If the courts could not look at the original version of the bill, then there was no way to compare the original purpose to the final purpose.[3]

In the 2005 *Pennsylvanians against Gambling Expansion* case, however, the Pennsylvania Supreme Court discarded its precedent and held that courts could entertain claims that laws violated the original-purpose requirement. When adjudicating such claims, courts now not only ask whether the title of the bill in final form accurately described the contents of the bill but also whether, after comparing the original purpose to the final purpose, "there has been an alteration or amendment so as to change the original purpose" (Pennsylvanians against Gambling Expansion Fund 2005, 408–409).[4]

Origination of Revenue Bills

Per Article III, §10, "All bills for raising revenue shall originate in the House of Representatives, but the Senate may propose amendments as in other bills." Unlike the single-subject and original-purpose clauses, the origination clause has an analogue in the U.S. Constitution, in Article I, §7, Clause 1. The purpose of the provision is to discourage the imposition of taxes by making the House—the chamber closer to the people—responsible for introducing measures raising taxes. The philosophy appears to be that taxation has a unique capability to exert tyrannical power over the people, and so the origination clause attempts to increase the barriers for such measures beyond the usual lawmaking procedures mandated for other types of legislation.

Pennsylvania had treated the origination clause as nonjusticiable (Mikell v. Philadelphia School District 1948),[5] but in the *Pennsylvanians against Gambling* case mentioned earlier, the Pennsylvania Supreme Court announced that it could in fact decide claims under the clause. The analysis in that case—both of the jurisdictional question and on the merits—was extremely cursory, however, and so it is unclear how a court will analyze such a claim in the future. In the *Pennsylvanians against Gambling* case, the court rejected the challenge to the law at issue because "the bill in fact originated in the House" (2005, 414). In the mock oral argument that you are about to see, the bill originated in the Senate, but the portion of the bill dealing with revenue was added as an amendment introduced in the House. Thus, we may have a conflict between the language of the constitution (which discusses the origination of "bills") and the apparent purpose of the clause (which might be thought to be satisfied where the House introduces the relevant language).

The Rules of Proceedings and Binding Future Legislatures

Article II, §11 grants each house of the General Assembly the "power to determine the rules of its proceedings." As relevant to the oral argument that will begin shortly, this provision raises the question of whether a statute may add to the procedures for passing bills. Specifically, the oral argument will consider whether a law should be invalidated due to the legislature's failure to comply with the Sunshine Law during the consideration of the bill.

This issue has not been litigated in Pennsylvania. Nevertheless, it does not strike me as a difficult one. It seems to me elementary that no legislature can bind its successors. Surely no law could require a supermajority to pass certain types of legislation—imagine a law that purported to require unanimous consent to pass a tax increase—and I know of no way to distinguish any other sort of procedural rule. Each house may determine its own rules, and those rules are open to reexamination by the house itself. If a house wishes to pass a law without complying with its own rules, then that decision should not be the business of the courts.[6]

Conclusion

I hope that these remarks serve as a useful introduction to the more detailed examination of these issues in which you are about to participate. There will be an opportunity for questions at the conclusion of the oral argument. Thank you for your attendance and your attention.

NOTES

1. That is what the U.S. Supreme Court did with the partisan-gerrymandering challenge to Pennsylvania's congressional districts in *Vieth v. Jubelirer* (2004), although there, too, the Pennsylvania Supreme Court has not let the lack of judicially manageable standards stop it from entering the political thicket (see League of Women Voters v. Commonwealth 2018).

2. Congress has the power to spend money "to pay the Debts and provide for the common Defence and general Welfare of the United States." U.S. Const. art I, §8, cl. 1. The United States Supreme Court has indicated that "in considering whether a particular expenditure is intended to serve general public purposes, courts should defer substantially to the judgment of Congress" (South Dakota v. Dole 1987, 207) and has gone as far as to suggest that "general welfare" might not be "a judicially enforceable restriction at all" (207n2).

3. See Pennsylvanians against Gambling Expansion Fund 2005, 408 (criticizing and overruling Consumer Party v. Commonwealth 1986).

4. This two-part inquiry is designed to protect the purpose of the original-purpose rule, which was "not . . . to avoid deception . . . but rather to preserve a regularized legislative procedure." Williams 1987, 106.

5. Note that the enrolled bill doctrine, were it still in effect, would prohibit the courts from analyzing the legislative history of a bill to determine where it "really" originated. The determinative consideration would be whether the enrolled bill itself specified that it was a House bill or a Senate bill. Cf. United States v. Munoz-Flores 1990, 408–410.

6. Wisconsin's Supreme Court so held earlier this year. State ex rel. Ozanne v. Fitzgerald 2011.

REFERENCES

City of Philadelphia v. Commonwealth. 2003. 838 A.2d 566 (Pa.).

Consumer Party v. Commonwealth. 1986. 507 A.2d 323 (Pa.).

Eskridge, William N., Jr., Philip P. Frickey, and Elizabeth Garrett. 2007. *Cases and Materials on Legislation: Statutes and the Creation of Public Policy*. 4th ed. St. Paul, MN: West Academic.

Kilgore v. Magee. 1877. 85 Pa. 401.

League of Women Voters v. Commonwealth. 2018. 175 A.3d 282 (Pa.).

Marcavage v. Rendell. 2008. 951 A.2d 345 (Pa.).

Mikell v. Philadelphia School District. 1948. 58 A.2d 339 (Pa.).

Payne v. School District of Coudersport Borough. 1895. 31 A. 1072 (Pa.).

Pennsylvanians against Gambling Expansion Fund, Inc. v. Commonwealth. 2005. 877 A.2d 383 (Pa.).

South Dakota v. Dole. 1987. 483 U.S. 203.

State ex rel. Ozanne v. Fitzgerald. 2011. 798 N.W.2d 436 (Wisc.).

United States v. Munoz-Flores. 1990. 495 U.S. 385.
Vieth v. Jubelirer. 2004. 541 U.S. 267.
Williams, Robert F. 1987. "State Constitutional Limits on Legislative Procedure." *Publius: The Journal of Federalism* 17 (Winter): 91–114.

Discussion Questions

1. What is the reason behind bills having a single purpose?
2. Why would the Constitution require bills to have titles that reflect their purpose?
3. What is meant by a bill's "original purpose"? Why is this sometimes a problematic concept?
4. What is the democratic argument behind the requirement that taxes originate in the House of Representatives?
5. How could one house of the Pennsylvania General Assembly illegally bind future sessions of the legislature?

Commonwealth Forum: Should Pennsylvania Adopt Direct Democracy?

YES

Direct democracy, such as through the initiative, popular referendum, and recall processes, allows citizens to place statutes and sometimes amendments to the state constitution on the ballot. Usually this requires the gathering of enough citizen signatures to put the proposal up for a popular vote. Similarly, the recall process requires gathering signatures to remove an elected official from office and hold another election according to the popular vote. Through these processes, citizens can overturn a law created by their legislature, put legislation on the ballot, or remove an unpopular politician from office, all while bypassing the usual legislative channels. Pennsylvania is one of just sixteen states, mostly clustered on the eastern seaboard, with no form of direct democracy.

From a purely democratic perspective, direct democracy in Pennsylvania would be the product of work on behalf of people usually shut out of the legislative process. Special interests have far too much influence in the legislature today, with money for campaign donations dictating the policy positions of elected officials. Furthermore, direct democracy creates more-informed citizens on policy issues. To prepare for voting, citizens must learn the ins and outs of various proposals. Additionally, direct democracy ensures that the will of the people is being exercised even if their elected representatives cannot or will not enact legislation to carry it out. For example, while gerrymandering directly affects the legislative process and which party controls the agenda, enacting legislation by popular vote would override the role of partisanship when drawing legislative boundaries.

NO

One of the fundamental tenets of American government is democratic rule by the people. Belief that citizens should consent to the laws that govern them is at the core of this belief. Pennsylvania government, like the national government, was constructed around the principle of representative democracy. Most of us do not have the time, or, frankly, the knowledge, to examine complex issues of public policy. To solve this problem we elect politicians to do our work for us. They examine issues through hearings and research, deliberate on the consequences of policy options, and then make decisions. We then hold them accountable for the full body of their work when they run for reelection.

Adopting direct democracy in Pennsylvania sounds like a great idea because it would give more "power to the people." However, in practice it would have numerous negative effects on the Commonwealth. Initiatives or referendums are passed when 50.1 percent of the voters approve a measure. What about the opinions of the remaining 49.9 percent? They get nothing. Representative democracy allows for compromise to make sure that multiple points of view are part of the policy-making process. Direct democracy also promotes making decisions on individual issues without thinking about their effect on the whole scope of what government does. Everyone wants lower taxes and more services. However, legislators and the governor are forced to think about the entire package of services provided to Pennsylvania and pass a balanced budget. Direct democracy doesn't force voters to link all of these issues together. The last, and probably worst, effect of direct democracy is to allow special interests one more vehicle to push their own interests. Well-funded groups, often from out of state, have successfully funded direct democracy campaigns in many states. Do we really want that in Pennsylvania?

For More Information

Initiative and Referendum Institute (http://www.iandrinstitute.org/index .cfm) is located at the University of Southern California. The institute is a nonpartisan educational organization dedicated to the study of the initiative and referendum.

National Conference of State Legislatures (http://www.ncsl.org/research/
elections-and-campaigns/initiative-referendum-and-recall-overview
.aspx) provides a useful overview of the process of direct democracy in
the United States. NCSL also tracks initiatives and referendums through
a database, at http://www.ncsl.org/research/elections-and-campaigns/
initiative-referendum-database-2014.aspx.

Democratic Delusions: The Initiative Process in America (Lawrence: University Press of Kansas, 2002), by Richard Ellis, explores the role of
money and outside interests in what he calls the Initiative Industrial
Complex.

Chapter 2
Gubernatorial Power

Governor Wolf's First Year

A Comparative Analysis

Paula A. Duda Holoviak

Thomas J. Baldino

Tom Wolf's first year as governor was dominated by the challenges of reaching a budget compromise with the Republican-dominated General Assembly. This chapter provides an overview of the difficulties and accomplishments of the first year of the Wolf administration. The chapter draws a historical comparison with seven other governors—George Leader, William Scranton, Raymond Shafer, Milton Shapp, Richard Thornburgh, Edward Rendell, and Tom Corbett (four Republicans and three Democrats)—and it concludes with some observations drawn from these previous governors' experiences that may inform the Wolf administration as it navigates its remaining years.

By the end of 2015, approximately 30 percent of the public rated Governor Tom Wolf's performance either good or excellent. But should the public's approval rating be the only assessment of the Wolf administration's first year in office? To evaluate his achievements, we need to assess objectively and carefully his accomplishments from both a legislative and managerial perspective and to compare them to his original list of first-year goals. Moreover, Governor Wolf's performance must be placed in a context that allows for comparison with previous governors, as it is important to understand the political, social, and economic environments in which a chief executive governs.

According to Governor Wolf's official blog, his first-year's theme was "jobs that pay, schools that teach, and a government that works" (Nicastre 2016). The governor's office cites twenty-seven specific accomplishments in his first year. Table 2.1 provides a summary of the results by category. Most notably, Governor Wolf expanded HealthChoices to provide 500,000 people with health insurance through Medicaid's expansion. He initiated online voter registration resulting in 61,000 citizens either switching party or newly registering online. He allowed the phaseout of the 171-year-old Capital Stock and Foreign Franchise Tax, which was implemented under Governor Tom Corbett, and he instituted a gift ban for all political appointees and state workers under his authority. He also created the Heroin Task Force to address the opioid addiction crisis spreading across the state (Bonner 2016).

Yet by December 2015, only about 30 percent of Pennsylvanians rated his performance as good or excellent, a rating comparable to those of Governors Ed Rendell and Tom Corbett at the conclusion of their first year in office (Giammarise 2016). (See Figure 2.1 for a comparison of four governors' approval ratings.) Unfortunately for Governor Wolf, his first-year accomplishments were overshadowed by failure to reach a budget agreement with the Republican-controlled General Assembly. Republicans believed that he had overused the media, because on many occasions Wolf held press conferences during which he criticized the Republican leadership. As Senate Majority Leader Jake Corman (R) put it, "His staff is still in campaign mode." The staff members referenced by Senator Corman were likely Wolf's chief of staff, Katie McGinty, and his policy director, John Hangar. Republicans generally

TABLE 2.1 GOVERNOR WOLF'S FIRST-YEAR ACCOMPLISHMENTS

Category	Accomplishment
Innovation	Online plow truck tracking
Economy	Elimination of Capital Stock Tax
Health care	Expansion of Medicaid
Infrastructure	Bridge repairs
Transparency	Ban on gifts for executive branch employees
Public safety	Heroin Task Force
State services	Elimination of means test for SNAP
Environment	Ban on drilling in state forests
Equality	Easier access to contract bidding
Education	76 Schools that Teach visits
Hunger/homelessness	Food Security Partnership

Source: Bonner 2016.
Note: With the exception of the elimination of the Capital Stock Tax, all accomplishments were achieved through executive action only.

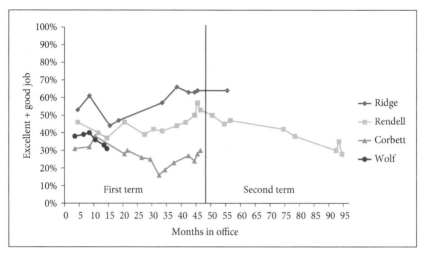

Figure 2.1 Comparison of Pennsylvania governors' job performance ratings. *(Source: Franklin and Marshall College 2016.)*

regarded both as excessively partisan, while many journalists and political analysts also noted their ideological passion rather than pragmatism, as well as their propensity to draw attention to their personal actions rather than working quietly and anonymously behind the scenes.

In fact, the majority of Wolf's accomplishments involved executive and not legislative action (Giammarise 2016; Comisac and Zwick 2016a, 2016b, 2016c, 2016d).[1]

The struggle over the Fiscal Year 2016 (FY16) budget was intense and dramatic and will likely be long remembered as a test of political wills between a Republican Party holding significantly large majorities in both houses of the General Assembly and claiming an electoral mandate for its small government/no taxes agenda (but whose leadership was relatively inexperienced),[2] and a novice politician in Governor Wolf, who also claimed a mandate because of his convincing victory over incumbent Governor Corbett. Both sides had reason to dig in their heels and test the mettle of the other, for to experience defeat in this first major confrontation could result in the losing side feeling marginalized and being viewed as weak by the press and the public. The resulting delayed budget was not a surprise. Research suggests that the factors most associated with late state budgets are divided government, a faltering economy, weak or no shutdown rules,[3] and the governor's request for higher taxes; all four factors were present in Wolf's first year (Klarner, Phillips, and Muckler 2010).[4]

Governor Rendell experienced his own budget battle with the legislature during his first year, 2003. He sent a minimal, first-stage FY04 budget that required no new taxes to the Republican-controlled General Assembly in order to have a budget submitted on time. He expected that the legislature would not act on it until several weeks later when he submitted what was effectively a large, supplemental budget proposal that required higher taxes to support additional spending, largely for new education and economic development programs. To his dismay, the General Assembly passed the frugal budget without even holding hearings, embarrassing the new governor. But Rendell learned a lesson, recovered, and worked with the legislature to pass most of his policy agenda, including tax increases over the next seven years (Giammarise 2016).

Compared to Rendell or to any other modern governor, Wolf's first budget proposal was extraordinarily ambitious. A former secretary of revenue under Rendell, Wolf sought a large increase in the state's personal income tax, a significant broadening of the sales tax base, the closing of loopholes in the state's business taxes, and a new extraction tax on Marcellus Shale gas. He also proposed sweeping property tax relief.

For Wolf, negotiations began cordially with each side presenting its priorities. Some areas for agreement and compromise appeared, particularly the desire to provide property tax relief. Important side issues such as privatizing and/or modernizing the state liquor system, addressing the yawning unfunded liability in the state's pension fund as well as reforming the pension system, imposing an extraction tax on Marcellus Shale gas, and increasing public school funding complicated the budget discussions. Both sides eventually agreed that a $1.2 billion budget deficit existed, but there were differences over how to eliminate the deficit. Republicans argued for more cuts in government spending, while Wolf and fellow Democrats in the General Assembly supported tax increases and additional state spending, especially to support public education. It is important to remember that state funding for public schools was the major issue that differentiated Governor Corbett and candidate Wolf in the 2014 campaign, with Wolf vowing to restore state school funding to the levels Governor Rendell had achieved at the end of his administration, albeit with the use of one-time federal stimulus aid. Wolf sought to add at least $1 billion more to the budget for education. When the budget talks stalled, with the threat of a government shutdown looming as the June 30 deadline approached, Republicans passed their own budget, which, in a highly unusual action, Governor Wolf vetoed in its entirety. Republicans claimed to be shocked, even though he had indicated that he would veto a Republican budget (Scolforo 2015a).

The 2016 fiscal year began without a budget and talks continued intermittently through the fall and into the winter behind closed doors. In February 2016, the governor was forced to propose a budget for FY17 without an enacted budget for FY16, the first time such an event had occurred since Governor Milton Shapp did so in 1971. However, Shapp's unfunded budget

Figure 2.2 Five Pennsylvania governors at the inauguration of Tom Wolf, January 20, 2015.
(Source: Office of Governor Tom Wolf.)

that year was the one that had been proposed by his predecessor, Governor Shafer. Wolf is thus the only governor since the 1968 constitution to have to propose a new budget without the enactment of his own current-year budget.

The governor, his staff, and surrogates criticized the Republicans publicly using rather caustic terms. Even more unusual, the governor's political apparatus began attacking Republican legislators in swing districts with direct mail to their constituents, infuriating the Republican Party (GOP) caucuses. Republicans felt that Wolf's tactics violated tradition in Harrisburg and responded with attacks on the governor. By December 2015, however, a budget deal between Wolf and the Senate's Republican leadership emerged, but when the House Republican leadership presented the budget to its caucus, the most conservative members killed the deal, because it would have required higher general fund taxes. Recognizing that if the budget and required tax legislation were brought to the House floor, they might pass with a combination of maverick Republicans and solid Democratic votes, Speaker Mike Turzai abruptly recognized a motion to adjourn. This time it was Wolf who felt shocked (Scolforo 2015a).

Without a budget, nonessential state services and operations were halted, including funding for public schools. Many school districts were forced to borrow money, while others reduced activities. The public backlash against the General Assembly and the governor over their failure to deliver a budget was vocal and harsh, but neither side appeared willing to concede. Pressure from parents, school boards, and teachers' unions moved a bipartisan majority of the legislature to pass a $30 billion no-frills budget, with no tax increases that became law without the governor's signature on March 28, an embarrassing and unprecedented outcome.[5] This made Wolf's budget late by 272 days, the second latest in Pennsylvania since 1956 (Stafford et al. 2012, table B1) and the second-to-last budget enacted in the nation in FY16.[6] Unfortunately, the budget simply delayed the impending deficit for FY17. Currently Pennsylvania faces a roughly $2 billion deficit for the fiscal year ending in June 2017 (Kiefer 2016).

In addition to failing to enact a budget for nearly a year, the governor also was unsuccessful on other important issues. His goal of a severance tax on natural gas did not materialize; in fact, the 2016 budget contained no new taxes. The GOP-controlled General Assembly passed one of its priorities, a pension reform bill, but Wolf vetoed it, drawing the ire of Republican leaders (Anderson 2015). While education funding did not increase, a revised school funding *formula*, developed by a bipartisan legislative commission established in the last year of the Corbett administration and cochaired by Republican legislators, was passed.[7]

Beyond the struggle to achieve a budget, Governor Wolf also committed several missteps that contributed to his administration's slow start and rocky relationship with Republicans in the legislature. The first was his firing of Eric Arneson, Governor Corbett's appointee to lead the Office of Open Records, which administers the right-to-know law, as well as also recalling twenty-eight nominations to boards, commissions, and judgeships announced by Corbett shortly before he left office (Worden 2015a). Arneson, a former spokesperson for the Senate Majority Caucus and a popular figure in the capitol, was instrumental in the design and passage of the Open Records Act in 2008. Arneson sued, and his case was heard by the Commonwealth Court, which found for Arneson. Of the other twenty-eight Corbett nominees, a compromise with the Republican leadership was achieved and twelve of Corbett's nominees were approved. However, on May 7, 2015, Senate Republicans refused to take action on Wolf's nominees (Levy 2015; Worden 2015b; Scolforo 2015b). Eventually an accommodation was reached, and Wolf's nominees were processed and confirmed, as well as more than thirty state judges to fill vacancies.[8]

The second miscue was naming Marcus Brown to lead the State Police. Brown, a state police commander from Maryland, generated controversy when he wore the Pennsylvania State Police uniform despite not graduating from the state's police academy and for pulling up lawn signs questioning his appointment. The Pennsylvania State Troopers Association and Senate Republicans requested that Wolf withdraw the nominee, but Wolf refused.

Then, on June 1, Wolf announced he would withdraw the nomination, but the Senate proceeded by a vote of 26 to 22 to reject the nominee. As Brown was an acting police commissioner, Wolf was not required to fire him, but he later moved Brown to the Department of Homeland Security and nominated Colonel Tyree Blocker, a retired State Police commander, for the commissioner's post (Couloumbis and Palmer 2015; Esack 2015).

So, given Wolf's political struggles and his unfinished agenda, how does the Wolf administration stand up under historical scrutiny? While the constitutional changes of 1968 altered the budgeting landscape, it is instructive to examine more closely several governors prior to the Pennsylvania Constitutional Convention—namely, governors George Leader (1955–1959), William Scranton (1963–1967), Raymond Shafer (1967–1971), Milton Shapp (1971–1979), Edward Rendell (2003–2011), and Tom Corbett (2011–2015). Leader was included because, like Wolf, he was a Democrat from York County who faced a Republican-dominated General Assembly. Scranton and Shafer's administrations operated under the pre-1968 state constitution, while Shapp was the first governor under the current constitution. Rendell and Corbett, as his two immediate predecessors, set the stage for Wolf and, in Corbett's case, dealt with the same political environment in the legislature.

Governor Leader came to power in an upset victory over the Republican lieutenant governor Lloyd H. Wood, winning 54 percent of the vote, the biggest Democratic sweep since 1857. Leader, however, faced deep economic and fiscal challenges. The unemployment rate in the state was the highest since the Great Depression at 8.8 percent (and as high as 15 percent in the coal and steel regions). He inherited a $58.2 million budget deficit from Governor John Fine's administration, and while the Democrats controlled the House during his first two years in office, the Republicans remained firmly in control of the Senate. Leader endured many epic budget battles during his four years in office. He first tried to balance the budget by enacting the highly unpopular personal income tax. The fight over the income tax proposal in his first budget went on for seventeen months. During this time, the press turned against the governor, claiming the tax would hurt the working class. Finally, in March 1956 a compromise was reached. The sales tax was raised to 3 percent, the corporate net income tax rose from 1 percent to 6 percent, and the gasoline tax rose one cent to six cents (Beers 1971; PHMC 2015a).

Leader's image was that of a progressive intellectual, a proponent of good government. He staffed his cabinet with college professors and policy wonks. He was a strong supporter of civil rights and the rights of the disabled. He angered his party by adding ten thousand civil service jobs to the state roster and weakening the patronage system. Among his accomplishments were the creation of the Department of Administration, the Pennsylvania Industrial Development Authority (PIDA), and reform of the state's mental health hospital system. Although author Paul Beers dubs him "Mister Clean," his administration was rife with scandal and he lost his bid for the U.S. Senate in 1958 (Beers 1980).

Governor Scranton came to office after eight years of Democratic dominance of the executive branch as well as much of Pennsylvania and national politics. He was adept at melding the image of traditional Republican values to a modestly liberal economic agenda. The Republicans retook control of both the Senate and House, giving Governor Scranton a legislative advantage. Scranton wisely allowed the legislature to avoid the issue of a statewide income tax. In his first year in office, he increased state spending by 38 percent and capital debt by nearly one-third, but managed to fund the increased spending with politically palatable sales and business taxes, including taxes on liquor and cigarettes. With the extra millions, he increased school subsidies and teacher salaries, opened vocational technical schools and community colleges, and expanded the PIDA. All of these legislative victories must be viewed in the light of single-party government and a very robust Pennsylvania economy. In fact, Pennsylvania gained 528,000 jobs from 1963 to 1970, with an unemployment rate of 3.6 percent in 1966.

Governor Shafer took office in 1967 with an unblemished political career, victorious in elections for district attorney, state senator, lieutenant governor, and, finally, governor. His last electoral success, however, proved to be a failure for the Commonwealth. When Shafer became governor, the state was running a deficit of $1 million per day. Although Shafer had a majority in the General Assembly during his first two years in office, he failed to remedy the government's fiscal ills by having a state income tax passed. According to statistics from the Pennsylvania Economy League, by 1969 Pennsylvania was running a $400 million deficit and was $242 million in debt. Shafer's experience mirrors that of the current governor. Shafer was unable to pass a budget for sixteen months (248 days, second longest after Governor Leader's first budget), and he was unable to convince the General Assembly to increase taxes to close the state's budget deficit. The legislature refused to confirm Shafer's appointments. Many blamed his inability to compromise or engage in legislative horse trading. But Shafer was unfailingly moderate in his politics, continuing and enlarging the Scranton legacy in education, welfare, and conservation. Many, however, viewed his administration as a failure, leaving the Commonwealth on the brink of bankruptcy. Though Shafer was the major force behind the Constitutional Convention of 1968, he wisely chose to have no role at the convention (Beers 1980; PHMC 2015c).

Following the 1968 constitutional reforms, Milton Shapp became the first two-term governor in Pennsylvania's history. An idealist with no elective office experience, he was a self-made millionaire. Unfortunately, his administration, particularly in its second term, was riddled with corruption. Despite his tireless efforts in 1972 following the flooding caused by Hurricane Agnes, and his ability to handle the financial woes of the Commonwealth, he was perceived as an outsider and was highly unpopular within his own party by the end of his second term. Nevertheless, he had notable legislative successes, including enactment of the first personal income tax; the establishment of a state lottery to fund free public transportation for senior citizens and property tax relief for low-income seniors; no-fault auto insurance; strong consumer protection laws; legislation to protect the rights of the mentally ill; the establishment of the Clean and Green Program to preserve agricultural farmland; and an environmental amendment to the Pennsylvania Constitution. These were all ranked among the most important laws of the Pennsylvania General Assembly under the 1968 constitution in a 2010 Temple University survey of current and former legislators, political scientists, and journalists. Indeed, the personal income tax was ranked as the single most important law of the modern era in the survey (Stafford et al. 2012). Conversely, Shapp failed to achieve property tax reform, privatize liquor stores, or establish a free Pennsylvania Turnpike.

In 1970 the Democrats attained majorities in both houses of the General Assembly, which allowed Shapp to quickly push through his preferred progressive income tax early. However, it was overturned by the Pennsylvania Supreme Court as a violation of the "uniformity clause" of the Pennsylvania Constitution. As noted above, Shapp and the Democratic legislature then enacted the flat tax that is still the Commonwealth's most important revenue producer. Pennsylvania was the forty-third state to adopt an income tax. Shapp used the veto liberally, but he was also overridden fifteen times. Governor Shapp's battles with the legislature on everything from abortion restrictions to the death penalty continued to the end of his second term (Beers 1980; PHMC 2015b).

In the twenty-first century, with Pennsylvania's two most recent governors, the issues remain much the same, but the political arena has been forever changed because of the 24/7 news cycle, easier access to previously unavailable government information, passage of the Open Records Act, emergence of social media as a political force, and the increasingly divisive and polarized politics on both left and right. Reforming property taxes, achieving equitable funding for basic and higher education, reforming the criminal justice system, and protecting the environment persist on Pennsylvania's twenty-first-century political agenda. In the past, governors were better able to control the distribution of their messages, as the number of news sources that covered Harrisburg were relatively few, while today any person or group can gather information and post it online at any time. The rise of the Tea Party in Pennsylvania, changing political alignments in Philadelphia's suburban counties, and the rightward drift of previously Democratic counties in southwestern Pennsylvania led to an east-west, conservative-liberal divide.

Governor Rendell faced many of the same problems as his twentieth-century predecessors. Confronting a General Assembly in Republican hands, his first budget was completed six months late, with the enactment of school funding and a personal income tax increase making Pennsylvania the last state in the nation to finish its budget. (See discussion of Rendell's 2003 budget above.) In fact, Rendell never managed to complete a budget on time; the 2009 budget was also the last in the nation to be passed. However, when the ink dried on a giant supplemental appropriation that completed the first Rendell budget, it included $1 billion in new revenues and a 10 percent increase in the state income tax. Rendell used administrative cuts to create $1.75 billion in savings, which he used to increase funding for the state's public schools. Rendell was legendary for his larger-than-life personality, his willingness to speak frankly with the media on nearly any topic, and his ability to wheel and deal with the legislature. In the end, despite many political differences with the General Assembly, his accomplishments included eliminating or cutting property taxes for the Commonwealth's senior citizens, bringing casino gambling to the state, increasing education funds, particularly for preschool education, and bringing Sunday liquor sales to the state store system.

Despite his many noteworthy successes, however, he failed on several major issues that remain unresolved today. He could not expand the sales tax, privatize the Pennsylvania Turnpike to raise additional revenue, or consolidate Pennsylvania's 501 school districts to 100 districts. Perhaps Rendell's most troubling failure was his unwillingness to seek a severance tax on Marcellus Shale gas shortly after the rapid expansion of drilling and production from the new wells (*PennLive* Editorial Board 2011).

Governor Corbett was elected to office with a reputation as a strong state prosecutor and corruption fighter. As Pennsylvania's attorney general, he empaneled a grand jury that indicted legislators of both parties and issued a strident—and many thought gratuitous—report blasting the General Assembly's culture and operations. He thus began his term as governor with a legislature that, although controlled by his party, regarded him as hostile to the institution. His relationships with legislators of both parties remained strained throughout his term. He departed office as Pennsylvania's first governor to lose reelection since the 1968 constitutional reforms that allowed the state's governor to serve two terms. He campaigned as a pro-business fiscal conservative and made the "no new taxes" pledge championed by Grover Norquist's organization, Americans for Tax Reform.

Corbett's legacy is mixed at best. While he did cut state taxes, he also reduced funding for public education and social services to balance the budget, though in his last year, he did substantially increase the state's subsidy to basic education.[9] In the end, he increased a variety of state fees and raised the state's excise tax on auto fuels to fund a $2 billion transportation program designed to repair the state's deteriorating roads and bridges. He also accepted the federal offer to expand Medicaid under the Affordable Care Act, although only after obtaining a waiver that critics said left millions of federal dollars on the table and provided far less coverage for poor and work-ing-class families. Achieving four of his major objectives—pension reform, liquor privatization, property tax elimination or reform, and the sale of the state's lottery system to raise several billion dollars in new revenue—proved elusive, however, perhaps because of his reserved character and inability to communicate effectively with the public, at least in the opinion of many Republican legislators. During his administration the state's credit rating was downgraded four times (Associated Press 2014).

Despite the many difficulties he faced—some self-generated and others inflicted by the General Assembly—Wolf's first year cannot be assessed as a complete failure or a success when compared to the first year of the governors who preceded him. In our opinion, Governors Leader and Shafer (both pre-1968 constitutional reforms) and Shapp (post-reform) had exceptionally chal-lenging first years and survived to govern with reasonable success for the re-mainder of their terms. Governors Scranton (also pre-reform) and Rendell and Corbett (post-reform) experienced first-year difficulties but eventually achieved many of their policy goals. Only Scranton's first year accomplished a great deal without notable conflict. Wolf's first year falls somewhere between those governors whose first years were the most difficult—namely, Leader, Sha-fer, and Shapp, and Scranton, Rendell and Corbett, whose first years are gener-ally regarded as triumphal. But it is important to remember that the relative success or failure of a governor's first year does not preordain the remaining three years of a governor's term. The person occupying the office can learn and adapt his or her governing style and strategies so that he or she survives the first year to achieve legislative victories and win reelection to another term.

Are there any general conclusions that we can draw from an examina-tion of the accomplishments and failures of the Commonwealth's governors since the 1950s? The following are a few conclusions and observations:

- It does not appear to be an advantage to present oneself as a po-litical outsider. Additionally, a successfully business career does not appear to translate into a successful political career.
- A working relationship with the General Assembly is critical. Compromise is essential, as is a willingness to listen to and accept as legitimate the concerns of the legislature's members. Of course, this assumes that members of the General Assembly are willing and able to compromise. Knowing when to "hold 'em and fold 'em" is key, and having something to trade is even more important.
- Social media's influence must be considered at every turn. It can make or break a governor, and, like the forces of nature, it cannot be controlled. Every legislative office can be its own public relations operation, which makes it very difficult for the governor to control the message that the public and the traditional media outlets receive.

- Government corruption is corrosive and will quickly diminish the legitimacy of a governor's administration and undermine its credibility with the public.
- While political division is nothing new to Pennsylvania politics, the intense polarization confronting the Wolf administration has taken division to a new level. The transformation of the General Assembly's membership since the pay raise vote and the Bonusgate scandal of 2006–2007 has dramatically increased the difficulty of finding common ground with the legislature.

It should be noted that if a major disaster or tragedy occurs during the first few years in office, and *if* the response to the disaster is handled properly, a governor may benefit. For example, after just eight months in office, Governor Scranton faced a national tragedy and political upheaval with the assassination of President Kennedy. Governor Shapp dealt with Hurricane Agnes and the total devastation along the Susquehanna River, including the flooding of the Governor's Mansion. Governor Richard Thornburgh experienced the nation's first nuclear disaster at Three Mile Island in 1979. And of course, Governor Ridge had to respond to the devastation and the public's fear following the 9/11 attacks, which included the downing of Flight 93 in Somerset County, Pennsylvania.

During emergencies, the public turns to the governor for leadership and will rally behind a governor who demonstrates competence, composure, and decisiveness. This improves the governor's chances of winning a second term. However, any natural disaster or emergency disrupts the normal flow of business in the capitol and possibly across the entire state, causing a governor to delay or entirely eliminate one or more major items from the governor's policy agenda. Few governors would wish for such catastrophes to occur on their watch. To date, while Governor Wolf has experienced political challenges, most particularly from the Tea Party wing of the Republican-controlled legislature, he has yet to face a significant disaster, tragedy, or even severe economic downturn, though a winter snowstorm that stranded motorists on the Pennsylvania Turnpike did prove embarrassing.

Governor Wolf's legacy thus far is mixed. Unless he can resolve some of the unfinished business of the Corbett administration—namely, pension reform, property tax reform, closing the budget deficit, and education funding reform—future generations may evaluate the Wolf administration as less than successful. Political corruption and much-needed campaign finance reform continue to dog the system generally, as does a largely ineffective legislative branch.

NOTES
This article was previously published as Paula A. Duda Holoviak and Thomas J. Baldino, "Governor Wolf's First Year," *Commonwealth* 18, no. 2 (2016). © 2016 The Pennsylvania

Political Science Association. ISSN 2469-7672 (online). http://dx.doi.org/10.15367/cjppp .v18i2.113. All rights reserved.

1. In fairness, President Obama was also criticized for attempting to govern by executive action, given his difficulties in persuading a Republican Congress to move on his legislative agenda, a reflection of the polarized state of American politics.

2. New to their roles were Senate Majority Leader Jake Corman, Whip John Gordner, Appropriations Chair Pat Browne, and House Speaker Mike Turzai, Majority Leader Dave Reed, and Whip Bryan Cutler.

3. Pennsylvania's shutdown rules, bringing vital spending to a halt without enacted appropriations, were greatly weakened by the 2009 Supreme Court decision *Council 13, Ex Rel. Fillman v. Rendell* (986 A. 2d 63 [2009]), which effectively relieved pressure on the governor and legislature to agree on a budget by continuing to fund most state programs.

4. For a fuller overview of the struggle to achieve a state budget, see Comisac and Zwick 2016a, 2016b, 2016c, and 2016d.

5. According to the Pennsylvania Policy Database, at http://www.cla.temple.edu/ papolicy, only four bills since 1979 have become law without the governor's signature, none having the significance of the general appropriations act. Such rare actions sometimes reflect a governor's judgment that a veto would be overridden.

6. Only Pennsylvania under Governor Wolf and Illinois under Governor Bruce Rauner lacked an FY16 state budget in the spring of 2016. Wolf and Rauner were both business executives new to elective office, who faced legislatures controlled by the opposition party. Although most state programs were operating, Rauner's budget was still incomplete at year's end.

7. The new school funding formula was widely praised by school officials and education advocates. The Wolf administration and the advocates lost an effort to delay its implementation until after the Corbett administration's school spending cuts were restored. The new formula will incrementally increase funding each year, leaving in place large inequities in the distribution of school resources in Pennsylvania accumulated over many years.

8. An anonymous source within the Wolf administration provided information about the agreement between Wolf and Senate Republicans.

9. Governor Corbett argued that his last budget did increase state support for basic education to record levels, because he used state money rather than the federal stimulus funds that Rendell had used. The stimulus money eventually ended, leaving the public schools short of money.

REFERENCES

Anderson, Christian. 2015. "Gov. Wolf Vetoes GOP Pension Reform Bill." *PennLive*, July 9. Available at http://www.pennlive.com/politics/index.ssf/2015/07/gov_wolf_says _hell_veto_gop_pe.html.

Associated Press. 2014. "What Will History Say of Gov. Tom Corbett's Tenure in Pennsylvania?" *PennLive*, December 25. Available at http://www.pennlive.com/politics/ index.ssf/2014/12/what_will_history_say_of_gov_t.html.

Beers, Paul. 1971. *The Republican Years: The Scranton-Shafer Era of Change and Controversy from 1963 through 1970.* Harrisburg, PA: Stackpole Books.

———. 1980. *Pennsylvania Politics Today and Yesterday: The Tolerable Accommodation.* University Park: Pennsylvania State University Press.

Bonner, Krystal. 2016. "27 Results from Governor Wolf's First Year in Office." Commonwealth of Pennsylvania, January 21. Available at https://www.governor.pa.gov/ blog-27-results-from-governor-wolfs-first-year-in-office.

Comisac, Chris, and Kevin Zwick. 2016a. "Capitolwire: Wolf Year-One Review, Part
    1—The Budget Impasse and PA's New Era of Gridlock." *Capitolwire*, April 4. Avail-
    able at http://www.capitolwire.com.
———. 2016b. "Capitolwire: Wolf Year-One Review, Part 2—A Good Start Deteriorates
    Quickly." *Capitolwire*, April 5. Available at http://www.capitolwire.com.
———. 2016c. "Capitolwire: Wolf Year-One Review, Part 3—'Too Many Cooks in the
    Kitchen.'" *Capitolwire*, April 6. Available at http://www.capitolwire.com.
———. 2016d. "Capitolwire: Wolf Year-One Review, Part 4—The Ill-Fated Compromise,
    a Glimpse of Things to Come." *Capitolwire*, April 7. Available at http://www
    .capitolwire.com.
Couloumbis, Angela, and Chris Palmer. 2015. "Senate Rejects Wolf's State Police
    Nominee." *Philadelphia Inquirer*, June 9. Available at http://www.philly.com/philly/
    news/politics/20150609_Wolf_pulls_nominee_for_State_Police_commissioner
    .html.
Esack, Steve. 2015. "PA Senate Rejects Tom Wolf's Nominee for State Police Commis-
    sioner." *Allentown Morning Call*, June 9. Available at http://www.mcall.com/news/
    nationworld/pennsylvania/mc-pa-marcus-brown-psp-senate-0608-20150608-story
    .html.
Franklin and Marshall College. 2016. "Franklin and Marshall College Poll: Summary
    of Findings." Available at https://www.fandm.edu/uploads/files/92489569924931096
    -february-2016-franklin-marshall-college-poll.pdf.
Giammarise, Kate. 2016. "What Defined Tom Wolf's First Year in Office." *Pittsburgh
    Post-Gazette*, January 20. Available at http://www.post-gazette.com/news/state/
    2016/01/20/Budget-fight-overshadows-Gov-Wolf-s-first-year-in-office/stories/
    201601200016.
Kiefer, Francine. 2016. "Gridlock in States: Why They're Mimicking D.C." *Christian
    Science Monitor*, April 8. Available at https://www.csmonitor.com/USA/Politics/
    2016/0408/Gridlock-in-states-why-they-re-mimicking-D.C.
Klarner, Karl E., Justin H. Phillips, and Matt Muckler. 2010. "The Causes of Fiscal Stale-
    mate." Paper presented at the Annual Meeting of the American Political Science
    Association, Washington, D.C.
Levy, Mark. 2015. "Republicans Begin Casting Critical Eye on Wolf's Nominees." *The
    Reporter*, January 22. Available at http://www.thereporteronline.com/article/RO/
    20150122/NEWS/150129921.
Nicastre, Mark. 2016. "Looking Back on Governor Wolf's First Year." January 15. Avail-
    able at https://www.governor.pa.gov/blog-looking-back-on-governor-wolfs-first
    -year/.
PennLive Editorial Board. 2011. "Gov. Ed Rendell: In Large Part Two-Term Governor
    Did What He Said He Would Do." *PennLive*, January 14. Available at http://www
    .pennlive.com/editorials/index.ssf/2011/01/gov_ed_rendell_in_large_part_t.html.
PHMC (Pennsylvania Historical and Museum Commission). 2015a. "Governor John
    Sydney Fine." August 26. Available at http://www.phmc.state.pa.us/portal/com
    munities/governors/1951-2015/john-fine.html.
———. 2015b. "Governor Milton Jerrold Shapp." August 26. Available at http://www
    .phmc.state.pa.us/portal/communities/governors/1951-2015/milton-shapp.html.
———. 2015c. "Governor Raymond Philip Shafer." August 26. Available at http://www
    .phmc.state.pa.us/portal/communities/governors/1951-2015/raymond-shafer.html.
Scolforo, Mark. 2015a. "Pennsylvania's Budget Train Wreck Unfolded over Past Year."
    New Castle News, October 5. Available at http://www.ncnewsonline.com/news/

pennsylvania-s-budget-train-wreck-unfolded-over-past-year/article_48a37fde
-6a9b-11e5-bb88-bffbd5ac2d51.html.
———. 2015b. "Wolf, Senate GOP Leaders Face Off over Fate of 12 Nominees." *Pocono Record*, May 8. Available at http://www.poconorecord.com/article/20150508/ NEWS/150509408.
Stafford, Richard A., Joseph P. McLaughlin, Jr., Michelle J. Atherton, Megan Mullin, and Nathan Shrader. 2012. *A Discussion of Topics Related to the Continuing Evolution of the Pennsylvania General Assembly*. Vol. 4 of *The Temple Papers on the Pennsylvania General Assembly*. Philadelphia: Temple University Institute for Public Affairs.
Worden, Amy. 2015a. "Governor Wolf Fires Open Records Director and Recalls Corbett's Nominations." *Philadelphia Inquirer*, January 22. Available at http://www .philly.com/philly/news/politics/20150123_Wolf_fires_open_records_director_and _recalls_Corbett_s_nominations.html.
———. 2015b. "Wolf and GOP Resolve Nominee Dispute." *Philadelphia Inquirer*, February 26. Available at http://www.philly.com/philly/news/politics/20150226_Wolf _and_GOP_resolve_nominee_dispute.html.

Discussion Questions

1. What were some political blunders during Governor Wolf's first year that could have led to an approval rating of 30 percent?
2. What contributes to a delayed state budget?
3. Should a Democratic governor work closely with a Republican legislature to do the basic work of government—for example, passing a budget? How important are cross-party relationships to governing?
4. What current developments in politics and communication might contribute to the loss or changing nature of executive power?
5. What are the key components to a successful term as governor? What might keep a governor from accomplishing stated goals?

Commonwealth Forum: Do Businesspeople Make Good Chief Executives?

YES

Citizens look to governors to create jobs and economic development in their states. Overall trade policy is negotiated between Washington, D.C., and other countries. However, much of the competition for development within the United States takes place between different states and metropolitan regions. Governors are at the forefront of convincing businesses to relocate to their states, incubating the development of new technologies and industries, and creating tax and regulatory schemes that are attractive to business. Governors with business experience have an advantage over career politicians because they have real-world experience in creating jobs and understanding the effects of government policies on the private sector. They also are able to view government operations with a set of fresh eyes, unlike individuals who become governor by the standard practice of working their way through the political system. Business practices of focusing on good customer service provision and cost efficiencies help governors streamline and rationalize government programs that are often designed around what is politically possible rather than best practices.

Businesspeople often successfully run for governor by arguing that they are not part of the entrenched political system. They are above the partisan rivalries and conflicts that grip contemporary American politics. They do not owe favors or paybacks to other politicians and special interests because they have not spent their careers in the political system. This allows governors with a business background to be results-oriented. This focus on policy outcomes, rather than partisan points, makes "CEO" governors the best qualified people to be a state's chief executive.

NO

Government is not a business, so why would a business executive be a better leader of government than a politician or someone with government experience? The idea that government should be run like a business is a myth that will not die. The differences between business and government are glaringly obvious. For one, the primary motive of business is to earn a profit. The primary goal of government is to serve the citizens. Second, businesses can choose with whom they interact and their clientele. Governments exists to serve all the people. Third, businesses have a strictly top-down structure, with good reason. Governments function on the basis of compromise on many levels, as they must weigh the outcomes of policies on the basis of how they would affect many groups and interests. Furthermore, executives in government work for the people, not the other way around. Finally (but by no means the only other reason), business decisions are private and, once made, require no public disclosure. Governments undergo constant criticism from the public and the press, and they function in plain view.

Two recent examples show the inadequacy of business executives in the highest position of state government. First, Governor Bruce Rauner of Illinois was elected in 2014 with an extensive business background leading investment firms. However, the state went without a complete budget through fiscal years 2016, 2017, and into 2018. Rauner's leadership has meant government dysfunction. Recent GOP presidential candidate and former governor of Florida Jeb Bush went straight from business into public office. Under his leadership from 1999 to 2007, spending ballooned by 45 percent, but taxes were cut largely for the wealthy and corporations, increasing debt by over $8 billion. Such results would not serve a business well, let alone the public sector.

For More Information

The **National Governors Association (NGA)** (http://nga.org) represents the interests of the nation's fifty-five governors of states, commonwealths, and territories. Through the NGA, governors share best practices, learn from each other, and develop policy solutions. Its website has numerous news items and reports as they relate to the role of the state executive.

Rutgers University Center on the American Governor (http://governors .rutgers.edu/) promotes research and discussion on the history and current role of governors with archived reports, videos, and analysis.

The Best Job in Politics: Exploring How Governors Succeed as Policy Leaders (Thousand Oaks, CA: CQ Press, 2012), by Alan Rosenthal, explores the workings of state executives through interviews with governors and legislators.

A Legacy of Leadership: Governors and American History (Philadelphia: University of Pennsylvania Press, 2008), edited by Clayton McClure Brooks, presents the position of governor in historical context, demonstrating how the role has changed over time as a result of culture, the economy, and world events.

Chapter 3
Tax Policy

Commonwealth Forum

Should Pennsylvania Abolish the Property Tax for Schools?

In November 2015, the Pennsylvania Senate narrowly failed to pass legislation abolishing the local school property tax and replacing it with state revenues raised by higher income and sales tax rates and the extension of the sales tax to a range of goods and services now exempt. The legislation, supported by dozens of citizen tax reform groups across Pennsylvania, was defeated 25–24 when Lieutenant Governor Michael Stack cast a tie-breaking vote against an amendment embodying the changes.

State Senators David Argall and Judith Schwank were principal sponsors of the legislation and vowed to continue the fight. Indeed, legislation to replace, reform, and reduce the property tax, particularly for schools, has been proposed and debated for decades, and some relief measures have been enacted, but the tax remains the principal levy to fund schools in Pennsylvania and in most states. Citizens in Pennsylvania and nationally consistently tell pollsters that it is the worst tax, and few if any elected officials will defend the levy, except on the pragmatic grounds that replacing it would require unrealistically large increases in state taxes.

Commonwealth invited Senator Argall, chair of the Senate Republican Policy Committee, and Jon Hopcraft, the committee's executive director, to summarize the argument that the tax is an antiquated and unfair levy and should be abolished. We invited Dartmouth College economist William A. Fischel, a nationally recognized expert who attended Pennsylvania public schools, to summarize his argument that, compared to statewide taxes, the local levy provides voters—even in households without schoolchildren—with stronger incentives to support high-quality public schools.

Yes, Abolish the Property Tax: It Is the Worst Tax for Schools

David G. Argall

Jon Hopcraft

A t the start of his career in 1890 at Columbia University, Edwin Seligman deemed the property tax "the worst tax known in the civilized world" (Brunori et al. 2006). One hundred twenty-six years later, Seligman's declaration would be met with raucous applause at town hall meetings across much of Pennsylvania.

The property tax is one of the oldest taxes in history—Athens levied a land tax in 596 BC (Jennings 2015). In 1982, former Pennsylvania Senate Majority Leader John Stauffer hypothesized that the first complaint about real estate taxes was likely submitted in Athens in 596 BC.

Article III, §14 of the Pennsylvania Constitution requires, "The General Assembly shall provide for the maintenance and support of a thorough and efficient system of public education to serve the needs of the Commonwealth."

We would challenge anyone today to argue that Pennsylvania's current school property tax system actually promotes a "thorough and efficient system of public education."

Think what has changed in Pennsylvania education since the first school property tax was enacted in the 1830s: Teachers are no longer paid partly in vegetables, our children no longer learn in one-room schoolhouses, teachers are much better educated, and students have moved from chalk and slate to textbooks and computers, but taxpayers still pay for public education through an outmoded, archaic, and unfair property tax.

Today, Pennsylvania school districts receive most of their funding from local property taxes with the state and federal governments contributing approximately 45 percent. Again, let us quote the late Senator Stauffer, who served in the Pennsylvania General Assembly from 1965 to 1988 and summed it up best: "Although [the property tax's] use has become nearly universal, it is the most unfair, fastest-rising and most capricious tax. Property tax assessments and reassessments have become bywords for political manipulation." According to the input we have received at countless town hall meetings, the situation has not improved since Senator Stauffer's unsuccessful efforts to reform the school property tax system in the 1980s.

This debate has gone on for decades in the Pennsylvania General Assembly, with the key question being "What is the best way to fund our public schools?"

In 1953, Governor John Fine enacted the state Sales and Use Tax at 1 percent. While this tripled state aid for education, it failed to kill off school property taxes (PHMC 2015a). In 1971, Governor Milton Shapp won a long-fought battle with the legislature and created the state income tax at 2.3 percent, dubbed the "Emergency Income Tax." Shapp increased aid to public schools and also signed a bill into law creating the Pennsylvania State Lottery with the intent to provide property tax relief to senior citizens (PHMC 2015b), but it failed to kill off the school property tax. In 2004, Governor Ed Rendell legalized casino gaming with a portion of the revenue dedicated toward property tax relief, but the hated school property tax continued to grow. In 2006, the approval of Act 1 tied allowable school property tax increases to inflation for the first time. The exemptions in Act 1, however, have allowed school districts to raise property taxes above the Act 1 index. In 2014, the state granted exceptions to 164 public schools across the Commonwealth to raise their property taxes above the Act 1 index (Frantz 2014). Since 2008, nearly one-third of the state's five hundred public school districts annually received exceptions from the state to raise taxes above the Act 1 limit (Welton 2015).

The pattern over the last six decades is clear—any temporary tax becomes permanent and any tax relief effort is temporary. Because of the state government's inability to prevent school property taxes from rising each year, the calls to *eliminate*—not reform—this hated tax continue to grow louder each year.

Why do people across Pennsylvania hate the school property tax? Here's one major reason: From 1993–1994 to 2012–2013, while the average annual regional consumer price index increased approximately 2.5 percent, the annual average school district property tax increased by nearly *double* the inflation rate at 4.9 percent. In other words, over that period, as Figure 3.1 indicates, the consumer price index cumulatively increased by 61 percent while the school property tax increased by 146 percent (Independent Fiscal Office 2013). The annual increases to school property taxes continue to outpace any other economic indicator despite Act 1 limitations. This is why so many people show up at town hall meetings across Pennsylvania to demand the elimination of school property taxes. Tweaking this hated tax or reforming this unfair and archaic system is *not* what people are requesting. They are demanding its complete elimination.

Article VIII, §1 of the Pennsylvania Constitution requires, "All taxes shall be uniform, upon the same class of subjects, within the territorial limits of the authority levying the tax, and shall be levied and collected under general laws." The subjective nature of the school property tax flies in the face of the uniformity clause.

Today, property owners are subject to higher property taxes based on a variety of outmoded factors, including when the property was purchased, upgrades to the interior and/or exterior of a dwelling, reverse appeals, additions to the dwelling, changes to the productive use of the land, among sev-

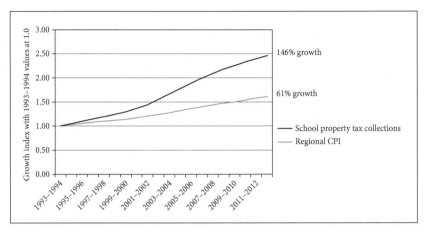

Figure 3.1 Historic trends in school property tax collections and regional consumer price index. *(Data Source: Independent Fiscal Office 2013.)*

eral others factors. Cherry-picking homeowners based on the sale of or up-grades to the property not only discourages individuals from purchasing property in certain school districts but also removes any incentive to improve properties because of the threat of future tax increases. The school district property tax is, at best, only remotely tied to an individual's ability to pay. Is this really how we want to fund the education of Pennsylvania's students in the twenty-first century? The only way to eliminate the unfairness of the school property tax system is to kill it off once and for all.

The plan to eliminate school property taxes in Pennsylvania was first developed and drafted by more than seventy grassroots taxpayer advocacy groups from across the state, known as the Pennsylvania Coalition of Taxpayer Associations. The coalition brought us a plan that would eliminate— not reduce—school property taxes in Pennsylvania by shifting to an increased Personal Income Tax (increasing the rate from 3.07 percent to 4.95 percent) and an increased and expanded Sales and Use Tax (increasing the rate from 6 percent to 7 percent and broadening the tax base). Each year, school districts would receive a cost of living adjustment tied to the State-wide Average Weekly Wage. The plan would also allow school districts to raise additional revenue through a local Personal Income Tax or Earned Income Tax increase contingent on voter approval. To put that in perspective, thirty-four other states require school districts to receive voter approval to levy or increase the local tax rate (Paul 2015).

Opponents frequently argue that income and sales taxes are too volatile for school funding. They usually fail to mention, however, that Pennsylvania's overall state budget receives over 70 percent of its revenue from the Personal Income Tax and Sales and Use Tax. Why should we require school districts to depend on hated and unfair property taxes when the state has long since decided that the sales and income taxes are much fairer and more appropriate taxes to meet our needs?

The plan created by the Pennsylvania Coalition of Taxpayer Associations is a shift from an unfair, archaic school property tax to a hybrid income and sales tax–based approach. When Pennsylvania voters are asked, they agree with this concept. Here's a sampling of the polling data: Harper Polling determined that Pennsylvanians believe that the property tax is the worst tax in Pennsylvania (50 percent)—eclipsing the combined dislike of income (27 percent) and sales (14 percent) taxes (Harper Polling 2015). Local tax reform continues to be a key priority statewide, narrowly trailing education funding as the top issue for Pennsylvania voters (Klinger 2015). During a telephone town hall event on October 6, 2015, with Berks and Schuylkill County residents, participants overwhelmingly supported elimination (81 percent) over reduction (11 percent) and caps on future growth (8 percent). KQV Radio in Pittsburgh in April of 2012 found that 85 percent of their listeners support a plan to eliminate school property taxes; the *York Dispatch* in May of 2012 asked a similar question, with 73 percent support of complete elimination; the *Easton Express Times* surveyed readers in March of 2015 asking about supporting a state budget deal or school property tax elimination, with 84 percent supporting the latter.

Figure 3.2 Inside view of the Pennsylvania State Capitol rotunda. *(Source: Photo by Bestbudbrian, courtesy of* Wikimedia Commons.*)*

This proposal, Senate Bill 76 and House Bill 76, would change our archaic school property system to one more in line with what taxpayers can afford to pay. Property owners would no longer bear the primary burden of funding public schools. Utilization of the income and sales tax will broaden the tax base, creating fairness and uniformity in taxation. Urban areas with population out-migration would no longer be tied to an eroding tax base for future revenue needs. Instead, more than 12.7 million Pennsylvanians plus tourists and other visitors would contribute to the state's public education system.

After a comprehensive review, the Pennsylvania Independent Fiscal Office determined that eliminating school property taxes would provide the largest relative tax cut to retired homeowners and increase disposable income for homeowners (Independent Fiscal Office 2012). Seniors and homeowners of all ages continue to be the strongest advocates for this legislation.

When the plan was first introduced in the state Senate in 2011, it garnered the support of roughly one-quarter of the Senators. After considerable grassroots lobbying across Pennsylvania, the number of Senate cosponsors has doubled. The plan was reintroduced in 2013 by fourteen Republicans and eleven Democrats, and again in 2015 with one-half of the Senate cosponsoring the measure. On November 23, 2015, the Senate debated this proposal for the first time in history. The result was a 24–24 tie vote, which was then defeated by the lieutenant governor's vote against the measure.

How can we finally resolve this decades-long debate and eliminate our archaic school property tax system? We are now meeting with the proponents and opponents of the measure to find ways to improve the bill. Every day, we are searching for that one additional vote that we need to secure passage in the Senate and send it to the House for its consideration.

We now face a unique window of opportunity in Harrisburg. Franklin and Marshall College Professor G. Terry Madonna and consultant Michael Young believe that this issue could unite—not further divide—state government leaders during this era of extraordinary partisanship in Harrisburg. In an often quoted column titled "RIP: The School Property Tax," Madonna and Young (2015) wrote:

Pennsylvania's property tax, like property taxes in many other states, is a fossilized artifact from the 19th century that faltered badly in the 20th century and failed spectacularly into the 21st century. . . . Now in the 21st century, talking about "reforming" the 19th century property tax really is just rearranging the deck chairs on the Titanic long after the iceberg has been hit. The property tax cannot be reformed— but it can be abolished. . . . Both sides really want the same thing here—a sane tax system in support of a stable revenue source for schools. Realizing that comity of interest is half the journey. Getting rid of the property tax means Wolf wins, the GOP wins—and most important of all, the long-suffering taxpayers of Pennsylvania win.

Homeownership has been the bedrock of the American Dream, but how can one achieve true homeownership when you are merely renting it from a school district? Eliminating the 1830s school property tax system and replacing it with a broader, fairer, and more equitable system will not only remove one of the biggest hurdles to achieving the American Dream; it will finally bring Pennsylvania's public education financing system into the twenty-first century.

If you do not believe us, come with us to our next town hall meeting. The constituents of the 29th Senatorial District would love to share their thoughts with you on this issue.

REFERENCES

Brunori, David, Richard Green, Michael Bell, Chanyung Choi, and Bing Yuan. 2006. "The Property Tax: Its Role and Significance in Funding State and Local Government Services." George Washington Institute of Public Policy Working Paper 27. Available at https://gwipp.gwu.edu/files/downloads/Working_Paper_027_PropertyTax.pdf.

Frantz, Jeff. 2014. "Pa. Granted Exceptions Allowing 164 School Districts to Raise Property Taxes More than 2.1 Percent." PennLive, May 2. Available at http://www.pennlive.com/midstate/index.ssf/2014/05/school_property_tax_act_1_exec.html.

Harper Polling. 2015. "Pennsylvania Statewide Poll." Available at http://harperpolling.com/polls/pennsylvania-statewide-poll-May-2015.

Independent Fiscal Office. 2012. "Analysis of HB 1776 and SB 1400 of 2012." Available at http://www.ptcc.us/pdf/ifo_property_tax_analysis_final_public_release_092512.pdf.

———. 2013. "Analysis of Proposal to Replace School Property Taxes: House Bill 76 and Senate Bill 76 of 2013." Available at http://www.ifo.state.pa.us/getfile.cfm?file=/Resources/Documents/SR2013-07.pdf.

Jennings, Marianne M. 2015. Real Estate Law. 11th ed. Boston: South-Western College.

Klinger, Jason. 2015. "Franklin and Marshall College Poll: Voters Support Medical Marijuana, Suspension of Death Penalty." June 18. Available at http://www.fandm.edu/news/latest-news/2015/06/18/franklin-marshall-college-poll-voters-support-medical-marijuana-suspension-of-death-penalty.

Madonna, G. Terry, and Michael L. Young. 2015. "Politically Uncorrected: RIP: The School Property Tax." PoliticsPA, March 24. Available at http://www.politicspa.com/politically-uncorrected-rip-the-school-property-tax/64671/.

Paul, James. 2015. "For Property Tax Relief, Give Voters Control." Commonwealth Foundation, November 13. Available at http://www.commonwealthfoundation.org/policyblog/detail/for-property-tax-relief-give-voters-control.

PHMC (Pennsylvania Historical and Museum Commission). 2015a. "Governor John Sydney Fine." August 26. Available at http://www.phmc.state.pa.us/portal/communities/governors/1951-2015/john-fine.html.

———. 2015b. "Governor Milton Jerrold Shapp." August 26. Available at http://www.phmc.state.pa.us/portal/communities/governors/1951-2015/milton-shapp.html.

Welton, Allison. 2015. "What Is Act 1 and How Did It Impact Property Taxes and School Funding?" *Keystone Crossroads*, June 22. Available at https://whyy.org/articles/what-is-act-1-and-how-did-it-impact-property-taxes-and-school-funding.

No, Keep the Property Tax: It Is the Best Tax for Schools

WILLIAM A. FISCHEL

The local property tax is an important part of funding public school systems in most states. It should be clear from the outset that it would be unwise to rely *entirely* on local taxes of any sort to fund a system of public schools. Some school districts contain a disproportionate number of poor and disadvantaged students, and such districts may need state assistance to give their children an adequate education. State mandates for special-needs students should also be accompanied by funds to pay for the additional expense. But aside from these exceptions, a properly and fairly administered system of local property taxation gives local voters—even those without school-age children—the right incentives to provide a thorough and efficient education.

The Basic Argument for Property Taxes

Here is the basic economic argument, which is a distillation of an important paper by Stanford's Caroline Hoxby (1999). Suppose that the local school superintendent, after consulting with principals and teachers, decides that the local high school needs to hire a group of teachers to teach in a newly created science, technology, engineering, and math (STEM) program. The voters are asked, directly in a referendum or indirectly through the school board, to finance this program with an increase in local property taxes.

In most communities, almost two-thirds of the voters will not have any direct interest in this because they have no children in schools (Kurban, Gallagher, and Persky 2012). An increase in property taxes will seem quite unpalatable to them. Considered in isolation, the tax increase would lower their home values (Do and Sirmans 1994).

But the superintendent points out that the STEM program will make the school district more attractive to families with school-age children. If the STEM program has this effect, it will raise the value of existing homes, which offsets the adverse effect of the property tax rise. This will apply even to voters who currently have no children in school, as long as their homes could be purchased by a family with children. If the offsetting rise is greater than the reduction caused by the tax, most voters would regard this as a desirable program. And from an economic standpoint, a net gain in the value of homes is an indicator that the program is efficient (Brueckner 1982).

It also follows that if there are no gains in home values from the program, or there are net losses, then the project is inefficient—the costs are registered as being less than the benefits. In this case, local property taxation provides incentives to reject boondoggles, since the net effect of the tax increase and the misconceived project will reduce home values. Local property taxation encourages local voters and their school boards to accept cost-effective projects and reject those that are losers in the eyes of home buyers.

That is the basic theory: Local property taxation subjects school spending to an effective benefit-cost test. The rest of this response briefly addresses evidence supporting this theory and adds a personal, Pennsylvania story to illustrate some overlooked advantages of local control.

Evidence from Economic Studies

The connection between school quality, property taxes, and local home values has been established in hundreds of studies, starting with a pioneering study of New Jersey cities by Wallace Oates (1969). Controlling for differences in location, size, and condition of the homes, Oates found that levels of school spending and property taxes affected—were "capitalized in"—the average value of houses in each community. He concluded that this provided a test for the efficiency of local decisions: "For an increase in property taxes unaccompanied by an increase in the output of local public services, the bulk of the rise in taxes will be capitalized in the form of reduced property values. On the other hand, if a community increases its tax rates and employs the receipts to improve its school system, the coefficients indicate that the increased benefits from the expenditure side of the budget will roughly offset (or perhaps even more than offset) the depressive effect of the higher tax rates on local property values" (Oates 1969, 968).

Studies since then have shown that voters are actually motivated by the connection between their property's value and the effects of the program (Sonstelie and Portney 1980). Homeowners are especially attuned to local public decisions because so much of their personal wealth is tied up in their homes (Fischel 2001). That local voters without children still support schools because of their beneficial effects on property values is well established (Hilber and Mayer 2009).

The discipline of local funding from property taxes and the encouragement it provides for local improvements explains why states that rely more on locally controlled property taxes have better schools. Thomas Husted and Larry Kenny (2000) found that states that reduced their reliance on local property taxes and increased state funds ended up with lower SAT scores and other indicators of overall educational quality. Joshua Hall (2007) concluded that Ohio districts that relied more heavily on property taxation performed better than those that got more money from the state. In my own review of a national study of SAT scores and state financing that ranked states from highest to lowest, I found that "in their top ten, none had more than 50 percent state funding. In the bottom ten, all but three states had more than 50 percent state funding" (Fischel 2002, 98).

The most dramatic and long-lasting experiment in school finance centralization—and rejection of local property tax financing—occurred in California in 1978. The state's voters approved Proposition 13, which cut most property taxes by more than half and left funding for the public school system almost entirely up to the state (O'Sullivan, Sexton, and Sheffrin 1995). Because of this tax revolt and because the state's court had severely constrained most local districts' ability to use local funds, California provides what economists call a "natural experiment" in school finance (Fischel 1989). It was "natural" in that Proposition 13 was sudden and unexpected by most state and local officials.

The results of this clean shift from local to state funding could not be more stark. Total spending declined, educational quality declined, and more-affluent families abandoned the system for private schools. Spending in the poorest districts was increased somewhat, but the gap in test scores between the affluent and poorer districts did not narrow at all (Brunner and Sonstelie 2006).

The local property tax also has the advantage of stability. In 2012 North Dakota voters were invited to eliminate the local property tax and substitute for it the state's swelling revenue from oil extraction (fracking) taxes (Davey 2012). The voters rejected this plan overwhelmingly, and it turned out to be a wise choice: Oil prices have since tumbled, and the state's school spending would have suffered as well. Voters may not love the property tax when considered in isolation, but they appear to realize that it is a more dependable source of revenue for services they care about.

Local Control: A Family Story

As an economist, I have emphasized the economic benefits providing for public education through local taxation. It has a long history in America, and it flourished during the period in which the American high school became the world leader in education (Goldin and Katz 2008). But local control of education through the property tax also has a less quantifiable aspect. Political scientists have mentioned the community-building aspects of local education finance. Alvin Sokolow observes, "In its traditional and relatively unlimited version, the property tax also contributes to representative democracy in two interconnected ways: (1) by giving locally elected officials the discretion to allocate resources in a fashion that represents community priorities; and (2) by engaging citizen-taxpayers directly in the actions of government" (1998, 182). I illustrate this with a family story.

I grew up in Lower Saucon Township, just outside of Bethlehem, Pennsylvania. The home my parents built and that my four siblings and I were raised in was then (in the 1950s) in a semirural area. The township schools were mostly remnants of one-room schools of the nineteenth century. Although they were not run as traditional one-room schools (all ages in one room), most of them were "doubled up" with two grades per room.

Despite the antiquarian appeal of the system, my parents were not too pleased with this arrangement, and my mother persuaded my dad to run for the school board. Despite a retiring personality and a complete absence of campaign activity, he won the election. He and other new board members helped consolidate the elementary schools into a new facility that offered a much better education (one grade per classroom). After twelve years on the board, he declined to run again. One of my proudest moments for my dad was when a delegation of neighbors arrived one evening to try to persuade him to run again.

I would be projecting too much on this to say that Dad was motivated by a concern for property values. He did own a fair amount of land and paid property taxes on it, but his chief concern was for the education of his children and that of other children in the township. The point I want to make is that this virtue does not run contrary to the financial incentives of a system that ties local schools to local property taxes. Had the state of Pennsylvania built and paid for all public schools from statewide taxes, it is more than possible that education would have progressed much more slowly.

Harvard economists Claudia Goldin and Larry Katz (2008) contrast the robust expansion of locally financed American education in the early twentieth century to the lagging European system, which was centrally financed. In Europe, advances in education standards had to wait until a national consensus was reached. In America, local school directors like my dad could seize the initiative and move the system ahead with only local approval. Such initiatives would be noticed by other districts, who would worry that they might fall behind (and have their home values decline). This benign competition results in more experimentation and keeps education in the forefront of public issues. The property tax as an institution helps make "doing good" match up with "doing well."

NOTE

This article was previously published as "*Commonwealth* Forum: Should Pennsylvania Abolish the Property Tax for Schools?" *Commonwealth* 18, no. 1 (2016). © 2016 The Pennsylvania Political Science Association. ISSN 2469-7672 (online). http://dx.doi.org/10.15367/cjppp.v18i1.81. All rights reserved.

REFERENCES

Brueckner, Jan K. 1982. "A Test for Allocative Efficiency in the Local Public Sector." *Journal of Public Economics* 19 (December): 311–321.

Brunner, Eric J., and Jon Sonstelie. 2006. "California's School Finance Reform: An Experiment in Fiscal Federalism." In *The Tiebout Model at Fifty*, edited by William A. Fischel, 55–93. Cambridge, MA: Lincoln Institute of Land Policy.

Davey, Monica. 2012. "North Dakota Considers Eliminating Property Tax." *New York Times*, June 11. Available at http://www.nytimes.com/2012/06/12/us/north-dakota-voters-consider-ending-property-tax.html.

Do, A. Quang, and C. F. Sirmans. 1994. "Residential Property Tax Capitalization: Discount Rate Evidence from California." *National Tax Journal* 47 (June): 341–348.

Fischel, William A. 1989. "Did Serrano Cause Proposition 13?" *National Tax Journal* 42 (December): 465–474.

———. 2001. *The Homevoter Hypothesis: How Home Values Influence Local Government Taxation, School Finance, and Land-Use Policies*. Cambridge, MA: Harvard University Press.

———. 2002. "School Finance Litigation and Property Tax Revolts: How Undermining Local Control Turns Voters Away from Public Education." In *Developments in School Finance, 1999–2000*, edited by William J. Fowler, Jr., 77–128. Washington, DC: National Center for Education Statistics.

Goldin, Claudia, and Lawrence Katz. 2008. *The Race between Education and Technology*. Cambridge, MA: Harvard University Press.

Hall, Joshua. 2007. "Local School Finance and Productive Efficiency: Evidence from Ohio." *Atlantic Economic Journal* 35 (September): 289–301.

Hilber, Christian A. L., and Christopher Mayer. 2009. "Why Do Households without Children Support Local Public Schools? Linking House Price Capitalization to School Spending." *Journal of Urban Economics* 65 (January): 74–90.

Hoxby, Caroline M. 1999. "The Productivity of Schools and Other Local Public Goods Producers." *Journal of Public Economics* 74 (October): 1–30.

Husted, Thomas A., and Lawrence W. Kenny. 2000. "Evidence on the Impact of State Government on Primary and Secondary Education and the Equity-Efficiency Trade-Off." *Journal of Law and Economics* 43 (April): 285–308.

Kurban, Haydar, Ryan M. Gallagher, and Joseph J. Persky. 2012. "Estimating Local Redistribution through Property-Tax-Funded Public School Systems." *National Tax Journal* 65 (September): 629–652.

Oates, Wallace E. 1969. "The Effects of Property Taxes and Local Public Spending on Property Values: An Empirical Study of Tax Capitalization and the Tiebout Hypothesis." *Journal of Political Economy* 77 (November–December): 957–971.

O'Sullivan, Arthur, Terri A. Sexton, and Steven M. Sheffrin. 1995. *Property Taxes and Tax Revolts: The Legacy of Proposition 13*. New York: Cambridge University Press.

Sokolow, Alvin D. 1998. "The Changing Property Tax and State-Local Relations." *Publius: The Journal of Federalism* 28 (January): 165–187.

Sonstelie, Jon C., and Paul R. Portney. 1980. "Take the Money and Run: A Theory of Voting in Local Referenda." *Journal of Urban Economics* 8 (September): 187–195.

Discussion Questions

1. What would be the benefits of eliminating the property tax in Pennsylvania? Who would the change benefit the most?

2. What sources of revenue would replace the property tax if it were eliminated? Why do Argall and Hopcraft argue that these funding mechanisms would be better for education?

3. Why does Fischel argue that the property tax is the best way to fund education?

4. How can Fischel look at the same funding system as Argall and Hopcraft and reach a completely different conclusion?

5. Who should be most responsible for funding education in Pennsylvania? The state or local governments?

Chapter 4
Energy Policy

Leaving Money on the Table

Pennsylvania Exceptionalism in Resisting Energy Severance Taxes

RACHEL L. HAMPTON
BARRY G. RABE

Nearly all energy-producing states elect to adopt and sustain a tax on the extraction of their oil and gas resources through so-called severance taxes, generating significant revenue for general as well as specialized state funds. Political support for such taxes generally crosses party lines and endures across multiple partisan shifts in the political control of a state. This reflects numerous features that tend to make these taxes quite popular and durable across election cycles. This long-standing pattern, however, faces one major exception: Pennsylvania's enduring reluctance to follow the path of other major energy-producing states and adopt such a tax. This article explores what it deems "Pennsylvania exceptionalism" as it seeks to address the issue of why one leading energy-producing state would refrain from tax adoption in contrast to every other such state. It places particular emphasis on the past decade, in which natural gas in shale deposits has triggered a dramatic expansion of production in Pennsylvania and ongoing political controversy over whether or not a severance tax should be adopted.

Energy production in the United States is not a new phenomenon. Large-scale oil drilling formally began before the Civil War in Pennsylvania and expanded to many other states by the turn of the twentieth century, alongside extensive extraction of coal and natural gas. By 1902, one oil well in Spindletop, Texas, had produced over 17 million barrels of oil, and the state has since remained a leading producer of both oil and natural gas. Texas and many other energy-producing states moved fairly rapidly to establish some tax on output, in some cases relying on this as a major revenue source. By the 1990s, though, many states assumed that their oil and gas production would plummet as supplies declined, likely leading to reduced reliance on severance tax revenue in the future.

The mid-2000s, however, saw the development of hydraulic fracturing and horizontal drilling techniques that allowed many states to tap into previously unavailable resources, such as oil and natural gas found in shale deposits. In some cases, states with long energy extraction histories got a new lease on life as major energy producers. North Dakota, for instance, experienced a boom of oil extraction starting around 2006. Such development created significant growth in the state's economy as its gross domestic product rose and unemployment rates dropped. The state's population grew for the first time in decades (Rabe and Hampton 2016), with particularly significant growth in localities near shale development. Other states, such as Colorado, Oklahoma, and Texas, also fit this pattern. But perhaps no state has stood out as has Pennsylvania in this new era of energy production. The state assumed a prominent role in the debate over hydraulic fracturing as it pursued its substantial natural gas deposits embedded in the Marcellus Shale. The state also experienced a significant economic boom related to expanded fracking, while it gained national notoriety over controversies related to the practice, including possible risks to water, land, air, and public health. In many respects, Pennsylvania emerged as a leading face of hydraulic fracturing, reflected in popular films and considerable media attention.

But despite changes in energy production throughout the United States, many states that engaged in the industry preserved the status quo, especially regarding their fiscal regimes (Rabe and Hampton 2015). More specifically, states mostly maintained existing taxes on the extraction of their oil and gas resources. These severance taxes are not a foreign concept to production states; in fact, they are the norm for nearly all petro-states in the United States, except Pennsylvania. Such broad acceptance of these taxes makes it arguably more intriguing that a "poster child" of the hydraulic fracturing movement does not have one.

This article explores the status of severance taxation in the United States. It describes these taxes and considers why most states—including all other major oil and gas producers—employ them. It further focuses briefly on their structure and use, while also touching on any perceived benefits and consequences, before turning to the question of why only one state has not enacted such a tax.

In particular, this article responds to the question of why Pennsylvania, a major player in the U.S. energy sphere, has failed to go where virtually every other oil- and gas-producing state has gone before in neglecting to enact a severance tax. It notes that the state's exceptionalism—its failure to implement a severance tax—spans the three governorships that have existed during the time of increased natural gas production in the state starting in the mid-2000s. This article also addresses the consequences of such a decision, including direct defiance of public support for a severance tax and a loss of realizing potential revenues from it during difficult fiscal times in Pennsylvania.

Severance Taxes

At its core, a severance tax is a tax on the extraction of a nonrenewable natural resource like timber, uranium, or coal. But most significant in terms of total revenue, severance taxes are levied on the extraction of oil and natural gas. Such taxes are levied in some form in thirty-eight states, and, of the top fifteen oil- and gas-producing states, all employ a severance tax except Pennsylvania (see Table 4.1).

Severance taxes are also levied in states regardless of partisan control of state government, and the taxes have survived through the exchanging of party control. Alaska has had a long-standing severance tax amid numerous Republican governors and legislatures as well as occasional Democratic leaders. North Dakota political leanings have similarly been relatively

TABLE 4.1 TOP OIL- AND GAS-PRODUCING STATES

Top oil-producing states	Severance tax?	Top natural gas–producing states	Severance tax?
Texas	Yes	Texas	Yes
North Dakota	Yes	Pennsylvania	No
California	Yes	Oklahoma	Yes
Alaska	Yes	Louisiana	Yes
Oklahoma	Yes	Wyoming	Yes
New Mexico	Yes	Colorado	Yes
Colorado	Yes	New Mexico	Yes
Wyoming	Yes	Arkansas	Yes
Louisiana	Yes	West Virginia	Yes
Kansas	Yes	Ohio	Yes
Utah	Yes	Utah	Yes
Ohio	Yes	Alaska	Yes
Montana	Yes	North Dakota	Yes
Mississippi	Yes	Kansas	Yes
Illinois	Yes	California	Yes

Sources: U.S. Energy Information Administration 2016; U.S. Energy Information Administration 2014a; National Conference of State Legislatures, n.d.

conservative, with Republican domination of both executive and legislative branches during much of recent decades. North Dakota has two overlapping taxes, adopted in 1953 by the legislature and another adopted in 1980 via ballot proposition and constitutional amendment. During Republican administrations, both North Dakota and Alaska also pursued constitutionally backed trust funds that allow each state to set aside tax revenues for permanent protection. Texas has maintained its severance taxes across eras of Republican, Democratic, and split-party government control, as has been the case in Arkansas, Colorado, Louisiana, New Mexico, and West Virginia, among others.

State oil and gas severance taxes are diverse in scope and form. They are referred to not only as severance taxes but also as production or conservation taxes, based either on the market value of the resource or the volume produced. These taxes range from rates that may be considered lower, like 1.3 percent of value, as is the case in Mississippi,[1] to rates as great as 10 percent of production value of oil, as in North Dakota. Of course it is misleading to consider only the rate of value or volume taxed because states also employ certain tax structures that include incentives and deductions that may lower the effective tax rate. Thus, for example, the Alaskan severance tax appears high in its net rate (35 percent), but this is deceptive, given the way it actually applies the tax (on net as opposed to gross value), and given its generous program of tax credits, which in recent years has exceeded total tax revenue.

Political Attractiveness of Severance Taxes

Almost every major energy-producing state employs a severance tax. But why would so many states adopt such a tax, given the general controversy surrounding taxation and tremendous variation in how states establish taxes to address their fiscal needs? While many other taxes face almost guaranteed opposition, as demonstrated by the divisive state debates over proposed gasoline excise tax increases and carbon tax adoption, the severance tax is almost universally accepted. There seems to be a political agreement across the American states—with few exceptions—that if you extract oil or gas, you put a tax on what is removed from below the surface of the ground. In subsequent sections, we explain the political appeal of these taxes.

Early Precedents

A number of states have had severance taxes for some time. In many instances, this began before multiple states and nations produced much oil and gas, thereby giving them considerable latitude in imposing a tax on a commodity that was in great demand amid uncertain supply options. In Texas, for instance, the severance tax on oil was adopted in 1907, and it established an early and visible model that could be replicated as neighboring states or states in other regions tapped their own fossil fuel deposits in subsequent decades. Indeed, the Texas precedent demonstrated that a severance tax was politically feasible and quite popular. It also established a precedent to set aside some revenues for specific programs and build a constituency through trust funds for elementary, secondary, and higher education, setting the stage for diffusion of these ideas across many states.

Easy Money and Tax Displacement

The most obvious reason a state might levy a tax on the extraction of oil and gas is for the considerable revenue that it might generate. Severance taxes are generally straightforward to adopt and implement, concentrated on points of production from drilling, so they can be fairly simple in their design and operation and do not require creation of a major staff to implement. More-over, they offer the possibility of generating significant funds for a state that could substitute these revenues for other taxes, perhaps allowing mainte-nance of lower rates for highly unpopular taxes on income or sales. States have several options in setting up these taxes, whereby they can tax either the market value of the oil and gas that is extracted, the volume that is pro-duced, or some combination of these two (Brown 2013).

Revenues from severance taxes can be quite large in the states that pro-duce significant amounts of oil and gas (see Table 4.2). For North Dakota, severance tax collections amounted to over $3 billion in 2014. That same year, severance tax collections generated over $2 billion for Alaska and $6 billion for Texas. Standing alone, these revenues are significant, but they are also important in context; many oil- and gas-producing states rely on sever-ance taxes to make up a significant portion of their total state tax revenue. In North Dakota, that $3 billion accounted for over 50 percent of the state's total tax collection. In Alaska, its severance tax made up over 70 percent of the state's total tax collection, while the percentage share in Texas was only 10 percent.

These revenues can fluctuate, given boom-and-bust cycles in production and commodity prices, as is further reflected in Table 4.2. However, sever-ance taxes have allowed some states to not only suppress rates of other taxes but also avoid adoption of contentious taxes in some cases as long as they provide some ongoing revenue. Neither Alaska nor Wyoming, for example, have an income tax and have generally produced sufficient revenue from energy extraction taxes to keep an income tax off their state agendas.

Opportunity to Earmark Revenue and Build a Constituency

Beyond generating substantial revenues for a state, severance taxes enable states to create and maintain funds directed to specific purposes such as education, or addressing environmental concerns tied to production. Most prominently, several oil- and gas-producing states allocate severance tax

TABLE 4.2 STATE SEVERANCE COLLECTIONS BY YEAR, 2005–2015 (CURRENT DOLLARS, THOUSANDS)

State	2005	2006	2007	2008	2009	2010	2011	2012	2013	2014	2015
Alabama	144,813	182,778	144,306	197,581	115,374	90,538	115,975	116,467	119,424	115,437	79,235
Alaska	925,699	1,274,642	2,436,660	6,939,040	3,829,564	3,355,049	4,238,789	5,787,360	4,016,966	2,456,212	105,233
Arizona	26,338	40,494	43,560	43,757	19,481	33,372	40,237	40,578	29,829	26,190	24,862
Arkansas	18,565	22,225	21,579	27,820	33,547	65,147	79,656	82,770	80,862	108,511	104,383
California	14,251	16,048	31,526	31,599	27,105	24,409	31,879	37,112	37,732	38,686	69,960
Colorado	145,114	212,753	136,888	151,474	285,015	71,436	146,690	175,090	147,732	245,087	292,683
Idaho	2,488	2,897	6,649	6,758	4,952	6,730	7,787	8,309	6,224	6,004	6,143
Kansas	117,424	149,676	132,281	168,696	142,658	102,878	122,152	132,907	73,806	124,883	148,077
Kentucky	228,848	281,581	275,313	293,334	355,985	317,146	342,320	346,050	269,786	241,989	220,613
Louisiana	711,766	716,396	904,164	1,035,695	911,433	758,469	729,260	885,982	834,116	862,150	731,330
Michigan	68,055	90,956	81,874	113,506	59,343	57,424	80,423	64,285	70,087	73,488	36,883
Minnesota	32,348	28,022	34,591	31,821	45,820	23,290	27,618	46,370	54,343	42,062	58,931
Mississippi	66,275	89,910	81,814	135,248	113,762	90,832	112,326	116,378	104,692	91,059	78,726
Montana	181,201	247,385	264,740	347,221	349,714	253,649	278,372	305,617	282,356	305,614	269,287
Nebraska	2,560	2,820	2,499	4,968	4,718	3,473	4,440	5,355	4,064	6,762	5,282

Nevada	39,691	44,526	62,178	74,130	145,450	182,752	272,240	303,038	290,448	111,395	121,604
New Mexico	712,539	923,304	942,354	625,938	931,832	654,752	804,586	768,106	713,998	1,066,343	1,001,741
North Dakota	262,339	346,672	391,337	791,692	827,417	1,136,553	1,883,816	3,187,112	2,457,530	3,293,053	2,849,324
Ohio	7,920	7,675	7,015	9,420	11,052	10,550	11,197	10,182	12,308	10,194	22,981
Oklahoma	762,506	1,059,919	942,148	1,184,765	1,067,182	743,686	830,662	848,947	515,981	679,406	556,546
Oregon	12,148	12,032	12,513	11,815	13,038	12,742	13,199	14,119	23,305	23,424	24,149
Pennsylvania	—	—	—	—	—	—	—	—	—	—	—
Texas	2,347,512	3,216,387	2,762,940	4,124,428	2,338,481	1,737,136	2,677,604	3,655,582	4,647,848	6,014,350	4,005,371
Utah	73,434	99,517	101,539	106,060	102,121	89,162	101,665	107,075	112,050	155,743	130,212
Washington	43,034	48,446	48,727	44,038	29,681	20,905	26,706	36,302	38,656	41,950	43,893
West Virginia	307,265	336,387	328,320	347,592	376,677	417,230	585,992	626,203	608,371	681,824	668,880
Wyoming	805,613	1,043,160	803,632	883,786	1,197,540	721,002	1,044,150	968,525	867,933	883,025	883,913
United States	8,131,573	10,567,667	11,063,600	17,808,329	13,438,451	11,071,812	14,692,766	18,752,729	16,493,248	17,780,808	12,603,072

Sources: National Conference of State Legislatures, n.d.; Richardson 2005; U.S. Census Bureau, n.d.

Note: Revenues include all types of severance taxes, not just oil and gas exclusively. U.S. Census Bureau data reflect the fact that severance taxes are taxes on the extraction of natural resources. Severance taxes may be applied to, among other resources, fisheries, coal, timber, uranium, and iron ore, in addition to oil and gas. Despite these other severance taxes, however, states that produce oil and gas receive the vast majority of severance tax collections. While Pennsylvania does not levy a severance tax on natural gas, oil, or coal, it does have what is called an "impact fee," as discussed later in this article. The impact fee collections in 2011–2015 were (in thousands) 204, 210; 202, 472; 225, 752; 223, 500; and 187, 712, far below what most other high-production states generate through severance taxes. See Act 13 Public Utility Commission, n.d.

revenues to what are known as trust—or permanent—funds, following on the pioneering effort in Texas from the early twentieth century. These funds are traditionally protected by state constitutions and thus are designed to feature greater longevity than other state funds created only through statute (Rabe and Hampton 2016). States that use trusts funds include Texas, New Mexico, Wyoming, Montana, Alaska, and, most recently, North Dakota, Utah, and West Virginia. As a result of these funds, oil- and gas-producing states may be able to better protect themselves against any boom-or-bust cycles that traditionally plague petro-states (Ross 2012).

This type of earmarking revenue from a specific tax can also create the opportunity for a state government to build a supportive political constituency through the targeted allocation of those funds. This linkage may foster considerable durability of the tax, given the recognition that its reduction or elimination could endanger a popular public benefit connected to the tax.[2] Alaska stands out as a prime example. After realizing how quickly any windfall from oil production would be depleted, Alaskan governor Jay Hammond pushed for a trust fund that was ultimately adopted through constitutional amendment in 1976 (Groh and Erickson 2012). To further protect the fund, Hammond created the Alaskan dividend system whereby citizens of Alaska are sent a check—sometimes in amounts as high as $2,000—from the Permanent Fund earnings each year (Moss 2012). Because of this allocation, citizens of Alaska have kept their eyes riveted on both the fund and the severance tax revenues that are allocated toward the fund, as evinced in debates that emerged starting in the mid-2000s. For decades, any suggestion of reduced tax rates has been linked in the public mind with a possible loss of dividend revenue and has proven to be extremely controversial. Other states have earmarked severance tax funds for popular programs, such as Wyoming's linkage with a significant scholarship program named after a popular former governor for students pursuing higher education at public institutions within the state.

Burden Shifting

Severance taxes are also attractive to energy-producing states because the burden of the tax is often passed along the production chain to out-of-state consumers (Mieszkowski and Soligo 2012). Many top-producing states— such as Alaska, Louisiana, Montana, Oklahoma, Wyoming, and North Dakota—are relatively low consuming states, meaning that more than 95 percent of their production is ultimately exported. Even major consuming states such as Texas and Pennsylvania export large amounts of the energy that they produce (U.S. Energy Information Administration 2014b). Severance taxes may thus be a relatively easy sell to constituents who might otherwise worry about the possible impact of a tax that is primarily applied to their consumption of energy.

This enables legislative supporters of a severance tax to claim political credit for imposing a cost on the removal of a natural resource that cannot be restored after use while knowing that most of the burden of any cost on consumption will be borne in other states or nations. Producing states thus face few political consequences from constituents about imposing price increases and also gain a possible political benefit by creating ways to spend the revenues for popular programs that they can sustain over time. There may well be parallels between the political attractiveness of severance taxes and other taxes that essentially export the costs, such as taxes imposed on vacations or business travel through hotel bills or rental cars. Dick Cheney recognized this as he defended high severance taxes while serving as Wyoming's representative in Congress during the 1970s (Powers 1982).

Political Constraints on Severance Taxes

The nearly unanimous rate of severance tax adoption among oil- and gas-producing states underscores the multiple factors that make them politically attractive despite their partisan control or geographic region. Their high political feasibility also translates into durability across various stages of implementation and multiple shifts of political leadership. No state has ever repealed an oil or gas severance tax that has been adopted, and relatively few have undertaken major rate reductions after initial adoption (Rabe and Hampton 2015). This has even endured into the shale era, when overall production has soared and states might be expected to consider repeal or rate reduction to lure or retain drilling within their boundaries, given increasing interstate competition to sustain and expand production.

Nonetheless, the shale era does underscore some of the challenges to sustaining or expanding severance taxes, given the possibility that such a tax might discourage industry from seeking further production in the state that employs the tax (Harrison 2006). This has led to some speculation that drilling firms might play one state against others in search of the lowest possible tax rates, along with the easiest paths to regulatory compliance, in making their location and investment decisions. Such arguments appeared, for example, in the Alaskan debates over its severance taxes during the last decade. State political leaders, including Republican governor Sean Parnell, expressed concern that Alaska would be outcompeted by states, like North Dakota, if its tax remained high, particularly given the relatively high cost of launching and sustaining drilling operations in remote Alaska and then moving its products to market. This resulted in significant tax reductions in 2013, though these proved highly controversial and contributed to Parnell's reelection defeat in 2014. But there is little evidence that states have pursued less-aggressive taxes in the shale era (Rabe and Hampton 2015), and some studies suggest that arguments claiming that reducing severance taxes will result in increased industry investment and production have little empirical foundation (Kunce 2003).

Severance taxes also threaten possible support to political officials from the oil and gas industry and their employees. States with a dominant energy-producing culture may compel politicians to curry favor with industry in search of possible campaign support or even employment after elected careers have ended or continue for part-time legislators. The questions of possible capture of state officials by local energy industries endure, albeit without much empirical evidence that this can block initial severance tax adoption, reverse such policies once created, or lead to significant statutory rate reductions over time. Instead, industry influence may be subtler, reflected in expanded state efforts to provide tax credits and economic development incentives or more flexible approaches to regulatory compliance. Overall, the political upside of severance taxes continues to outweigh the negatives, at least in the vast majority of state cases to date.

Pennsylvania Exceptionalism

This overall pattern of high political feasibility for severance taxes makes the Pennsylvania case unique and worthy of extended consideration, given its unique standing among oil- and gas-producing states as averse to such taxes. Since the Drake Well was first drilled in Pennsylvania in 1859 (Wile 2012; Yergin 2011), the state has been a major energy producer, including coal, oil, and natural gas, across many decades, with operations in many of the state's sixty-seven counties. While the state has also long extracted natural gas, and has used horizontal drilling techniques since 2003, it generally assumed that it was phasing out fossil fuel production in the late 1990s and early 2000s and increasingly turned toward development of renewables through regulatory mandates and tax incentives (Rabe 2007). It was not until around 2009 that drilling activity accelerated markedly (U.S. Energy Information Administration 2017a, 2017b), allowing the state to tap into the bountiful Marcellus Shale.

Since that time, the landscape and economic geography of Pennsylvania have shifted considerably, given the advent of the shale era and Pennsylvania's emergence as the second-largest natural gas–producing state, surpassed only by Texas. The number of producing gas wells in Pennsylvania increased from 57,346 in 2009 to over 70,000 in 2014, and total volume of natural gas production soared during these years (see Table 4.3). The oil and gas industry in Pennsylvania also saw substantial growth in both employment and wages. Employment in the oil and gas industry went from 5,829 in 2007 to 20,943 in 2012. The average annual pay in that same industry went from $60,870 in 2007 to $82,974 in 2012 (U.S. Bureau of Labor Statistics 2014). Pittsburgh was increasingly declared as the hub of industrial leadership of this expanding

TABLE 4.3 PENNSYLVANIA NATURAL GAS GROSS
WITHDRAWALS

Year	Natural gas gross withdrawal (million cubic feet)
2000	150,000
2001	130,853
2002	157,800
2003	159,827
2004	197,217
2005	168,501
2006	175,950
2007	182,227
2008	198,295
2009	273,869
2010	572,902
2011	1,310,592
2012	2,256,696
2013	3,258,042
2014	4,214,643
2015	4,768,848

Source: U.S. Energy Information Administration 2017b.

industry, and large industry-wide advocacy groups began to form in this shale play, such as the Marcellus Shale Coalition. Such regional organizations also included participation by Ohio and West Virginia firms, although Pennsylvania continued to dominate this activity, particularly after New York imposed an extended moratorium on fracking in 2015 after years of temporary halts due to environmental opposition. Industry and state government officials have likened Pennsylvania to a burgeoning natural gas superpower, potentially luring refineries and manufacturing firms eager to have proximity to abundant natural gas supplies.

The dramatic increase in production of natural gas in the state tied to hydraulic fracturing has entailed more gas production and jobs but also increased environmental risks to air quality and groundwater. Additionally, the state may face impacts from the use of diesel, forest disruption from pipeline construction, and methane leakage. A Pennsylvania State University study in 2016, for instance, found that the cost of environmental impacts would range from $162,000 to $755,000 per well, although it ultimately concluded that the economic benefits to the state from drilling in the Marcellus Shale would exceed any known environmental impacts (Considine, Considine, and Watson 2016).

Amid all of this production and growth—and environmental impact—however, the state has sustained its unique status as the only state that produces oil and gas but applies no severance tax to that extraction. This decision cannot be explained by any historic aversion to taxation, reflected in relatively high rates of sales and personal income taxes over an extended time. The state has shifted back and forth between various forms of Republican and Democratic control, although it routinely voted for Democratic presidential candidates between 1988 and 2012. It has not adopted any constitutional amendments, contrary to other states, to ban or restrict various forms of taxation and has generally ranked toward the middle of the pack among states according to their commitment to environmental protection (Rabe 2016b).

The uniqueness of the Pennsylvania system and its sustained opposition to a severance tax cannot be overemphasized. A quick comparison to the state's shale neighbors who are both heavily involved in energy production—West Virginia and Ohio—bolsters this idea that Pennsylvania has truly deviated from the American state norm on this issue: West Virginia and Ohio both levy severance taxes. West Virginia overcame aggressive coal industry opposition to a severance tax in the 1950s and subsequently established such taxes for oil and natural gas; it has also created a trust fund called the West Virginia Fund, although it receives a far smaller portion of state tax proceeds than most other trust funds, including those in Alaska, North Dakota, and Texas (Rabe and Hampton 2016). Ohio adopted a Resource Severance Tax on oil, natural gas, salt, and a variety of minerals in 1972. Consequently, Pennsylvania presumably has political and economic space to adopt some version of a tax without triggering huge losses of development to neighboring jurisdictions. Nonetheless, it remains the exceptional American case throughout the shale era. To understand this costly decision requires exploration into the political arena in which these decisions were made.

Severance Tax Aversion across Three Shale-Era Governorships

Pennsylvania's decision to refrain from a severance tax illustrates one state government option in the politics of economic development, whereby a state attempts to foster economic growth in a particular sector by either reducing or eliminating specific costs imposed on an industry through some form of taxation. The state has long struggled politically with boom-and-bust cycles that reflect its long-standing role as a major producer of fossil fuel energy alongside major development of manufacturing steel and other energy-intensive industries. During periods of decline in these areas, Pennsylvania has actively explored a wide range of development strategies that either would reverse these patterns of contractions or promote alternative forms of economic development, as has been the case in many other states (Brace 1993; Eisinger 1989; Hansen 1989). This has occurred across multiple decades amid various patterns of partisan control of state government.

One cornerstone of these various Pennsylvania economic development efforts has been attempting to promote as much fossil fuel development as possible by rejecting proposals to tax extraction. Some severance tax opponents contend that relatively high rates of corporate income and other taxes that cut across various industries may already impose significant tax burdens on energy-producing industries. This reflects a desire to use broader-based taxes in the state but also to use a nonseverance tax strategy to signal to the energy sector a strong desire to sustain legacy production as long as possible. This then pivoted toward a desire to sustain an anti-tax approach to promote expanded production once the shale era opened a possible path toward a return to national leadership in natural gas output and related use. In either instance, the absence of a severance tax has been seen as maximizing potential development of the resource.

However, the continuation of this policy during the past decade coincided with a growing partisan divide on the question of whether Pennsylvania should join the ranks of all other gas- and oil-producing states and adopt a severance tax. The governorships of Edward Rendell (Democrat, 2003–2011), Tom Corbett (Republican, 2011–2015), and Tom Wolf (Democrat, 2015–2019) have featured high-decibel and near-constant state political debate over the severance tax question, usually reflecting major partisan divides between anti-tax Republicans and pro-tax Democrats. This alignment varied somewhat, linked in part to whether or not drilling was occurring in a particular legislative district. But this was quite limited and leaves partisan affiliation as the best predictor of political response to numerous proposals to adopt some form of a severance tax.

Divided Partisan Control in the Rendell Era

This section reviews the Pennsylvanian odyssey of debating but rejecting severance taxes during this period, beginning with the Rendell era. First elected in 2003, Rendell was the first Pennsylvania governor to see the reemergence of a surge in shale gas production in the state. Rendell supported drilling but also endorsed a severance tax. He embraced legislation that would create a 5 percent tax on the extraction of natural gas and oil, though most Pennsylvania fossil fuel production involved only the former. This proposal was generally supported by Democrats in the legislature while it was strongly opposed by most Republicans. The Republican Party (GOP) retained control of the Senate throughout Rendell's entire governorship, a pattern that continued through the Corbett and Wolf administrations. In turn, the House was held by Republicans in 2005–2006 and then later between 2011 and 2016.

The highly partisan divide over a severance tax proposal was also linked to controversy over how to develop a regulatory system to oversee this new and expanding form of energy extraction (Rabe and Borick 2013). Rendell argued that other states had successfully adopted and maintained such a tax without harming production and that such a tax in Pennsylvania could help diversify the state's base of resources, which had been severely strained by the Great Recession. But in 2010, the governor pronounced the severance tax plan dead after protracted legislative debate. "It is irresponsible for Senate and House Republicans to refuse to compromise and simply turn their backs on these negotiations after days and weeks and months of work," he said. "Their clear unwillingness to change their previous proposal or to resolve differences with the House Democrats and with my administration makes it obvious that they have killed the severance tax in this legislative session" (Swift 2010). In response, Republican officials countered that any tax adopted during the formative period of shale development and expansion could drive energy extraction investment to other jurisdictions, particularly given the expanding set of drilling options as shale supply discoveries continued to expand around the nation and beyond. Some Republicans opposed a tax under any circumstances whereas others argued that it should be tabled during this period of rapid expansion but possibly be revisited in the future after development matured.

Unified Republican Control in the Corbett Era and the Emergence of the Impact Fee

Term-limited Rendell did not get the chance to further pursue his severance tax vision; Republican Tom Corbett was elected as his successor in 2010, with unified Republican control of the governorship and both legislative chambers during his single term. Having aligned himself heavily with the gas industry during his election and in earlier stages of his political career as attorney general, including substantial campaign donations, Corbett pushed aggressively for shale gas development as a centerpiece of a way to transform the Pennsylvania economy. In his first budget message as governor, in 2011, he said, "Let's make Pennsylvania the hub of this [drilling] boom. Just as the oil companies decided to headquarter in one of a dozen states with oil, let's make Pennsylvania the Texas of the natural gas boom. I'm determined that Pennsylvania not lose this moment. We have the chance to get it right the first time, the chance to grow our way out of hard days" ("Text" 2011). Corbett made no bones about his view that severance tax adoption was "un-American" and could destroy any prospect of Pennsylvania realizing its potential as a natural gas powerhouse (Rabe and Borick 2013, 329).

Corbett's plan to transform Pennsylvania into a natural gas superpower involved a multipart strategy that emerged in part from an advisory commission he convened early in his governorship. This would ultimately lead to legislation known as the Unconventional Gas Well Impact Fee Act (or Act 13), signed into law by Corbett in February 2012 after legislative votes that fell largely along partisan lines. The legislation represented one of the first efforts by any state to address numerous aspects of shale governance through one comprehensive statute, as many states had been relying primarily on earlier regulatory and tax policies applied to conventional drilling or piecemeal reforms of earlier policies (Rabe and Borick 2013). It included many new regulatory provisions, although it received national attention primarily for two reasons.

First, it formally expanded state government authority over numerous aspects of hydraulic fracturing, including many types of land-use decisions that might otherwise fall under local government control. This included such issues as restricting well site operating hours, limiting noise around drilling operations, and establishing conditions for screening and fencing around sites, even in cases where drilling took place near residential areas or small businesses. Pennsylvania had a long-standing tradition of substantial state deference to local authorities in most areas of zoning and land-use planning, including many issues linked to expansion of drilling. But Act 13 formally shifted that control to state authorities, with various responsibilities allocated to the Pennsylvania Department of Environmental Protection and related state agencies that generally did not regulate local land use. This represented a form of preemption designed to limit local resistance to expanded drilling, an issue that has also emerged in many other states where local and state views have clashed (Rice 2016). This was intended to make it as straightforward as possible for gas extraction proposals to secure needed permits and approvals to move ahead with new drilling operations. Act 13 would, however, ultimately produce prolonged litigation that led to a historic reversal in a 2013 State Supreme Court case, *Robinson Township v. Commonwealth of Pennsylvania* (2012), that would produce much subsequent uncertainty about the boundary of state and local roles that continued through 2016.

Second, Corbett attempted to honor his no-severance-tax pledge that had been a core part of his campaign with an alternative mechanism of an impact fee. This would represent the imposition of some annual costs on each drilling site during the early years of operation, set as a fixed annual fee rather than as a percentage of gross value of produced natural gas. It would decline over time despite the productivity of the well, and all revenue would be allocated through a formula to various state agencies and local governments where drilling would occur. The animating principle was that this was not a tax but rather a fee to help governments mitigate some of the "impacts" of shale development. A further political attraction was that this fee was likely to be set at a very low level when translated into a percentage of produced natural gas value. It thereby set a de facto rate that was far lower than most state severance taxes at its peak and would both decline and then disappear entirely over time, unlike all existing state severance taxes that remained in force over the full lifetime of production.

The impact fee plan also used revenue allocation as a way to build local government support for the fee, potentially serving to create a loyal political constituency that might then oppose any future severance tax. Most severance taxes allocate revenues on a statewide basis rather than concentrate them on jurisdictions where drilling occurred. In the case of the impact fee, the only Pennsylvania counties, municipalities, and townships that were eligible for any potential revenue were those that hosted drilling operations. The portions of impact fee revenue that would be returned to localities would be allocated on the basis of energy production. Local governments were able to use impact fee funds on a wide range of programs, including road repair and emergency services that were in some way linked to drilling (Weber and Harleman 2015).

Local governments, however, would have to make the political decision to actually authorize such a fee rather than the state, with the legislation simply giving them this option and avoiding any direct state responsibility for the levy. Therefore, proponents framed this as lacking state political fingerprints, with the fee approval decision made locally. If localities went forward with the impact fee, the state would then collect the revenue but make local allocation contingent on full local compliance with state regulatory

Figure 4.1 Marcellus Shale protest. *(Source: Marcellus Protest.)*

provisions, including restraint from any local efforts to add regulatory burdens linked to drilling that violated Act 13's state preemption provisions. This clause was applied almost immediately, with seven local jurisdictions in 2012 failing to receive any impact fee revenue because of state interpretation of some form of noncompliance. These jurisdictions alleged heavy-handed state government oversight, but they had no recourse despite having levied the impact fee within their boundaries.

The impact fee adoption did not quash subsequent debate over severance taxation. The fee did sustain Republican support in general, albeit with exceptions in some cases where GOP legislators represented districts without shale activity and thereby received relatively little revenue related to drilling in the state. It did little to deter Democratic support for a tax, most intensively in areas of the southeastern and south-central portions of Pennsylvania that lacked shale and received limited revenue transfer from the fee to localities. Nonetheless, there was never a serious effort to put a severance tax onto the legislative agenda for the balance of Corbett's term in office. This reflected unified Republican political control of state government and the argument of party leadership that a nontax fee was more than sufficient to cover any adverse impacts of natural gas drilling in the state while being sufficiently modest to give Pennsylvania energy producers a financial edge versus alternative state drilling venues.

Return to Divided Control in the Wolf Era

Corbett made Act 13 and his staunch support for expanded natural gas extraction a cornerstone of his 2014 reelection bid. All of the prominent candidates for the Democratic nomination endorsed some form of a severance tax, including eventual nominee Tom Wolf, who promised if elected to support a severance tax that he said could raise up to $1 billion annually (Cocklin 2014a, 2014b, 2015). The severance tax issue figured prominently in campaign advertising and candidate debates. In one exchange, Corbett emphasized that the impact fee was already bringing in revenue to state and local governments and that higher taxes would deter future energy investment. Wolf argued, "We have a God-given resource lying beneath our feet; we need to do everything in our power to make sure this benefits Pennsylvania. My severance tax is not meant to kill the goose that's laying the golden egg. I'm just saying, let's share some of that gold with the people of Pennsylvania" (Bravender 2014). Wolf won a decisive victory over Corbett by a 55 percent to 45 percent margin, which seemed likely to propel pursuit of severance tax adoption. However, Wolf had no measurable electoral coattails, as both chambers of the legislature remained in Republican hands and the GOP increased its overall margin in the Senate.

During his first two years in office, Wolf repeatedly championed various versions of a severance tax to replace the impact fee, with significant variations in rates that began at 5 percent on the value of gas at its wellhead in 2015 but increased to 6.5 percent the following year. This higher rate would have surpassed that of any state east of the Mississippi River, though it would have remained below many states to the west of that divide. In 2016, Wolf added a proposed supplement of a volumetric fee that would have also included a 4.7 cent surcharge for every thousand cubic feet and, in effect, assured higher rates when gas prices declined. This suggested some efforts to emulate the tax and fee combination that had long been in place in neighboring West Virginia, with considerable industry opposition despite its political durability. Wolf demonstrated willingness to adjust the technical terms of the proposal, including rates and the related fee, and generally retained solid but not unanimous support from Democratic legislators. He generally favored allocating revenues for education and local governments rather than any longer-term investments through a trust fund. But despite his various adjustments, Wolf gained virtually no traction among Republicans in either the House or Senate, reflecting their steadfast opposition to any extraction tax (Woodall 2016).

This has resulted in protracted partisan battles, with the lack of agreement on the severance tax leading to an extended failure to adopt a state budget. Pennsylvania had considerable precedent for late budget completion but the 2015–2016 delays were unusually long, ultimately lasting for nearly one year. These battles included aggressive use of vetoes by Wolf that prevented any spending for certain state government programs, with the severance tax controversy a primary point of contention. Wolf would ultimately back down and withdraw the tax proposal in order to secure a 2016 budget accord but vowed to return to this issue in future sessions. The state also faced extended partisan divides over a range of new environmental regulations on drilling operations established by the Wolf administration through interpretation of Act 13 and related statutes by the state Department of Environmental Protection. Opponents argued that any new severance tax would only compound the added costs imposed by these new regulations.

Severance tax opponents in the Wolf era were particularly emphatic that such a tax could be considered only if natural gas prices eventually rebounded after a period of significant decline during the mid-2010s. As in prior periods, some opponents suggested that a tax would never be acceptable whereas others held out the possibility of some reconsideration in the future. Divides were also evident over the extent to which Pennsylvania should rely on natural gas extraction and related development as a fundamental path for future economic growth or should it pursue economic diversification instead. Some Republicans were adamant that prices would bounce back and that the state could also lure substantial new manufacturing through tax credits and subsidies linked to new investment that made significant use of natural gas harvested in the Keystone State. One such proposal advanced by Republican House Speaker Michael Turzai, the Keystone Energy Enhancement Act, called for creation of Keystone Energy Zones that would offer highly favorable terms for such investment and arguably transform Pennsylvania along the lines of more energy-intensive states such as Texas.

Opponents also contended that Pennsylvania would lose its competitive edge to neighboring Ohio and West Virginia in the Marcellus Shale and Utica Shale plays if it followed their precedents and established a severance tax. Marcellus Shale Coalition president David Spigelmyer routinely noted in 2015 and 2016 that any severance tax adoption by Pennsylvania would trigger a major out-migration of drilling operations to other states, even though they all had some form of severance tax in place. In a representative comment, he observed in 2015 that a state severance tax would make the state "uncompetitive with Ohio, Texas, and Louisiana—China. Capital can move like water in Pennsylvania. It can move from Pennsylvania pretty quickly" (Cusick 2015). In particular, he anticipated movement to the immediate west of the state if a tax was adopted, noting that "you can line up at the border and watch rigs move into Ohio" (Lee 2015).

Both West Virginia and Ohio faced severance tax controversies of their own during this period, although neither adopted any changes in established taxes through the end of 2016. In West Virginia, Democratic governor Earl Ray Tomblin in 2016 lamented plunging severance tax revenues from gas, oil, and the state's iconic fossil fuel of coal and endorsed the idea of some reduction in these taxes in hopes that it might trigger a rebound for extraction. The West Virginia State Senate supported a bill to eliminate a volumetric fee similar to the one Wolf proposed for Pennsylvania that complements the severance tax. It also supported a reduction in its 5 percent severance tax on oil, natural gas, and coal production to 3 percent over a two-year period. Both of these failed to gain support in the lower House of Delegates, though this issue reemerged during the 2016 election and figured to resurface in subsequent years.

In Ohio, Republican governor John Kasich argued that Ohio's severance tax, which charges a fixed amount per unit of energy produced regardless of price (twenty cents per barrel of oil and three cents per thousand square feet of natural gas) and generally ranks among the lowest in the nation, represented a state failure to capture revenue that should be linked to the permanent removal of a natural resource. Much like Wolf, Kasich repeatedly advanced bills with a variation of higher rates between 2011 and 2016, ranging from 1.5 percent to 6.5 percent. He proposed that most of the revenue could be used to reduce other taxes, including rates for state personal income taxes. Kasich faced significant but not unanimous opposition from members of his own party in the legislature, and a Pennsylvania-like standoff ensued for several years without resolution, although it did not go so far as to delay budget agreements. In a comment representative of his views, Kasich said in 2015 that the current tax system is a "total and complete rip-off to the people of this state" (Krebs 2015). In 2016, he vowed frequently to continue his campaign to increase the severance tax and use revenues to provide personal income tax relief.

Consequently, Pennsylvania remained unique in refraining from severance tax adoption but found itself by 2017 nestled in a shale play where neighboring states continued to debate property tax rates and structure during an energy price decline. The question of severance tax adoption remained prominent on Pennsylvania's political agenda as Wolf entered the second half of his term in 2017; any further political standoff on this issue would likely only keep it prominent in subsequent election cycles. As a result, Pennsylvania and its immediate neighbors posed an important national test of the future political prospects for severance taxes.

Consequences of Pennsylvania Exceptionalism and Future Considerations

Much like other energy-producing states, Pennsylvania has not been immune from boom-and-bust economic cycles either historically or in the shorter time horizon of the shale era. It continues to face questions about the impact of natural gas development on its economy and environment in both the near and longer terms, with strong parallels to other states and nations that operate energy-centered economies. But Pennsylvania's unique stance on severance taxes creates a number of important considerations for the state, both in the near term and in coming decades, as it further explores development of its natural gas supplies.

General Revenue Forgone

First, the lack of a severance tax is costly to the state of Pennsylvania in terms of lost potential revenue and the need to use other taxes to cover its budgetary outlays. Thus far, the impact fee has generated slightly more than $1 billion for the state during its first five years of operation, with approximately 40 percent retained by the state and the remainder allocated to county and local governments. Wolf has projected, however, that a 6.5 percent severance tax would generate $350.9 million in revenue for the 2016–2017 fiscal year, leading up to $507.0 million for the general fund by the 2020–2021 fiscal year (Phillips 2016). The Pennsylvania Budget and Policy Center had much higher estimates in 2013, however, reflecting that revenue projections have declined as natural gas prices have dropped markedly (Pennsylvania Budget and Policy Center 2013). There are no reliable published estimates of whether Pennsylvania secures added drilling and related economic stimulus because of its nontax approach.

As in the case of state severance tax revenues, Pennsylvania impact fee revenues have declined in recent years. Revenues peaked at $226 million in fiscal year 2013, slipped to $188 million for fiscal year 2015, and were projected to drop to an estimated $129 million to $171 million for fiscal year 2016. In addition to the fact that total revenues are considerably lower than most other severance tax states, despite the state's massive natural gas production (see Table 4.2), impact fee revenue is most abundant in years immediately after drilling begins rather than over the entire production life of each well when the fee is phased out and then eliminated even if drilling continues. So it is susceptible to significant fluctuations as the sheer amount of new drilling moves up and down, as it has in recent years. As a result, revenue production will decline markedly over time despite overall output unless there is a constant pace of new drilling (Environmental Law Institute and Washington and Jefferson College Center for Energy Policy and Management 2014).

This consequence is especially considerable in light of Pennsylvania's ongoing budget crisis. Other major energy-producing states with a severance tax, such as Alaska and North Dakota, have also struggled with major deficits, given oil price busts, although these reflect both declining severance tax revenues and the decision to suppress other taxes, given severance tax dependence. In turn, other states that have considerable energy production and a severance tax, such as Texas and California, have had less-significant budget problems, given their more diversified statewide economies and tax bases (Saha and Muro 2016). As of 2017, there were no long-term fixes in sight for the Pennsylvania budget after a patchwork of increases in tobacco taxes, partial privatization of liquor sales, a one-time tax amnesty program, a loan from a medical malpractice insurance fund, and anticipated expansion of gambling and related taxes were used to attempt to close an immediate budget gap.

Earmarked Revenue Foregone

Just as Pennsylvania is missing out on the opportunity to collect substantial revenues, it is also forgoing opportunities to use them to address negative consequences from drilling or prepare for longer-term challenges. In Colorado and North Dakota, considerable amounts of severance tax revenue are placed in special funds for related programs such as land reclamation, water conservation, and alternative energy development (Rabe and Hampton 2015). As Pennsylvania Budget and Policy Center officials stated in 2010, "Legislative inaction has left the environment unprotected in the Marcellus Shale region of the state. It has passed the local costs of increased drilling on to state and local taxpayers" (Swift 2010). The absence of a severance tax also precludes the possibility of setting aside some portion of oil- and gas-production revenues for long-term uses through the creation of a trust fund. In

North Dakota, 30 percent of annual severance tax revenues are deposited in a state Legacy Fund for investment and gradual allocation once state oil resources have been depleted; other states have continued to experiment with their own versions of this approach (Rabe and Hampton 2016).

The Resiliency of Severance Taxation as a Pennsylvania Agenda Issue

The sustained rejection of severance tax proposals over the last decade demonstrates the steep political hurdles to adoption. But it also indicates a kind of resilience for this issue, with an enduring base of political support that is unlikely to disappear. Alongside the view that Pennsylvania should refrain from severance taxation and use this unique feature to try to expand extraction and related development is a continuing counterargument that the state should attempt to extract some lasting revenue value from the permanent loss of its fossil-fuel-based natural resources. This reflects in part a long Pennsylvania history with the aftermath of energy-production booms, including long-term environmental damage linked to extensive coal mining operations that remain a challenge in many parts of the state and a desire to mitigate any potential risks with supplemental revenue.

This debate is unlikely to disappear at any point in the near future and would likely continue even if Pennsylvania adopted some form of a tax. Indeed, public opinion analysis suggests a significant base of public support for some form of a severance tax in the state, a remarkable finding, given the ongoing state political opposition to such a tax and the general lack of public enthusiasm for new taxes. Between February 2014 and February 2016, the Muhlenberg Institute of Public Opinion conducted four surveys of Pennsylvania residents and found consistently that 62 percent to 63 percent of respondents favored the adoption of a severance tax with 25 percent to 29 percent opposed and the remainder not sure (see Table 4.4). These surveys also found that respondents were far more likely to say that such a tax would not encourage drilling firms to leave the state, including a 48 percent to 36 percent margin in February 2016 (see Table 4.5). This is consistent with earlier survey findings from Muhlenberg on this issue, suggesting a sustained majority of support across the last two governorships and periods of both surging and declining natural gas prices (Brown et al. 2013).

Future Severance Tax Prospects

A prolonged pattern of suppressed prices for natural gas does not necessarily mean reduced production, given the continued industry success of refining extraction technologies and practices that reduce the sales price necessary to allow them to generate a profit. Indeed, Pennsylvania natural gas production set a record in 2015, reflecting continued growth in output despite sus-

TABLE 4.4 PENNSYLVANIA SURVEY RESULTS FOR SEVERANCE TAX QUESTION

Q: *Many states have created "severance taxes" in which drillers pay a tax that is based on the value of natural gas and oil that they extract from below the ground. Pennsylvania does not currently have such a tax. Do you think that Pennsylvania should adopt such a tax or not?*

Year	Should adopt	Should not adopt	Not sure/refused
February 2014	62%	29%	9%
February 2015	63%	25%	13%
October 2015	63%	28%	9%
February 2016	62%	28%	10%

Source: Muhlenberg College Institute of Public Opinion, "Fracking Related Questions: Summary 2011–2016" (in authors' possession).

TABLE 4.5 PENNSYLVANIA SURVEY RESULTS FOR FIRM DRILLING QUESTIONS

Q: *Please tell me if you strongly agree, somewhat agree, somewhat disagree, or strongly disagree: Increasing taxes on natural gas drillers in Pennsylvania will lead drilling firms to leave and so should be avoided.*

Year	Strongly agree	Somewhat agree	Somewhat disagree	Strongly disagree	Not sure
2011	11%	22%	23%	28%	16%
2012	16%	16%	30%	34%	4%
2015	18%	20%	26%	29%	8%
2016	21%	15%	23%	25%	25%

Source: Muhlenberg College Institute of Public Opinion, "Fracking Related Questions: Summary 2011–2016" (in authors' possession).

tained price reductions (Cocklin 2016b). In turn, possible expansion of natural gas exports, including liquefaction and transport to other continents, converges with growing domestic demand for the fuel as an alternative to coal and suggests that the national appetite for natural gas is not going to disappear at any discernible future point. Moreover, there does not appear to be any political constituency in the state capable of securing a political majority through a campaign to halt or place a New York–like moratorium on drilling and leave natural gas in the ground.

Consequently, fracking will in all likelihood continue in Pennsylvania alongside ongoing debate over regulatory policy and severance taxes. Other issues such as the fairness of royalty payments to landowners and the levels of bonds that drillers are required to post have also remained contentious in recent years, including protracted litigation against some of the major gas-producing firms (Cocklin 2016a). There has also been periodic discussion in the legislature and among local governments to allow localities to impose property taxes on pipelines that run through their jurisdictions, as is allowed in numerous other states. However, the severance tax question remains a central point of contention not just in Pennsylvania energy policy circles but in state politics more broadly. In all other gas- and oil-producing states, the severance tax issue has long since been resolved, leading to taxes that have proven durable for decades and generations in most state cases. In those settings, the discussion of severance taxes links to issues of rates and revenue use. Only in Pennsylvania does the very question of severance tax adoption remain an open and contentious one.

NOTES

This article was previously published as Rachel L. Hampton and Barry G. Rabe, "Leaving Money on the Table: Pennsylvania Exceptionalism in Resisting Energy Severance Taxes," *Commonwealth* 19, no. 1 (2017). © 2017 The Pennsylvania Political Science Association. ISSN 2469-7672 (online). http://dx.doi.org/10.15367/com.v19i1.131. All rights reserved.

1. California, a top producer of crude oil, also has an unusually low severance tax rate. The state levies what is called an oil- and gas-production assessment that is set each year by the California Department of Conservation, imposed on each barrel of oil and each ten thousand cubic feet of natural gas produced in the state (California Department of Conservation, n.d.). Individual counties rather than state authorities, however, are responsible for collecting the ad valorem taxes. California might be the state most similar to Pennsylvania in its failure to create a statewide severance tax amid considerable controversy over drilling and simultaneous pursuit of a cap-and-trade system to reduce carbon emissions (Rabe 2018). In fact, severance tax debates have also simmered in California since the 1990s, including the most recent major effort to create an oil extraction tax that took place in 2014, with a proposal to allocate revenue for higher education. This generated a considerable constituency among University of California students but ultimately was not adopted (Smith and Kovitz 2014).

2. For an application of this approach in the case of carbon pricing, see Rabe 2016a.

REFERENCES

Act 13 Public Utility Commission. n.d. "Disbursements and Impact Fees." Available at https://www.act13-reporting.puc.pa.gov/Modules/PublicReporting/Overview.aspx (accessed February 20, 2018).

Brace, Paul. 1993. *State Government and Economic Performance*. Baltimore: Johns Hopkins University Press.

Bravender, Robin. 2014. "Gubernatorial Hopefuls Wrangle over Drilling Tax." *E&E News*, September 23. Available at https://www.eenews.net/greenwire/2014/09/23/stories/1060006297.

Brown, Cassarah. 2013. "State Revenues and the Natural Gas Boom: An Assessment of State Oil and Gas Production Taxes." National Conference of State Legislatures, June. Available at http://www.ncsl.org/research/energy/state-revenues-and-the-natural-gas-boom.aspx.

Brown, Erica, Kristine Hartman, Chris Borick, Barry G. Rabe, and Thomas Ivacko. 2013. "Public Opinion on Fracking: Perspectives from Michigan and Pennsylvania." Available at http://closup.umich.edu/issues-in-energy-and-environmental-policy/3/public-opinion-on-fracking-perspectives-from-michigan-and-pennsylvania.

California Department of Conservation. n.d. "*Assessment Process.*" Available at http://
www.conservation.ca.gov/dog/for_operators/Pages/assessments.aspx (accessed
January 4, 2017).

Cocklin, Jamison. 2014a. "Midterm Elections a Mixed Bag for Appalachian Basin's Oil,
Gas Industry." *Shale Daily*, November 5. Available at http://www.naturalgasintel
.com/articles/100311-midterm-elections-a-mixed-bag-for-appalachian-basins-oil
-gas-industry.

———. 2014b. "XTO Chief Critiques Appalachian States' Taxes." *Shale Daily*, September
25. Available at http://www.naturalgasintel.com/articles/99831-xto-chief-calls
-appalachian-state-regulations-outdated.

———. 2015. "With Wolf's Inauguration, Questions Loom for Pennsylvania NatGas
Industry." *Shale Daily*, January 16. Available at http://www.naturalgasintel.com/
articles/101063-with-wolfs-inauguration-questions-loom-for-pennsylvania-natgas
-industry.

———. 2016a. "Pennsylvania Lawmaker Proposes Costlier Bonds to Cover Shale Wells."
Shale Daily, August 30. Available at http://www.naturalgasintel.com/articles/107580
-pennsylvania-lawmaker-proposes-costlier-bonds-to-cover-shale-wells%20for%20
further%20discussion.

———. 2016b. "Pennsylvania Shale Production Increased Again Last Year," *Shale Daily*,
February 22. Available at http://www.naturalgasintel.com/articles/105435
-pennsylvania-shale-production-increased-again-last-year.

Considine, Timothy J., Nicholas B. Considine, and Robert Watson. 2016. "Economic and
Environmental Impacts of Fracking: A Case Study of the Marcellus Shale." *International Review of Environmental and Resource Economics* 9 (3–4): 209–244.

Cusick, Marie. 2015. "Déjà Vu All Over Again: Why the Shale Gas Tax Keeps Flaming
Out." *StateImpact*, November 25. Available at https://stateimpact.npr.org/pennsyl
vania/2015/11/25/deja-vu-all-over-again-why-the-shale-gas-tax-keeps-flaming
-out/.

Eisinger, Peter K. 1989. *The Rise of the Entrepreneurial State: State and Local Economic
Development Policy in the United States.* Madison: University of Wisconsin Press.

Environmental Law Institute and Washington and Jefferson College Center for Energy
Policy and Management. 2014. "Getting the Boom without the Bust: Guiding Southwestern Pennsylvania through Shale Gas Development." Available at https://www
.eli.org/research-report/getting-boom-without-bust-guiding-southwestern-pennsyl
vania-through-shale-gas-development.

Groh, Cliff, and Gregg Erickson. 2012. "The Improbable but True Story of How the
Alaska Permanent Fund and the Alaska Permanent Fund Dividend Came to Be."
In *Alaska's Permanent Fund Dividend: Examining Its Suitability as a Model*, edited
by Karl Widerquist and Michael Howard, 15–40. New York: Palgrave Macmillan.

Hansen, Susan B. 1989. "Targeting Economic Development: Comparative State Perspectives." *Publius: The Journal of Federalism* 19 (Spring): 47–62.

Harrison, Kathryn, ed. 2006. *Racing to the Bottom.* Vancouver: University of British
Columbia Press.

Krebs, Natalie. 2015. "No Taxation without (Oil and Gas) Representation." *CityBeat*, July
29. Available at http://www.citybeat.com/news/article/13002033/no-taxation-with
out-oil-and-gas-representation.

Kunce, Mitch. 2003. "Effectiveness of Severance Tax Incentives in the U.S. Oil Industry."
International Tax and Public Finance 10 (September): 565–587.

Lee, Mike. 2015. "Pa. Senate Wrangles over Whether to Tax Industry during a Downturn." *E&E News*, June 2. Available at https://www.eenews.net/energywire/stories/1060019482/print.

Mieszkowski, Peter, and Ronald Soligo. 2012. "United States." In *Oil and Gas in Federal Systems*, edited by George Anderson, 310–338. New York: Oxford University Press.

Moss, Todd, ed. 2012. *The Governor's Solution*. Washington, DC: Center for Global Development.

National Conference of State Legislatures. n.d. "State Severance Taxes." Available at http://www.ncsl.org/research/fiscal-policy/2011-state-severance-tax-collections.aspx (accessed January 4, 2017).

Pennsylvania Budget and Policy Center. 2013. "Pa.'s Marcellus Impact Fee Comes Up Short." Available at http://pennbpc.org/pa-marcellus-impact-fee-comes-short.

Phillips, Susan. 2016. "Wolf Proposes 6.5 Percent Tax on Marcellus Shale." *StateImpact*, February 9. Available at https://stateimpact.npr.org/pennsylvania/2016/02/09/wolf-proposes-6-5-percent-tax-on-marcellus-shale/.

Powers, Carol. 1982. "State Taxation of Energy Resources." *Boston College Environmental Affairs Law Review* 10 (2): 503–564.

Rabe, Barry G. 2007. "Race to the Top: The Expanding Role of U.S. State Renewable Portfolio Standards." *Sustainable Development Law and Policy* 7 (Spring): 10–16, 72.

———. 2016a. "The Durability of Carbon Cap-and-Trade." *Governance* 29 (January): 103–119.

———. 2016b. "Racing to the Top, the Bottom, or the Middle of the Pack? The Evolving State Government Role in Environmental Protection." In *Environmental Policy: New Directions for the Twenty-First Century*, 9th rev. ed., edited by Norman J. Vig and Michael E. Kraft, 33–57. Washington, DC: CQ Press.

———. 2018. *Can We Price Carbon?* Cambridge, MA: MIT Press.

Rabe, Barry G., and Chris Borick. 2013. "Conventional Politics for Unconventional Drilling." *Review of Policy Research* 30 (May): 321–339.

Rabe, Barry G., and Rachel L. Hampton. 2015. "Taxing Fracking: The Politics of State Severance Taxes in the Shale Era." *Review of Policy Research* 32 (July): 389–412.

———. 2016. "Trusting in the Future: The Re-emergence of State Trust Funds in the Shale Era." *Energy Research and Social Science* 20 (October): 117–127.

Rice, Carolyn. 2016. "The Struggle for Shared Governance in Hydraulic Fracking Policy: An Interstate Comparison of Texas, Oklahoma, and Colorado." Available at http://closup.umich.edu/student-working-papers/2/the-struggle-for-shared-governance-in-hydraulic-fracturing-policy-an-interstate-comparison-of-texas-oklahoma-and-colorado.

Richardson, James A. 2005. "Severance Tax, State." In *The Encyclopedia of Taxation and Tax Policy*, 2nd ed., edited by Joseph J. Cordes, Robert D. Ebel, and Jane G. Gravelle, 357–360. Washington, DC: Urban Institute Press.

Robinson Township v. Commonwealth of Pennsylvania. 2012. 52 A.3d 463 (Pa. Cmwlth.).

Ross, Michael. 2012. *The Oil Curse*. Princeton, NJ: Princeton University Press.

Saha, Devashree, and Mark Muro. 2016. "Permanent Trust Funds: Funding Economic Change with Fracking Revenues." Brookings Institution, April 19. Available at https://www.brookings.edu/research/permanent-trust-funds-funding-economic-change-with-fracking-revenues.

Smith, Taryn, and Bo Kovitz. 2014. "UC Students Lobby Higher Education Policies at State Capitol." *Daily Californian*, April 7. Available at http://www.dailycal.org/2014/04/07/uc-students-lobby-higher-education-policies-state-capitol/.

Swift, Robert. 2010. "Rendell Calls Gas Severance Tax Dead This Year." *Times-Tribune*, October 22. Available at http://thetimes-tribune.com/news/rendell-calls-gas-severance-tax-dead-this-year-1.1052137.

"Text: Gov. Tom Corbett 2011–12 Budget Address." 2011. *Pittsburgh Post-Gazette*, March 8. Available at http://www.post-gazette.com/news/state/2011/03/08/Text-Gov-Tom-Corbett-2011-12-budget-address/stories/201103080454.

U.S. Bureau of Labor Statistics. 2014. "The Marcellus Shale Gas Boom in Pennsylvania: Employment and Wage Trends." Available at http://www.bls.gov/opub/mlr/2014/article/the-marcellus-shale-gas-boom-in-pennsylvania.htm.

U.S. Census Bureau. n.d. "Annual Survey of State Government Tax Collections (STC)." Available at https://www.census.gov/programs-surveys/stc.html (accessed January 18, 2018).

U.S. Energy Information Administration. 2014a. "Rankings: Natural Gas Marketed Production, 2014." Previously available at https://www.eia.gov/state/rankings/#/series/47.

———. 2014b. "Table C10: Energy Consumption Estimates by End-Use Sector, Ranked by State, 2014." Previously available at https://www.eia.gov/state/seds/data.cfm?incfile=/state/seds/sep_sum/html/rank_use.html&sid=US.

———. 2016. "Rankings: Crude Oil Production, June 2016." Previously available at https://www.eia.gov/state/rankings/#/series/46.

———. 2017a. "Number of Producing Gas Wells." Available at https://www.eia.gov/dnav/ng/ng_prod_wells_s1_a.htm.

———. 2017b. "Pennsylvania Natural Gas Gross Withdrawals." Available at https://www.eia.gov/dnav/ng/hist/n9010pa2a.htm.

Weber, Jeremy, and Max Harleman. 2015. "Shale Development, Impact Fees, and Municipal Finances in Pennsylvania." Center for Metropolitan Studies *Policy Brief*, Winter 2015–2016. Available at http://www.metrostudies.pitt.edu/Portals/4/pdfs/82684_PolicyBrief_FINAL.pdf.

Wile, Rob. 2012. "153 Years Ago Today, an Unemployed Sick Man Drilled the First Modern Oil Well." *Business Insider*, August 27. Available at http://www.businessinsider.com/edwin-drake-first-modern-oil-well-153-years-ago-2012-8.

Woodall, Candy. 2016. "Does Gov. Tom Wolf Still Want a Severance Tax on Drilling?" *PennLive*, January 26. Available at http://www.pennlive.com/news/2016/01/other_states_with_severance_ta.html.

Yergin, Daniel. 2011. *The Quest: Energy, Security, and the Remaking of the Modern World*. New York: Penguin Press.

Discussion Questions

1. What is a severance tax? Why do states have them?
2. Is the presence of severance taxes related to party control in most states?
3. How much do severance taxes generate in oil- and gas-producing states? How much of state revenue do they generate?
4. If most Pennsylvania natural gas is exported (along with a possible tax on it), why does the state not have a tax?

5. Is a severance tax on gas likely in Pennsylvania in the future? Consider the revenue implications and environmental impacts.

Commonwealth Forum: Should State Government Subsidize the Economic Development of Natural Gas Facilities?

YES

The Pennsylvania Department of Community and Economic Development's website has an "Investment Tracker" that allows visitors to view economic development activities by the Commonwealth since 2000. The drop-down menu lists 322 programs that have been administered during this period. Like it or not, state government is in the business of economic development. The first component of competing nationally and internationally for jobs is by providing a favorable tax and regulatory environment. The second component is attracting individual firms through targeted tax breaks, infrastructure development, relocation assistance, and job training programs.

Pennsylvania has been hit hard by deindustrialization. However, the continued technological development of hydraulic fracturing practices has presented the state with a way to create more jobs by accessing oil and natural gas in the Marcellus Shale. The Commonwealth has decided to invest heavily in encouraging the growth of this industry. Pennsylvania is now the second-largest natural gas producer in the United States. At the end of 2016, 20,524 workers were directly employed in oil and natural gas production, and 54,547 were employed providing supplies to the industry. Pennsylvania Marcellus Shale development has resulted in $10 billion of investment to build or retrofit natural gas power plants. It has also attracted jobs through corollary businesses such as petrochemical plants and natural gas exporting facilities. Further, the impact fee levied on producers by the state raised $1.2 billion through the end of 2017. This money is disbursed to state agencies and local governments for infrastructure development, conservation programs, and, for some localities, tax cuts. Beyond economic development and tax revenues, cheap natural gas has lowered utility prices for residents of Pennsylvania. Given these results, how is it possible to argue against the Commonwealth's investment in this industry?

NO

Why should state government subsidize an already heavily subsidized industry? Estimates vary, but fossil fuels already receive a subsidy of around

$20 billion per year. The costs in terms of environmental degradation, poor health outcomes, and contribution to climate change are not included in the price of natural gas or any other fossil fuel. While natural gas burns cleaner than coal or oil, companies that produce it should not receive public dollars to pollute the air and water.

The Shell ethane cracker plant planned in Beaver County will receive the largest tax subsidy in state history, valued at $1.65 billion. Meanwhile, the plant will create only six hundred permanent jobs ($2.75 million per job!). Is such a massive tax expenditure really worth it? No wonder state government is experiencing such tough budget decisions and a $2 billion structural budget deficit. They're giving away the store. Such subsidies result in a raw deal for Pennsylvanians. Tax cuts for large, wealthy, multinational corporations mean state revenue must come from somewhere else, namely, average citizens.

To add insult to injury, parts of the plant are being built in Mexico and shipped to the construction site. Not only that, but of the estimated $100 million in steel needed to build the plant, manufacturers in Pennsylvania would be lucky to get a few crumbs. Most likely, the steel will come from China. So, Pennsylvania citizens are paying to advance the development of not only large profitable corporations, but other nations, too. One can only wish for such dedication from state government to the advancement of its own people as they have for the polluting fossil fuel industry.

For More Information

The **Pennsylvania Public Utility Commission** (http://www.puc.state.pa.us/filing_resources/issues_laws_regulations/act_13_impact_fee_.aspx) has an Act 13 (Impact Fee) website dedicated to providing information and resources related to the law and its collected revenues.

PowerSource (http://powersource.post-gazette.com/) of the *Pittsburgh Post-Gazette* is a special supplement on energy policy. It covers the Pittsburgh region's natural gas, coal, nuclear, and alternative energy sectors in context.

State Impact Pennsylvania (https://stateimpact.npr.org/pennsylvania/) is a product of member National Public Radio stations WITF and WHYY covering the topics of energy, the environment, and the economy. It was developed in response to the last decade's growing energy economy in the state.

The **Marcellus Shale Coalition** (http://marcelluscoalition.org/) provides information on natural gas from the perspective of the industries that are extracting it from the Marcellus Shale.

Chapter 5
Education Policy

What Would Student-Based Allocation Mean for Pennsylvania School Districts?

MARGUERITE ROZA

AMANDA WARCO

In recent months, policy makers across the country have been exploring state school financing formulas with the goals of promoting equity, transparency, and adequacy. Toward that end, state leaders are considering a new model for disbursing state education funds called student-based allocation (SBA)—one that would allocate funds on the basis of students. In fact, many states already have some sort of formula using students as the basis, although in practice, most essentially use a hybrid set of allocations such that the portion of funds allocated on the basis of students varies substantially across states. This analysis of fourteen states shows that among the sampled states, between 0 and 85 percent of all state and local funds is allocated on the basis of students. In Pennsylvania, after operating in the absence of a formal allocation formula for several years, the Basic Education Funding Commission (BEFC) was tasked with recommending a new finance scheme for funding the state's schools. In this paper, we outline the rationale behind SBA and investigate the extent to which the BEFC proposal would allocate funds on the basis of students.

One of a state's primary responsibilities is to divide up the public funds for K–12 schooling. Each state has a set of finance policies that together determine how the state and local funds are allocated so that districts can then apply them to schools and classrooms. Different states use a host of variables, formulas, and other mechanisms to determine how much each district receives. Because of the tremendous political lift involved in changing state formulas, they do not change much from year to year. Rather, states tend to layer new program funds onto the old model or make minor tweaks here or there to address the greatest pain points. Eventually, a formula may seem broken enough that a state tackles it from top to bottom.

Such appears to be the case in Pennsylvania, where a State Commission (called the Basic Education Funding Commission, or the BEFC) was tasked with developing a whole new state education funding formula. Of interest in Pennsylvania is a mechanism called student-based allocation (SBA), also known as weighted student funding. With SBA, state (or state and local) funds are deployed on the basis of students and student types (poverty, disability, etc.). Student-based allocation has garnered interest among state leaders largely for its promise to improve equity and transparency, while ensuring that districts with higher-needs students receive appropriately higher allocations. Further, as state leaders face both increasing costs and highly constrained resources, some state leaders are seeking SBA as a means to facilitate greater productivity and financial sustainability in their state education systems.

In this chapter, we outline the rationale behind SBA and investigate the BEFC proposal against that rationale. Drawing on data from Pennsylvania and other states' SBA systems, we compare Pennsylvania's current and proposed allocations to those of fourteen other states. And we analyze what the BEFC proposal would mean for the relative share of state funding allocated according to student versus district characteristics.

State Leaders Look to SBA to Enhance Equity and Productivity

The specifics of state funding formulas vary widely. But what many states have in common is incremental layers of formula iterations that can unintentionally work to create inequities among districts, hinder efficient use of public funds, and inhibit system-wide productivity. As states rethink their allocation systems, many are considering SBA as a way to tackle these three challenges.

Student-based allocation emerged in the United States two decades ago as a means for large districts to better deploy funds to schools.[1] The funding formula is student driven: A fixed dollar amount is set for each student type and funds flow on the basis of students, with higher-needs students generating incrementally more money. The funds remain flexible so that each locale can spend them as needed. This formula departs from traditional district allocations that tend to assign positions to schools (one teacher for every twenty-five students, one counselor for every three hundred students, etc.). Big districts like Houston, Boston, Baltimore, Denver, Cleveland, Chicago, and others now use SBA at the district level to distribute funds to schools.

More recently, state leaders have taken an interest in using SBA to push state (or combined state and local) funds to districts (or directly to schools) as illustrated in Figure 5.1. While some states do allocate a foundational per-pupil payment (a foundation formula), what sets SBA apart is that student need drives the variation in the fixed per-student amounts paid out. That weighted formula replaces a range of ways that states are funneling dollars to districts and schools beyond just their basic formula. For instance, some states drive funding for high-needs students through categorical allocations or designated program funding (such as funds for reading coaches, gradua-tion specialists, and so on). Separate state allocations are often layered on for designated efforts for science, technology, engineering, and math (STEM) initiatives, teacher bonuses, Advanced Placement (AP) coursework, text-books, and much more, creating opaque and complex allocations that may work to undo any equitable distribution created by the basic formula. Other states lean on funding formula mechanisms like hold-harmless provisions for enrollment decline,[2] adjustments for size and urbanicity, or to offset charter school growth. Several states, such as Delaware and Idaho, do not use a foundation formula at all but rather allocate staff positions based on student enrollment (and then reimburse districts for actual salaries of the allowable staff counts) or use some other arrangement altogether (like a grandfathering formula, where all districts get some percentage of their pre-vious year's allocation regardless of changes in the number of students served or the mix of student needs).[3]

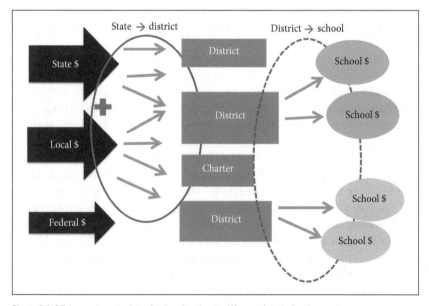

Figure 5.1 SBA can be used to deploy funds at different levels in the system.

Student-based allocation has surfaced as a solution to frustrations with existing state allocation formulas, which have been criticized for being:

- complex, opaque, and unfair
- too prescriptive, inflexible, and onerous in terms of compliance
- inequitable because districts get uneven revenues (often driven by the interplay of local and state monies) and districts with greater student needs do not receive sufficiently greater resources to meet their students' challenges
- inefficient and unproductive, since current formulas protect districts from making needed adjustments to changing enrollments or conditions

Proponents say SBA simultaneously addresses the complexity (district leaders know that an English-language learner will generate $X allocation, a homeless student will generate $Y), flexibility (schools can individualize resources to match their staff and students' strengths and needs), and equity concerns (students with greater needs trigger larger allocations).

Further, SBA is thought to replace policies that are considered inefficient with policies that promote productivity-enhancing adaptations. A criticism of some existing funding formulas is that they fund "phantom students" by delivering more funds to districts than would be justified by their actual enrollment (Roza and Fullerton 2013). These policies can take the form of:

- extra funds for declining-enrollment districts
- offsets for districts that lose students to charter schools
- small-districts subsidies
- minimum allotments for categorical allocations

In each case, the affected districts receive funds in excess of what they would receive if only the students on their rolls were funded. All told, these kinds of provisions drive more funds to some districts than are warranted under the total state enrollment figures and corresponding lower per-pupil allotments for all other districts (assuming limited state funds). Hold-harmless provisions, for instance, are also thought to insulate district leaders from making the adaptive (and therefore productivity-enhancing) changes (such as right-sizing but also adopting new delivery models) needed to better meet the size of the shrinking student rolls. In other words, the policies intended to protect these districts may be enabling a more sluggish response to changes that should be happening with enrollment fluctuations.

Nudging districts toward greater adaptability—the thinking goes—is important in a labor-intensive sector where costs will likely outstrip revenues in coming years. With labor costs rising faster than revenue streams, schooling could suffer from steady decline over successive years of incremental cuts, provided that services remain stuck in a fixed delivery model that does not adapt to the kinds of changes that have fueled productivity improvements in other service sectors (Roza 2013). To make productivity improvements, districts need to seek new delivery models that allow schools to do the most with scarce, but fairly allocated, resources.

In California, state leaders recently replaced a reportedly complex and onerous system of categorical funding with a student-based formula called the Local Control Funding Formula (LCFF) (see Freedberg 2013). For each district, the state determines the target spending, based on the mix of students and student types, and then applies the expected local funds toward that target. State funds then make up the difference. (Table 5.1 shows how much is allocated for each student by grade level and need.) Districts then have flexibility in how they apply funds, and then own the corresponding responsibility for improved outcomes. The LCFF is not a pure SBA model, however, as state leaders did leave a pool of funds in a hold-harmless provision to protect some districts from large losses in the first few years of implementation.

A similar model was proposed in Colorado, but the Colorado formula was tied to a ballot measure that was defeated at the ballot box in 2013 (Simpson 2013). In the last three years, leaders in Ohio, Illinois, Georgia, Arizona, and Delaware have also made proposals to advance SBA, and in some cases those are still pending.[4]

TABLE 5.1 CALIFORNIA'S STUDENT-BASED ALLOCATION FORMULA

Student types*	Allocation
Grades K–3	$7,557
Grades 4–6	$6,947
Grades 7–8	$7,154
Grades 9–12	$8,505
Limited English	+20%
Poverty†	+20%
Foster youth	+20%

Source: Data from California Department of Education 2015.
* In California, students receive the weight only once even if they fall into multiple categories. Often, in other state formulas, students receive the weight amount for each category that applies to them.
† High-poverty districts are also awarded a 50 percent weight for each poor student above 55 percent.

Concerns about Flexibility and Districts' Adaptability to Changes

This policy proposal is not without skeptics. Some worry that with greater local flexibility, districts would still yield to pressures from advantaged parents, unions, or other forces to spend money unwisely or in ways that ill serve the most disadvantaged students.

Others remain concerned that, since a student-based formula funds only students, it is not sensitive enough to differences in districts created by nonstudent factors. For instance, SBA formulas do not take into account the historic district enrollments (for shrinking districts), charter schools, small size, high transportation costs, and so forth. Skeptics worry that districts with these and other characteristics may be less equipped to serve students with the available funding. And finally, some worry that, if not clearly defined or limited, districts may have an incentive to overidentify certain types of students.

Pennsylvania's BEFC Tasked with Devising a More Sustainable State Allocation Formula

Plenty has been written about how Pennsylvania's existing formula is not a formula at all.[5] At one point, Pennsylvania did have a student-based formula on the books, but it has not been used in several years. Rather, recent years' state funding has been allocated by just adding a percentage each year to whatever each district received the year before, regardless of any changes in student rolls. Not surprisingly, growing districts are seeing per-pupil allocations fall, while districts that have lost students are now funded at higher per-pupil allocations.

Other changes in student needs are also not considered, including the rapid rise in the percentage of students in poverty. As the BEFC reports, the percentage of students eligible for free or reduced lunch has risen from 35 percent to 48 percent over the last decade (Basic Education Funding Commission 2015). Given the higher needs associated with these student characteristics, districts are understandably concerned about a state formula that ignores these changing student needs.

Much of the back and forth in Pennsylvania has also concerned the overall level of state funding and its interactions with local money. This article does not tackle the question of how much money was or would be put into the state formula, but rather focuses on the means of deploying it. However, also at issue is the constant worry that state sources will remain insufficient to meet the rising cost factors in Pennsylvania's districts. In Pennsylvania, like in other states, labor costs are outpacing state revenues, forcing trade-offs within districts that put pressure on the financing model. For instance, from 2004 to 2008, the benefits load on salaries (a number that should remain fixed if benefits were growing at the same rate as salaries) jumped from 30 percent to 37 percent.[6] With cost pressures mounting, and given the constrained nature of state funds, there is pressure for the state system to fund schooling in a way that helps promote productivity improvements.

The BEFC Proposal Would Deploy Funds by Both Student and Nonstudent Factors

Given the above conditions, the BEFC considered SBA for the state. In the summary report, the BEFC makes a proposal for a hybrid state allocation formula that involves divvying up state monies in ways that include elements of SBA while also driving a portion of funds to districts on the basis of nonstudent factors:[7]

a. *Student-based factors include poverty and English proficiency.* As the BEFC has outlined, poverty is a student factor relevant to learning. The BEFC's formula includes three types of poverty weights to take into account varying levels and concentration of poverty. Similarly, students with limited English proficiency are awarded an additional 60 percent allocation.

b. *The formula recognizes local revenue capacity.* Whereas an SBA model could include local funds in its generation of a per-pupil allocation, the BEFC formula applies a local income and capacity index (an index designed by the BEFC that takes into account district median income and property tax wealth), which works similarly to channel more funds to those districts with less local wealth.

c. *The BEFC's formula insulates districts from changing enrollment and corresponding financial implications.* Rather than base allocations on actual current-year student counts—as a pure SBA formula would—the BEFC bases allocation on a rolling three-year average. In doing so, districts with declining enrollment are funded for more students than actually attend the district, while some are not receiving funds for all the students on their rolls in a given year. The BEFC's rationale is to protect declining-enrollment districts, but at the same time, that adjustment for "phantom" students means declining-enrollment districts are not making the year-to-year adaptations justified by their enrollment changes.

d. *The BEFC channels higher per-pupil amounts according to district characteristics.* In the SBA design, district characteristics are not weighted, only *student* ones. The BEFC formula, however, factors in some district characteristics to its formula, including size, sparsity, and attendance at charter schools.[8] The result is that the dollar amount generated for a third-grade student with limited En-

glish proficiency in one district is different from that generated for
a student with the same characteristics in another district.

The BEFC Proposal Yields 37 Percent of Funds Driven on the Basis of Pupils

The BEFC-proposed formula, like those in other states, contains some elements of an SBA system and yet has some funding factors that do not involve
student types. Given that most states are some hybrid of different funding
formula types,[9] our team has been conducting an ongoing study (thus far in
fourteen states) to measure the portion of state and local monies delivered via
SBA.[10] Measuring progress toward full SBA can inform state policy makers as
they take stock of the current finance policies and set goals for future policies.

The study analyzed all state and local funds in each state and determined
the portion of any state and local funds deployed with a student-based formula. To be considered student based, the allocation had to deploy a fixed
amount of money on the basis of students or student types. The study considered all state and local public funds for K–12 education, excluding any long-
term obligations like debt for facilities.[11] The study then investigated the percentage that would be allocated if Pennsylvania swapped its current allocations
and instead deployed all its funds using the BEFC-proposed formula.[12]

Figure 5.2 captures the findings for each of the fourteen states including
Pennsylvania's allocations both in the current form and using the BEFC formula for all allocations. As is evident in the figure, states vary widely on the
portion of funds delivered on a student basis. New Jersey, California, and Minnesota all distribute more than 75 percent of the state and local funds on a
student basis. Delaware, Idaho, Tennessee, and Washington have low percentages, since these states deliver funding primarily through a staffing formula.

At present, none of the funds in Pennsylvania's existing model are delivered via SBA (hence the 0 percent), as the state is essentially using a hold-
harmless mechanism. If the state instead adopted the BEFC formula for all
its funding, that percentage would jump to 37 percent. Relative to the other
SBA states, that figure is low, although a substantial increase over its current
figure of 0 percent.

Why does the BEFC proposal only yield 37 percent of the funds delivered
via SBA? The nonstudent factors, such as charter schools and district size, are
partly to blame. A pure student-based formula would ignore district size and
the school type, and fund only the students. The responsibility for the district,
then, would be to craft delivery models that were more suited for smaller
enrollments or could transfer those same per-pupil allotments to charter
schools. Some schools already do this, relying on staff with multiple roles. For
instance, a principal of a small school might also teach a class, or instead of a
full-time gym teacher or nurse, the school might contract with a personal
trainer or nursing service in order to buy services in smaller increments.

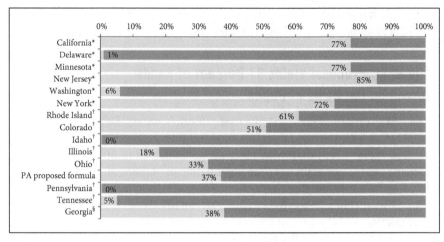

Figure 5.2 Portions of state and local education funds delivered via SBA.
Note: Reported figures augment analysis initially reported by Miller, Roza, and Simburg 2014, with authors' analysis based on publicly available state and local education funding sources, legislative language, and allocation reports.
* 2013–2014
† 2014–2015
§ 2015–2016

Another reason that the BEFC formula does not yield a higher percentage of funds delivered via SBA is that its basis is on the three-year rolling enrollment average and not actual current-year enrollment. Finally, the BEFC does not use a student basis for counting local funds toward its formula allocation (rather, it uses a local-capacity index). The result is that local funds together with state funds do not generate a predictable dollar amount for a particular student type. That dollar figure will continue to vary by district.

A Window of Opportunity in Pennsylvania

The reason that state education-finance formulas stay in place for decades is that the politics are challenging. Education tends to be the largest item in state budgets, and every locale has something to gain or lose with a potential formula overhaul. At the same time, when the window for change opens, legislators have an enormous responsibility, as the next formula will likely be in place for decades.

No one can say for certain what schooling will look like two decades from now, let alone understand how cost structures will be redefined. For instance, will population density be a moot factor given technological changes that might be able to group students in a shared course miles apart? Will the school year be redefined and staffing roles dramatically altered? For state leaders, designing an allocation system amid such uncertainty is tricky, particularly given that so many years may pass before there is the opportunity to modify the system. But the one thing we know will still be there in two decades are the students. Aligning money with the students offers some promise that a finance formula will be able to stand the test of time.

As Pennsylvania's leaders continue to explore solutions to its ongoing state financing issues, this is the moment to take stock of both the opportunity and the extent to which proposals meet the state's long-term goals. We can expect that leaders will have different opinions on what's best for Pennsylvania, and for how districts should be expected to operate with public funds. This analysis compares the existing and proposed state models with those in other states, to illustrate the range of solutions being generated in states across the country. As leaders size up their options and make decisions about the future of Pennsylvania's education-finance formula, understanding the scope and implications of the proposals before them is critically important.

NOTES

This article was previously published as Marguerite Roza and Amanda Warco, "What Would Student-Based Allocation Mean for Pennsylvania School Districts?" *Commonwealth* 18, no. 1 (2016). © 2016 The Pennsylvania Political Science Association. ISSN 2469-7672 (online). http://dx.doi.org/10.15367/cjppp.v18i1.82. All rights reserved.

1. For a more complete history and description on weighted state funding, see Roza 2014.

2. Here we refer to "hold-harmless provisions" as provisions that states include to prevent a year-to-year decrease in funds to a district. Most often, such hold-harmless provisions work to ensure that a district's total funding level does not dip below the previous years' level, despite decreases in actual student enrollment. For further discussion of the impact of this type of hold harmless, see Roza and Fullerton 2013.

3. For instance, Pennsylvania's formula does not take into account enrollment at all but rather works as a uniform percentage adjustment to the previous year's funding level.

4. See, for example, Smith and Snell 2015 and "Manar, Others" 2015.

5. For one example, see Pennsylvania School Funding Project, n.d.

6. These are our calculations based on National Center for Education Statistics data from 2004 to 2008. For additional discussion of rising labor costs, see Basic Education Funding Commission 2015, including testimony from Marguerite Roza on page 24.

7. Pennsylvania created a similar task force in 2013 to study the state's approach to special-education funding. That task force ultimately made recommendations to use a formula that would create three funding tiers for special-education students (based on what districts had been spending on those students in previous years) and adjust that funding according to district-based characteristics. In 2014–2015, the state amended the funding formula to allocate $19.8 million through the new formula. Since the formula amounts were tied to the previous years' funding levels, the formula is not student based. The BEFC was tasked with revising the Basic Education Funding calculation only, which does not include the special-education funding.

8. Charter schools are public schools that operate independently of school districts. Approaches to funding charter schools vary across states. In Pennsylvania, charter schools receive their funding through the district. The BEFC mistakenly considers percentage of district attendance in a charter in their weighted student formula as a "student" characteristic, rather than a characteristic of the district.

9. Hawaii is the closest to a pure SBA model, although the state has only a single district.

10. See an earlier reporting on a portion of these findings in Miller, Roza, and Simburg 2014.

11. Federal funds, which represent 9–12 percent of total K–12 revenues, were excluded from this analysis, as were funds for long-term debt and capital costs.

12. Note that at the time of writing, the legislature was not considering adopting the BEFC formula for all its funds, so the model here is a hypothetical policy model for future years.

REFERENCES

Basic Education Funding Commission. 2015. "Report and Recommendations." Available at http://basiceducationfundingcommission.pasenategop.com/files/2014/08/final-report-061915-.pdf.

California Department of Education. 2015. "Local Control Funding Formula Overview." Previously available at https://www.cde.ca.gov/fg/aa/lc/lcffoverview.asp.

Freedberg, Louis. 2013. "Reform of California's School Finance System Likely." *EdSource*, June 4. Available at http://edsource.org/2013/governor-brown-eyes-yet-another-education-victory/32907.

"Manar, Others Detail Proposed Changes to Education Funding in Illinois." 2015. *Illinois Business Journal*, February 7. Available at http://www.ibjonline.com/local-business-headlines/1180-manar-others-detail-proposed-changes-to-education-funding-in-illinois.

Miller, Larry, Marguerite Roza, and Suzanne Simburg. 2014. "Funding for Students' Sake: How to Stop Financing Tomorrow's Schools Based on Yesterday's Priorities." *SEA of the Future* 3 (May): 19–31.

Pennsylvania School Funding Project. n.d. "Pennsylvania's Historic School Funding Problem." Available at http://www.paschoolfunding.org/the-problem/pennsylvania%E2%80%99s-historic-school-funding-problem/ (accessed January 22, 2018).

Roza, Marguerite. 2013. "Leveraging Productivity for Progress: An Imperative for States." *SEA of the Future* 2 (May): 8–17.

———. 2014. "Weighted Student Funding." In *Encyclopedia of Education Economics and Finance*, edited by Dominic J. Brewer and Lawrence O. Picus, 835–838. Los Angeles: Sage.

Roza, Marguerite, and Jon Fullerton. 2013. "Funding Phantom Students." *Education Next* 13 (Summer): 8–16.

Simpson, Kevin. 2013. "Voters Reject Big Tax Hike, School Finance Measure Amendment 66." *Denver Post*, November 5. Available at http://www.denverpost.com/breakingnews/ci_24462841/voters-reject-big-tax-hike-school-finance-measure.

Smith, Aaron, and Lisa Snell. 2015. "Moving toward Transparent and Student-Based Funding Reform in Georgia." *Georgia Public Policy Foundation*, December 4. Available at http://www.georgiapolicy.org/2015/12/moving-toward-transparent-and-student-based-funding-reform-in-georgia/.

Discussion Questions

1. What are the basic elements of student-based allocation (SBA)?
2. How do the authors define a hold-harmless provision? What does the term mean in relation to education finance?

3. What are some of the common criticisms of SBA? Are these positions valid?
4. What are some examples of student-based factors and district-based factors when considering how much to fund schools?
5. Why is it so hard to change education funding formulas?

Commonwealth Forum: Should Pennsylvania End the Practice of Hold-Harmless Funding?

YES

Pennsylvania's policy of hold-harmless education finance ensures the same level of funding since 2015 for each of the state's five hundred school districts no matter how many students are enrolled in that district. Instead of funding students, in other words, the state funds districts. No other state in the country abides such a practice. If another state does not fund on a per-student basis, they either smooth the transition from year to year using rolling averages, or dedicate a certain percentage of the previous year's higher allocation. Not a single state guarantees continuous level funding from a previous date. The state's hold-harmless practice was even more egregious between the 1991–2008 and 2011–2015 periods, when there was no explicit education funding formula. Pennsylvania's newest funding formula enacted in 2016 dedicates only *new* dollars to the formula, not the earlier levels of funding. In effect, this results in stranding resources in districts that no longer need them, while denying students in growing districts and students in districts with higher need from receiving an equitable distribution of state taxes.

Public dollars dedicated to education should follow a logical pattern of distribution according to the basic characteristics of students and the district. For example, rural districts have high transportation costs because of sparsity, and urban districts have costs related to a higher number of English-language learners. Pennsylvania's education-finance system still does not take these factors into account, since the vast majority of dollars are still allocated based on out-of-date student counts from the early 1990s. That politicians in the legislature continue this system because of election ramifications is indefensible.

NO

In *Reynolds v. Sims* (1964), Chief Justice Earl Warren wrote a classic defense of the idea of one person, one vote. He stated that "legislators represent people, not trees or acres. Legislators are elected by voters, not farms or cities." For the purposes of drawing legislative districts, geography does not matter. Unfortunately, it does for school districts. The United States is a highly mobile society. People are constantly seeking better economic opportunities and are willing to move to find them. For 67.3 percent of Pennsylvania school districts, this has meant a declining population over the twenty-year period ending in 2014. The loss of residents often means lower property ownership and property values, resulting in less revenue for schools. Fewer students does not automatically mean precipitous declines in costs. State and federal mandates, pension financing, and the fixed costs of school facilities all continue to put pressure on school districts. Rural areas in particular face problems of achieving economies of scale because of low population density and high transportation costs. The hold-harmless provision of the Commonwealth's school funding system have helped keep these school districts afloat.

Hold harmless is not the problem with education funding in Pennsylvania. The state's reliance on local revenue to fund schools should be the real focus of reform. In fiscal year 2015 the state spent $10.5 billion on elementary and secondary education. Sounds like a lot, right? Not when considering that local governments spent $16.2 billion. Stated differently, Pennsylvania paid 36.9 percent of education costs and local governments 56.5 percent. Nationally, states pay 47.1 percent of education costs. In fiscal year 1973, the Commonwealth's share of education spending was 50.96 percent. If the state rededicated itself to funding at least half of the costs of education, hold harmless would not even be an issue.

For More Information

The **Pennsylvania Department of Education** (http://www.education.pa .gov) provides public statistics on enrollment, the budget, student test scores, and a host of other information.

A comprehensive analysis of the hold-harmless education-finance policies of the fifty states can be found through research done by the **Center on Regional Politics** at Temple University (http://www.cla.temple.edu/ corp/files/2014/12/HH-Policies-Policy-Brief.pdf).

The **Education Law Center** has a wealth of resources on school funding in the state (https://www.elc-pa.org/).

The **Commonwealth Foundation** is clearly opposed to the practice of hold harmless in its analyses and opinion pieces (https://www.common wealthfoundation.org/).

Chapter 6
Demographics and Public Policy

More Trouble Ahead for Public School Finance

The Implications of Generational Change in Pennsylvania

Maureen W. McClure

Vera Krekanova

Pennsylvania's generational transitions will be rockier and more expensive for education finance than is publicly acknowledged. Debates over both the necessity for and the affordability of tax increases already frame state education budget debates. Education policy and planning data, especially at regional and local levels, tend to be isolated from other sector-wide and cross-sectoral data. This study explores the examples of tax-capacity and workforce-quality data and concludes that two issues state, regional, and local education policy makers cannot ignore are increased dependency ratios and a smaller workforce with fewer economic opportunities. Aging seniors increase dependency ratios, are less mobile, and enjoy lighter tax burdens, putting greater public responsibilities on the labor force. Younger, educated workers have heavier tax burdens and are more likely to leave for younger states with less-heavy tax burdens.

For the last thirty years, education finance policies in Pennsylvania were framed largely in terms of battles over expenditures. This, for the most part, included resources related either to access (inequalities, needs, adequacy, etc.) or to choice (charter schools, accountability, etc.). In contrast, in more centralized education systems internationally, discussions about education's contributions to provincial and national development and consequent revenue generation were popular. In the much more decentralized United States, development policy left education largely relegated to the margins. In the Commonwealth, some local school districts were highly engaged in regional workforce development issues, but over the last few decades, state interest in them has been limited. Education policies have focused instead on the contributions of classroom instruction and the structures of its delivery systems.

Why, then, is regional workforce development so important now? Without sustainable growth in the state's tax capacities, it will be difficult for Pennsylvania to manage its growing problems of aging taxpayers, relatively poor youth, and pension obligations. One well-known concern is the threat to economic growth that may be presented by unprecedented shifts in the shapes of state populations. Florida's population is growing. Pennsylvania's is flatlined. Given the irreversibility of many of these demographic shifts, without offsetting economic growth, they are likely to threaten education's revenue streams. The state's shifts in the internal distributions of its age cohorts are linked to the stability of the education sector's abilities to meet its future obligations.

The impacts of shifts in the state's population shapes on its tax capacities have been more carefully considered in other sectors, such as rural and urban development. The education sector not only needs to integrate other sectors' existing analyses and projections, it also must take greater responsibility for more transparent reporting of its contributions to development beyond the schoolhouse door. The reasons are clear. Growth is essential to offset increasing demands for services. The education sector competes at the state level with other development sectors. Is the growth of populations with limited incomes making the state a more expensive and less competitive place to live? If so, how is education helping to mitigate these problems and promote growth? And how can these issues be more widely incorporated into local or state strategic planning for education and workforce development?

These shifts need more-nuanced analyses when considering education finance policy. For example, what are the potential threats to workforce quantity and quality? In terms of quantity, baby-boom retirees have relatively few workers in the taxpaying age cohorts just behind them. In terms of quality, many of today's workers lack job stability, earn low wages, have few benefits, and face limited paths to upward mobility. The connections between education, development, and growth are not easily measured. These relationships are instead both historically messy and wickedly contested. They cannot, however, be ignored.

The state needs to better assist its Department of Education (PDE) in its efforts to provide better access to sector-wide, as well as cross-sector, data and analyses. State, regional, higher-education institutions (HEIs), and Local Education Agency (LEA) planning can benefit from this improved access.

Prologue

Pennsylvania's generational transitions will be rockier and more expensive for education finance than is publicly acknowledged. Debates over both the necessity for and the affordability of tax increases already frame state education budget debates. State policy's costing, data collection, and analysis capabilities, however, have not yet been either well integrated or broadly disseminated for use in strategic planning across the education sector. This includes the PDE, HEIs, and LEAs. In Pennsylvania, LEAs include career and technical centers, charter schools, intermediate units, school districts, special program jointures, and state juvenile correctional institutions.

The PDE's data collection and access capacities have greatly improved over the years. The department has come a long way from compliance data tapes sitting in isolated offices to online, multiyear data that are easily downloaded from their website. Education's contribution to revenue generation and development issues (tax capacities, workforce quantity and quality, economic growth, quality of life, etc.) are, however, only marginally referenced.

Currently, the PDE has only limited requirements for data related to costing, revenue generation, tax burden, or contributions to community stability, growth, and workforce development in their mandated strategic planning for school districts. Consequently, PDE access to multisector data and analyses in these areas have not yet been made easily available, visible, or deeply integrated within the education sector and across other sectors.

Demographic concerns are central. They can be framed as the problems of growing dependencies. As the state's dependency ratios rise, so do the risks for the state's tax capacities, perhaps especially for the education sector. Total dependency ratios very roughly compare the economically active and inactive. Young-age and old-age ratios are also popular. The dependency ratio is calculated as follows:

65 or older + 14 or younger ÷ Total working-age population (15–64)

The scale and rate of population aging have been triggering anxieties among policy makers (and the public) about the financial capacity of societies with populations over sixty-five surpassing the populations under fifteen (Beard et al. 2011). Dependency ratios can only be rough measures, as population behaviors are, of course, much more complicated. For example, the intensity of the dependency is not measured (many over sixty-five work, many of working age cannot work, etc.), but these issues can be addressed elsewhere by workforce-quality data.

Data are available to help refine dependency ratios and their consequences for shifting tax capacities and workforce development. Given rising costs and riskier returns, the education sector increasingly needs to more visibly justify public investments in it. One way is to demonstrate the sector's connections to Pennsylvania's growth risks, tax, and workforce capacities. To what extent are the state's fewer young families both poorer and less prepared for higher education, and thus educationally more expensive than their parents' generation?

Pennsylvania's major sectors such as education, health, and infrastructure need to make their contributions to state and local development much more visible for two reasons. First, as a direct contribution, education prepares the next generation for the inheritance of civil society. It is essential. Second, as an indirect contribution, the generational security required for economic growth can often be overlooked. Public education not only grapples with problems of student achievement, it also supports families' and communities' efforts to raise children who can govern civil societies and make their way in changing economies.

These cooperative, generational efforts reach beyond the important needs for standards and accountability. A larger generational question is what ethical roles and responsibilities Pennsylvania has in helping students, families, and communities consider what it means to be a U.S. citizen in an increasingly complex international political economy. A smaller generational question is what are the ethical roles and responsibilities of schools in avoiding misaligned regional and state workforce quality.

Workforce quality, as it is used here, refers to:

- levels of employment (full-time, part-time, etc.)
- levels of workforce capital (human, social, and cultural)
- levels of income

As workforce quality shifts and enrollments decline for a while statewide, it cannot be business as usual for education planning and funding policies.

The state's education funding policies and practices need to reflect a more nuanced understanding of the state's taxpayers. While state public policy debates have acknowledged the growing impacts of generational transitions on tax bases, greater support is needed not only for local analysis, planning, and management but also for greater public visibility for these critical issues. As the Commonwealth's shifting population reshapes its political economy, it creates problems that are both too difficult to be easily solved and too important to be ignored.

Education: Losing Its Fan Base?

It is already well known that the baby-boom cohort (born about 1946–1964) is leaving the workforce for retirement, placing new fiscal burdens on the state in two ways. First, they visibly place demands on state expenditures. This burden comes primarily in terms of health care and public pension payouts.

There are not only more of them; they are living longer. Without sufficient economic growth, the additional payouts needed to cover these retiree costs may threaten education budgets. Second, retirees in Pennsylvania do not pay income taxes on their pensions. This places downward pressure on tax capacities at the very time demands on it are increasing. It also puts pressure on economic growth to offset this downward pressure. Third, the baby-boom generation is creating scale problems because as they leave income-tax-generating jobs for retirement, they are being replaced by cohorts of fewer people.

In addition, the Generation X cohort (born about 1965–1980) may not generate as much in income taxes, not only because there are fewer of them but also because many of the jobs held by those retiring, including higher-paying ones, are being eliminated (Newhook 2015; Powell 2013).

Younger cohorts, Generation X, millennials (also known as Generation Y or the Echo Generation, born about 1981–1995), and Generation Z (born about 1996–2015), have grown, or are growing into, labor markets more challenging for many than the ones their parents faced when they were young (Carnevale, Hanson, and Gulish 2013; Taylor 2014).

The growing state impacts of generational transitions on tax bases are better known in Harrisburg than in LEAs and HEIs. This means creating more public forums for education and development debates on the consequences of shifting population shapes. For example, it seems unlikely that most school districts have incorporated the Independent Fiscal Office reports into their state-mandated strategic plans. Nor have many conducted a nuanced analysis of the tax-capacity consequences of changing demographics within their own districts. The Commonwealth's shifting population shapes and rising dependency rates are creating problems for the education sector that are too difficult to respond to in a sector-isolated approach (McClure, Sabina, and Krekanova 2016).

Historically Unique

What is raising the urgency levels for local, regional, and state education policy makers now? Two things: uniqueness and complexity. First, the scale of population shifts in many developed countries is historically unique. The baby boom began in the aftermath of World War II and ended roughly with the widespread availability of reliable birth control measures in the early 1960s. This generational cohort was not only much larger than those before; it was also living longer. A major event such as the baby boom is a "black swan," meaning it has high historical impact and is without precedent (Taleb 2010). This means approaches to strategic planning designed in the late twentieth century no longer hold as well as they did before. For example, a needs-based focus on access to and quality of resource expenditures may overlook a capacity-based analysis of revenue-generation projections.

Current population shapes in the United States and other nations are already radically different from more-traditional images of population pyramids still present in countries such as Mexico. In comparison, the U.S. population pyramid has for some time looked a little more like a lumpy rectangle (see Figure 6.1). The lumps were created by the aging boom and its echo generation. In a larger sense, these problems are only temporary, as the population is already shifting again. Temporary, however, as it is used here, is measured in decades. These shifts have significant consequences for both educational revenues and expenditures and will last for some time. This is not news. Neither is its absence from education-sector planning.

Pennsylvania today is wealthier in data than in strategy. The state has already aged. Aging means rising interest in sectors other than education. It also means there are large numbers of taxpayers and voters who are currently leaving the labor force and perhaps leaving behind a degree of interest in voting for and ability to pay for increased taxes for education.

More Limited Pathways for the Young

As boomers retire, many jobs are either disappearing or will not be filled because of a "skills gap" some young people face, as they are unprepared for

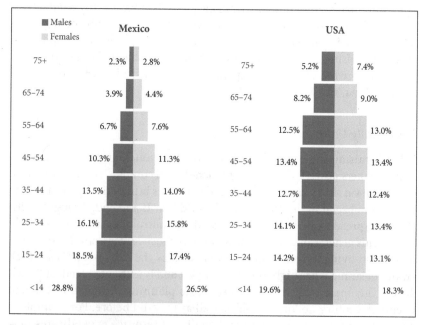

Figure 6.1 Population pyramids, 2015. *(Data source: U.S. Census Bureau* International Data Base, *at https://www.census.gov/data-tools/demo/idb/informationGateway.php.)*

high-skill, high-wage jobs (Schleicher 2013; Symonds, Schwartz, and Ferguson 2011). In the past, young workers with limited educations could informally develop skills through experience on the shop floor. This allowed them to work their way up from a working-class existence to a more stable middle-class life. Today, however, there are fewer shop floors to create the informal education paths needed for upward mobility. There are instead many more dead-end, low-skill, low-wage jobs with limited access to paths leading to middle-skill, middle-wage jobs (Center for Workforce Information and Analysis 2015).

Can Pennsylvania Eschew Perverse Incentives?

Today's younger citizens are poorer, needier, and may be more likely to be thought of as "other," not us. For example, more than 39 percent (approximately 1.04 million) of Pennsylvania's young children live in low-income families (National Center for Children in Poverty 2017). Despite sincere efforts to legislate better access to better education, the consequences of large inequalities remain to be overcome. How will elected officials balance investments in the young, who are less likely to vote, against seniors, who are more likely to show up at the polls? Will teachers' unions be able to offset senior voters? The voting rates among twenty-five- to forty-four-year-olds are below 50 percent but almost 70 percent among those over age sixty-five (File 2014).

Pennsylvania continues to focus its investments on K–12 classroom instruction under an assumption that it will translate into a future functioning labor market. This may or may not be true. Largely absent is attention to tax base stability. Where are the critical public and private investments needed both for labor market access and for the continuous, active workforce "up-skilling" to meet the demands of a twenty-first-century political economy (and state budgets) (Carnevale, Hanson, and Gulish 2013; Mérette 2007)?

Unfortunately, by the time problems created by weak education-sector investments in local and state growth and development rise to critical visibility, it may be too late to mitigate the damage created. Too often the more complex the problem, the more likely policy makers are to mandate policies with visible, accountable short-term returns, even when longer-term investments in development and economic sustainability may be more valuable (Levin et al. 2009). As part of a state with rapid aging and limited growth, the education sector in Pennsylvania has to help generate growth and development that can be highly competitive not only in attracting and starting businesses but also in competing to attract and keep mobile young families with middle- to high-skilled labor.

As we begin to look at Pennsylvania's population dynamics, we can only scratch the surface. The provision of public education to ensure opportunity for the next generation is part of our social contract. The private sector can do its part and make critical contributions, but it cannot take responsibility for the security of generational transitions. The next decades will test our social contract. The education sector can no longer simply contend over expenditures on the basis of need. It also has to show that the current generation's resources are being invested well in the next. We need to batten down the hatches so the state can better weather this passing storm.

Generational Threat to Revenue Stability

How big is the problem? In Pennsylvania, never before did the number of older people surpass the share of population below the age of fifteen. Today, however, the cohorts of sixty-five and over and under fifteen are almost equal (see Figure 6.2). In five years, the share of older people will outweigh the share of children by 2.4 percentage points. In ten years the difference grows to 4.8 percentage points, and in twenty years the gap grows to 6.8 percentage points.

Aging and its impact on education finance is not only an issue of a rapid increase in the number of older people; there are also amplifying trends with complex economic, political, and social implications for families and communities. As more and more older people continue to live longer, as in the rest of the United States, Pennsylvanians' lifespans are becoming extended by an entire extra generation. Consequently, family composition, housing arrangements, and lifestyles now need to change to accommodate a four-generation society with an unprecedented number of middle-aged adults with living parents (Findsen and Formosa 2011; Taylor 2014).

Pennsylvania as Canary: Already Older

Pennsylvania already ranks fourth in the United States for the percentage of those sixty-five and over (West et al. 2014). Indeed, all age cohorts over forty-five are significantly larger in Pennsylvania than in the rest of the nation (see Figure 6.3). The eighty-to-eighty-four cohort is 23 percent larger than the national average, and the eighty-five-and-older cohort is 34 percent larger.

To compound the problem, younger cohorts, for the time being, are smaller in Pennsylvania than in the rest of the United States. The state's highest gap is among those age zero to five. The zero-to-five cohort is 10 percent, and the five-to-ten cohort is 9 percent, smaller than the national benchmark. The entire older half of Pennsylvania's population (over forty-five years old) is larger (by 9 percent), and the entire younger half (under forty-five years old) is smaller (by 7 percent), than the same groups on the national level. This substantial 16 percent gap leaves the state with fewer people to carry heavier demographic burdens than those in other states.

This demographic deficit problem is even more urgent when we consider troubling high school and college dropout rates, persistent child poverty

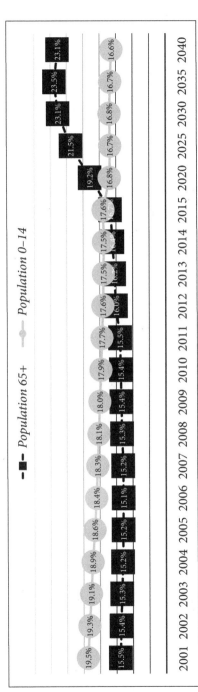

Legend:
- ■ - Population 65+
- ◆ - Population 0–14

Data series (Population 65+, black squares):
2001: 15.5%, 2002: 15.4%, 2003: 15.3%, 2004: 15.2%, 2005: 15.2%, 2006: 15.1%, 2007: 15.2%, 2008: 15.3%, 2009: 15.4%, 2010: 15.5%, 2011: 16.0%, 2012: 16.2%, 2013: 16.8%, 2014: 17.6%, 2015: 19.2%, 2020: 21.5%, 2025: 23.1%, 2030: 23.5%, 2035: 23.1%

Data series (Population 0–14, grey circles):
2001: 19.5%, 2002: 19.3%, 2003: 19.1%, 2004: 18.9%, 2005: 18.6%, 2006: 18.4%, 2007: 18.3%, 2008: 18.1%, 2009: 18.0%, 2010: 17.9%, 2011: 17.7%, 2012: 17.6%, 2013: 17.5%, 2014: 17.5%, 2015: 17.6%, 2020: 16.8%, 2025: 16.7%, 2030: 16.8%, 2035: 16.7%, 2040: 16.6%

X-axis: 2001 2002 2003 2004 2005 2006 2007 2008 2009 2010 2011 2012 2013 2014 2015 2020 2025 2030 2035 2040

Figure 6.2 Share of Pennsylvania population by age cohort, 2001–2040. *(Data source: U.S. Census Bureau American FactFinder database, at https://factfinder.census.gov/faces/nav/jsf/pages/index.xhtml; Behney et al. 2014.)*

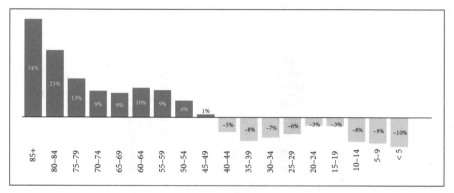

Figure 6.3 Pennsylvania population compared to U.S. population by share of age cohort, 2015. *(Data source: U.S. Census Bureau* American FactFinder *database, at https://factfinder.census.gov/faces/nav/jsf/pages/index.xhtml.)*

Note: Positive numbers denote higher-than-national-average concentration of population within a particular age cohort; negative numbers denote lower-than-national-average concentration of population within a particular age cohort.

rates, and youth unemployment rates. All of these shrink the size of the workforce available to support growing dependency ratios. Thus policy makers need to start addressing out-migration issues now by planning how to attract and keep younger cohorts.

Those who are most able, however, are also often the most mobile. They can take their families and leave for less-expensive states with more job opportunities, younger populations, and lighter tax burdens. Better assessments of this potential problem and other disruptive possibilities and their consequences for the education sector are needed. Developments in big data analytics may now allow for superior multisectoral analyses to better inform decision support and planning across a wide range of related issues.

Population Shifts and the Hiccup Problem

Pennsylvania's future is now (see Figure 6.4). In 2001, the population over forty-five was already estimated to be 39 percent. In 2015, the estimate had grown to 45 percent. In contrast, the under-twenty-five cohort accounted for only 33 percent in 2001 and, by 2015, even less, at 31 percent.

What about the core of working-age adults in the middle? Over the last fifteen years, the core of Pennsylvania's population shifted from a thirty-five-to-fifty-four cohort to a forty-five-to-sixty-four cohort. During this time the youngest cohort shrank noticeably. These shifts are likely to have consequences for the state's tax base.

Today's population pyramids look significantly different than fifteen years ago and they continue to morph. In 2040, about the time many children born today will have graduated from college and will be getting married,

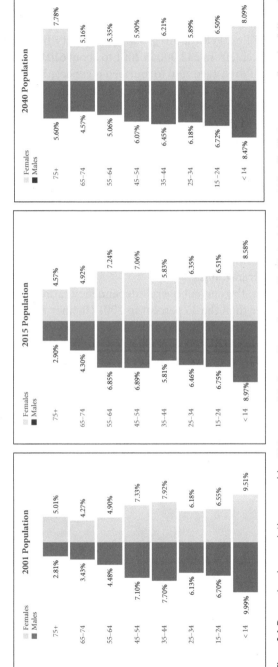

Figure 6.4 Pennsylvania population pyramids. *(Data source: U.S. Census Bureau American FactFinder database, at https://factfinder.census.gov/faces/nav/jsf/pages/ index.xhtml; Behney et al. 2014.)*

starting families, and buying homes, significant changes to the Pennsylvania population composition will have occurred. In terms of relative size, there will be a much narrower difference between the age cohorts (see Figure 6.4). The population aged sixty-five and older will have grown 71 percent, from 1.9 million to 3.3 million. Within this group, those eighty-five and older will have grown 152 percent, from 242,000 in 2001 to about 610,000. Meanwhile, the population of children aged zero to fourteen is expected to decline about 2 percent, from 2.40 million to 2.34 million. Additionally, over 40 percent of these children are likely to be raised in low-income families, communities, and school districts. Many of these children are not likely to be well prepared for higher-education success.

Growing Risks for Education Policy: Generational Dependency Issues

Also, perhaps because these problems have little historical context, they lack a policy infrastructure to manage them. There are few lobbyists either for the development contributions of the education sector or for a generational interest in successful transitions.

In Pennsylvania, the current overall dependency ratio is 34.2 percent. This is slightly lower than the 35 percent in 2001 (Behney et al. 2014). Even small, one-tenth of a point shifts can be significant. This decrease, however, is only temporary. By 2020, the dependency ratio is estimated to be 35.9 percent, and by 2040, 39.7 percent (Tucker 2012). Aging will drive all of the increases in dependency ratios (see Figure 6.5). These rapidly growing old-age dependency ratios are signaling major issues for public policies that include education (Rudawska 2010).

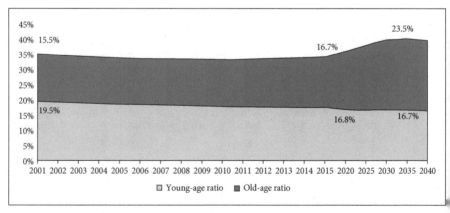

Figure 6.5 Dependency ratio in Pennsylvania (per 100 working-age persons), 2001–2040. *(Data source: U.S. Census Bureau American FactFinder database, at https://factfinder.census.gov/faces/nav/ jsf/pages/index.xhtml; Behney et al. 2014.)*

Pensions: Who Will Be Able to Pay in the Future?

Very visible in the media is the state's chronic issue of public pensions. How can Pennsylvania meet its constitutional obligations without compromising the quality of life of the rest of its citizens (Beard et al. 2011)? It may already be too late to avoid problems. Voters from the private sector with fewer retirement benefits are likely to be both reluctant and unable to pay increasingly higher taxes to fund public pensioners, even though they are currently obligated to do so by the state constitution as it has been interpreted by the courts.

Some state and LEA policy makers claim limited future problems because the marginal increases in local pension contributions start to decline in a couple of years. In 2001, however, there was one pensioner for every four workers in Pennsylvania. Soon there will be only three. Without major inmigration, within a generation only 2.5 Pennsylvanian workers will be available to support one pensioner. Those 2.5 workers will also be likely to be caring for their families, worrying about housing costs and health care, and/or paying off college loans (Tucker 2012). With over 40 percent of these 2.5 workers now growing up under low-income conditions, what will be their opportunities? What kind of education investment do they need today, and what kind of jobs will they need tomorrow so they can manage these future complex fiscal responsibilities?

Generational Security and a Fraying Social Contract

Generational security is a slowly growing issue. For many decades, there was the assumption of a social contract that justified transfers of public funds to the young and elderly on the basis of solidarity among the generations (Samorodov 1999; Taylor 2014). A generational solidarity principle anticipated that those participating in the labor market would contribute a share of their gross salary toward the income of retirees in exchange for a promise that the next generation would do the same. Today's changing demographics raise the potential for political conflict among current generations who find themselves in very different predicaments in the solidarity arrangement.

The large cohort of older workers who dutifully contributed to the pensions of the previous generation is becoming dependent on the contributions of a much smaller, younger, poorer, and less-well-educated generation. For example, since 2000, the earnings of Pennsylvania's youngest cohorts grew by about 30 percent. In contrast, the earnings of the state's oldest cohorts grew by more than 50 percent over the same period, also starting from a larger base. Some but not all of the following is to be expected because of experience. The current average earnings of those twenty-five to thirty-four are 34 percent smaller than the earnings of those thirty-five to forty-four, and 41 percent smaller than the earnings of those forty-five to fifty-four. This of course may shift with age, but in the meantime, it may crimp spending on large-ticket items such as housing.

Disparate Economic Power within and across Groups

In addition to the political economy tensions across generational cohorts, there is also the issue of disparate economic power both within and across groups. For example, dependency ratios are based solely on age. Age cohorts are assumed to be monolithic consumers of public services. First, the dependency ratios assume similar levels of needs within and across dependent groups (children and the elderly). Second, they assume similar earning abilities within the working-age population. These cohort numbers generally do not incorporate other mitigating factors such as gender, disabilities, and poverty.

To understand the more complex tax-capacity risks created by the shifting demographics of Pennsylvania, it is important to consider additional variables such as gender in the policy mix. For example, the number of females in Pennsylvania surpasses the number of males in every age category above thirty-five. Among the population age eighty-five and older, there are more than twice as many women as men. Women also account for 60 percent of the eighty-to-eighty-four cohort and 56 percent of the seventy-five-to-seventy-nine cohort. This trend, and its effects on revenue generation, is likely to become more pronounced the older the population grows.

Women not only live longer; they tend to have less financial security because of a lifetime of unequal and inadequate access to education and economic participation (Beard et al. 2011). This compounding effect may reduce tax capacities while increasing demands and costs for services. For example, many want to stay in their homes longer but lack resources for property tax increases to support schools. So they vote to keep school taxes down.

Education Cannot Ignore Workforce Quality

Dependency ratio growth, therefore, has significant consequences for education, both for the competition for expenditures and the stability of tax capacities. It is important to consider not only the size of dependencies but also the quality of workforces. Dependency ratios alone cannot account for workforce quality. How many people may have full-time jobs with little pay? How many are discouraged, disabled, or stay at home by choice? While a range of descriptive data is widely available (Independent Fiscal Office 2016; Behney et al. 2014), their use in state, regional, HEI, and LEA education policy and planning remains limited.

Workforce Quality: Employed, Unemployed, Discouraged, and Not in the Labor Force (Voluntary and Involuntary)

Workforce-quality indicators are often overlooked as a measure of return to public investments in education, despite their availability. For example, as of December 2015, there were approximately 6,140,000 employed and 306,000 (4.8 percent) unemployed adults in Pennsylvania (Center for Workforce Information and Analysis 2015). The current labor force participation rate in Pennsylvania is only 62.5 percent, about the same as in the United States generally (Bureau of Labor Statistics 2018; Center for Workforce Information and Analysis 2015).

The four largest sectors employed about one-half of available jobs: health care and social assistance sector (17 percent), government (12 percent), retail trade (11 percent), and manufacturing (10 percent). It is important that the pipeline of younger workers under twenty-five is only about one-half the size of those fifty-five and older (Center for Workforce Information and Analysis 2015). Almost 47 percent of Pennsylvania's employed workforce is now forty-five or older, a significant increase from 37 percent in 2001 (see Figure 6.6). The cohort of employed workers age twenty-five to forty-four accounted for only 40 percent, and only 13 percent were under twenty-four. In only the last fifteen years the share of the state's active workforce who are sixty-five and older almost doubled, while the size of the three youngest cohorts each decreased by 2 percent. Traditional assumptions of generational replacement simply no longer hold. These dynamic changes have consequences for revenue generation.

In August 2015 Pennsylvania ranked thirty-first in national unemployment at 5.4 percent (Center for Workforce Information and Analysis 2015).

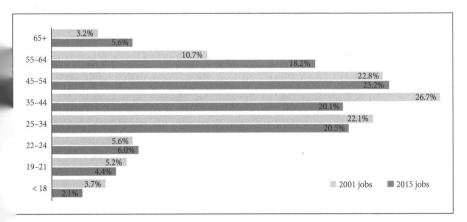

Figure 6.6 Distribution of jobs in Pennsylvania by age cohort, 2001–2015. *(Data source: Bureau of Labor Statistics 2015.)*

Unemployment was higher for males (5.7 percent) than females (4.6 percent). The youngest workers experienced the highest unemployment rates—11.8 percent for those sixteen to nineteen and 10.5 percent for those twenty to twenty-four. In contrast, the unemployment rate of workers fifty-five and over was only 3.7 percent. The average length of unemployment among all dislocated workers was thirty-one weeks. One-third of the unemployed, approximately 107,000, were considered long-term unemployed (they had been out of work for more than twenty-six weeks) (Center for Workforce Information and Analysis 2015).

Discouraged Workers. Employment and unemployment are not the only two variables, as there are many people who do not participate in the current labor force. Discouraged workers, for example, are those who both want and are available for work but have not found it. They have looked for work during the past year but not in the last four weeks. There are approximately twenty-eight thousand discouraged workers in Pennsylvania, or about twice the 2007 prerecession level. Almost 60 percent of the discouraged workers are males, and 40 percent are between the ages of twenty-five and fifty-four (Center for Workforce Information and Analysis 2015).

Not in the Labor Force: People with Disabilities. Those who are voluntarily not in the labor force include those under 65 who are retired, stay-at-home parents, caregivers, and the like. Those who are involuntarily not in the labor force include the disabled, as well as those who are institutionalized (Bureau of Labor Statistics 2015).

Approximately 820,000 working-age Pennsylvanians (11.2 percent) are classified as having one or more disabilities. The employment rate of people with disabilities in Pennsylvania is only 33.6 percent, and only about 20 percent of them are working full-time. An additional 11 percent of people with disabilities are actively looking for work (Erickson, Lee, and Von Schrader 2014).

The problem, therefore, is more complicated than it may appear to be at first. The working-age population that is unemployed or unable to sustain participation in the labor market quietly adds to the dependency levels. In other words, it increases the pressure on the state's expenditure and weakens its revenue base. The resulting employment-to-total-population ratio in Pennsylvania is currently 59.2 percent. For every ten people who are working, there are six who are not (Center for Workforce Information and Analysis 2015). Further, not all of those who are working have good jobs.

Workforce Quality: Compensation

The average annual wage in Pennsylvania in 2015 was $63,000 (United States was $72,641), but the median is only $43,400 (United States was $53,657) (Bureau of Labor Statistics 2015). More than one-half of Pennsylvanians

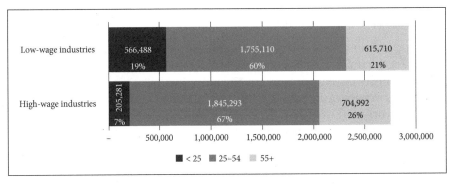

Figure 6.7 Jobs in Pennsylvania by age of worker and wage sector, 2015. *(Data source: Bureau of Labor Statistics 2015.)*

(52 percent) are employed in industries with average wages below even the $63,000 benchmark. Without access to manufacturing and other middle-skill, middle-wage jobs, today's younger workers (under twenty-five) are significantly more concentrated in the low-wage industry sectors with limited upward mobility, such as accommodation and food services, retail, or arts, entertainment, and recreation. These younger workers are underrepresented in the high-wage industry sectors such as utilities, mining, even information. Older workers (fifty-five and older), conversely, are more concentrated in the high-wage industry sectors than in the low-wage sectors (see Figure 6.7).

Workforce Quality: Part-Time Work

In addition to those who are not working and those in low-paying jobs, approximately 279,000 Pennsylvanians are working part-time for economic reasons. Economic reasons mean they have stated they would prefer full-time work and are working part-time only because full-time jobs are not available. This alone represents between 4.5 percent and 5.0 percent of the employed. Prior to the recession, people working part-time for economic reasons comprised between 2.5 percent and 3.0 percent of the state's employed. Women working part-time for economic reasons have historically been about one-half percentage point higher than men (Center for Workforce Information and Analysis 2015). In times of significant shifts at both ends of the population, the labor market opportunities available to the demographic core (active workforce) are critical to both the state's fiscal performance and successful generational transitions.

In sum, the state's tax capacities may be more fragile than the education sector currently assumes. Dependency ratios both identify and mask generational needs and abilities to pay. Moving forward, more attention is required to assess the risks to education's revenue-generation sources.

Workforce Transition Problems

Aging in Pennsylvania presents a significant risk to the supply side of labor market dynamics. First, the numbers of older workers significantly surpasses the numbers of younger workers. Second, the current pipeline of younger workers cannot easily substitute for the human and social capital skills of aging workers (Dychtwald, Erickson, and Morison 2004). In addition to poorly matched work experiences and skills, there are significant differences in preferences for sectors and occupations between the two age groups.

For example, in Pennsylvania the highest concentration of older workers (age fifty-five and older) is in teaching and training, management, and office and administrative occupations. The highest concentration of adult workers age twenty-five to fifty-four is in computer, legal, and construction occupations. And the highest concentration of the youngest workers (under twenty-five) is in food preparation and serving, sales, and personal care occupations. Younger workers may be working their way through school, or may not yet have landed a job for which they are qualified. Nevertheless, these jobs are often less likely to build toward careers and upward mobility. When these low-wage jobs become low-wage occupations, they generate weak career trajectories. As a consequence, this can result in weak competition for jobs across cohorts because of differences in knowledge, skills, and experiences. Consequently, there is a limited substitutability between them (Eichhorst et al. 2013; Samorodov 1999).

Education Policy for Pennsylvania's Population Scale and Shift Problems

The problems created by the sheer scale of population shape-shifting lack precedent. Paying attention to dependency ratios and workforce quality is important in education policy because they influence revenue-generation issues such as total tax burden and tax effort willingness. Too often in the past, school taxes have been treated as independent factors rather than as interdependent with other sectors of local and state taxation and development. Taxpayers experience their sum of taxes more than their individual parts. Dependency ratios can affect a district's or a state's willingness to tax across the public sector, making education a development competitor with health, transportation, and other areas.

Challenges to Personal Incomes. Baby boomers aging out of the labor force are destabilizing the state's already delicate balance between active and inactive workers. Increasing numbers of retirees are turning to Social Security with limited savings to manage their own retirements and health care. In addition to retirees with limited savings, the state is called on to support public education pension payouts. These are not insignificant. Where can Pennsylvania turn for additional resources? Not to retirees on limited incomes with limited savings. Not to the high-wage jobs left unfilled by retirees. Not to the young in low-wage jobs. Not to unemployed, discouraged, or part-time workers. Not to those voluntarily or involuntarily (disabled) not in the labor force. Will the state's economic growth pull us out? Let us hope.

Challenges to Property Taxes. Personal incomes are not the only revenue policy area that becomes complicated with increasing dependency ratios. Market values may be affected as well. What will be the demand for suburban homes when many baby-boomer retirees are ready to sell and fewer young people are available and/or able to buy? A younger generation of millennials is postponing marriage, childbearing, car and home buying for up to ten years later than their parents' generation (Taylor 2014). Many face large education debt loads and consequently have less available for mortgage payments. High debt loads are to be expected in a state like Pennsylvania, which has some of the highest public higher-education in-state tuition costs in the United States (Friedman 2016). Further complicating these generational transitions are the problems of the market's financial interest rates, which, since the Great Recession, have been held deliberately low as an economic stimulus. This stimulus, however, came in the form of a massive interest rate subsidy. For the older generation it meant lower returns on their savings accounts, CDs, and other investments. For the younger generation it meant lower interest rates for big-ticket items such as homes and cars. Even with the lower interest rate subsidies, recovery was slow. Why? The young had fewer discretionary resources, making it difficult for them to take advantage of lower interest rates (e.g., school loan debt had higher interest rates than other items). Young people are also paying larger shares of their incomes for housing (Taylor 2014). All of these issues may eventually affect Pennsylvania's market valuations of taxable properties in some school districts.

Is Relief on the Way?

Not likely. Two issues that state, regional, and local education policy makers cannot ignore are increased dependency ratios and a smaller workforce with fewer economic opportunities for at least the next decade or so. Together they help make the state less competitive in national and global markets. First, the state cannot deport aging seniors who increase dependency ratios, putting greater public responsibilities on the labor force. Raising taxes to meet public demand for services risks making the state less competitive in the marketplace. While seniors enjoy lighter tax burdens and are likely to be less mobile, younger workers have heavier tax burdens and are more mobile. Younger, more educated people are more likely to leave for younger states with less-heavy tax burdens.

Pennsylvania is an aging state with many small school districts that already have relatively few taxpayers. Now many of them are aging out of personal income taxes, buying less, and voting to keep taxes down so they can stay in their homes. Will this contribute to an increasingly lower-quality workforce and make the state even less competitive? In the face of these challenges, Pennsylvania needs to better invest in children from low-income families today so they have opportunities to successfully access a civil society and prosperous economy tomorrow (Carnevale, Hanson, and Gulish 2013).

Today, education policy makers and planners need to broaden their views beyond instructional accountability in the classroom and better manage the empirical realities and trajectories that add risk to revenues. The state's demographics and workforce-quality data are well known, but these data have not yet been visibly incorporated in the PDE's funding policies or in its directives for regional and local strategic planning. This continues despite growing uncertainty and risk. The longer education policy makers avoid addressing the uncertainty inevitably being created by these shifts, the more difficult responses may be in the future.

Why now? The die is already cast. The players for 2040 are already on the stage. Children born today will be only twenty-five in 2040. They may still be in the workforce in 2080. The Commonwealth needs to carefully review its social contract for generational succession. Schools may be like businesses in some ways, but markets may not be the only, or the best, framework for managing long-term generational security issues.

So What Is the Road Forward?

Education policy and planning data, especially at regional and local levels, tend to be isolated from other sector-wide and cross-sectoral data. Two examples are tax-capacity and workforce-quality data, even though they are well known and available. The road forward is to support PDE's efforts to include data that focus on education's contribution to development in state funding policies, and support for regional and local workforce planning and policy. Deeper integration of the state's data silos and more-visible promotion of accessible finance research reports could help the education sector think beyond classroom tests to its contributions to Pennsylvania's economic and civic development.

The sector's current focus on "the greater need" marginalizes its greater contribution. This includes the mapping of the networks of interdependence that are created by districts' changing demographics, revenue-generation sources, and workforce quantity and quality. How do these contexts fit in institutional budgeting, strategic planning, and collective bargaining contracts?

Of course, sector-wide and cross-sectoral issues are messy and are wick-edly difficult to model. Ignoring the mess for the tidiness of test scores, how-ever, may land Pennsylvania's education policy makers and planners in the classic dilemma found in the "keys and the streetlight" story. Someone finds a person looking for keys under a streetlight. Pitching in, neither has any luck.

"Where did you lose your keys?" the one inquired.

"In the park," the other responded.

"Then why look here?"

"Because the light is better here."

Understanding education's development relationships with tax capaci-ties and workforce quality means working in much dimmer light than more-traditional measures of classroom accountability using test scores. It is worth it. The good news is that more than many other states, Pennsylvania has many resources on which to draw.

NOTE

This article was previously published as Maureen W. McClure and Vera Krekanova, "More Trouble Ahead for Public School Finance: The Implications of Generational Change in Pennsylvania," *Commonwealth* 18, no. 1 (June 2016). © 2016 The Pennsylvania Political Science Association. ISSN 2469-7672 (online). http://dx.doi.org/10.15367/cjppp.v18i1.84. All rights reserved.

REFERENCES

Beard, John R., Simon Biggs, David E. Bloom, Linda P. Fried, Paul Hogan, Alexandre Kalache, and S. Jay Olshansky. 2011. *Global Population Ageing: Peril or Promise?* Geneva: World Economic Forum.

Behney, Michael, Sue Copella, Jennifer Shultz, Debbie Bowalick, Aaron Koontz, Larry Meyers, and Michael Kotovsky. 2014. "Pennsylvania Population Projections, 2010–2040." Available at http://www.rural.palegislature.us/documents/reports/Popula tion_Projections_Report.pdf.

Bureau of Labor Statistics. 2015. *Quarterly Census of Employment and Wages.* Washing-ton, DC: U.S. Department of Labor.

———. 2018. "Employment Situation Summary." *Economic News Release*, February 2. Available at http://www.bls.gov/news.release/empsit.nr0.htm.

Carnevale, Anthony P., Andrew R. Hanson, and Artem Gulish. 2013. *Failure to Launch: Structural Shift and the New Lost Generation.* Washington, DC: Center on Educa-tion and the Workforce.

Center for Workforce Information and Analysis. 2015. "PA Monthly Workstats." De-cember. Available at http://www.workstats.dli.pa.gov/Research/Pages/default.aspx.

Dychtwald, Ken, Tamara Erickson, and Bob Morison. 2004. "It's Time to Retire Retire-ment." *Harvard Business Review* 82 (March): 48–57.

Eichhorst, Werner, Tito Boeri, Michela Braga, An De Coen, Vicenzo Galasso, Maarten Gerard, Michael Kendzia, et al. 2013. "Combining the Entry of Young People in the Labour Market with the Retention of Older Workers." IZA Research Report No. 53. Available at http://www.iza.org/en/webcontent/publications/reports/report_pdfs/ report_pdfs/iza_report_53.pdf.

Erickson, William A., Camille Lee, and Sarah Von Schrader. 2014. "2012 Disability Status Report: Pennsylvania." Available at http://www.disabilitystatistics.org/status Reports/2012-PDF/2012-StatusReport_PA.pdf.

File, Thom. 2014. "Young-Adult Voting: An Analysis of Presidential Elections, 1964–2012." Available at http://www.census.gov/prod/2014pubs/p20-573.pdf.

Findsen, Brian, and Marvin Formosa. 2011. *Lifelong Learning in Later Life: A Handbook of Older Adult Learning.* Rotterdam: Sense.

Friedman, Jordan. 2016. "10 Colleges with the Highest Tuition for In-State Students." *U.S. News and World Report*, May 3. Available at http://www.usnews.com/education/best-colleges/the-short-list-college/articles/2014/10/28/10-colleges-where-in-state-students-pay-the-most-tuition.

Independent Fiscal Office. 2016. *Economic and Budget Outlook: Commonwealth of Pennsylvania.* Harrisburg, PA: Independent Fiscal Office.

Levin, Kelly, Benjamin Cashore, Steven Bernstein, and Graeme Auld. 2009. "Playing It Forward: Path Dependency, Progressive Incrementalism, and the 'Super Wicked' Problem of Global Climate Change." *IOP Conference Series: Earth and Environmental Science* 6 (50): 502002. Available at http://iopscience.iop.org/article/10.1088/1755-1307/6/50/502002.

McClure, Maureen W., Lou Sabina, and Vera Krekanova. 2016. "Adequacy: A Comparative Study of Generational Financial Interests in Florida and Pennsylvania." Paper presented at the Annual Meeting of the National Education Finance Conference, Jacksonville, FL.

Mérette, Marcel. 2007. "Substitution between Young and Old Workers in an Ageing Context." Paper presented at the International Conference on Policy Modeling (EcoMod), Sao Paulo, Brazil.

National Center for Children in Poverty. 2017. "Pennsylvania Demographics of Young, Low-Income Children." Available at http://www.nccp.org/profiles/PA_profile_8.html.

Newhook, Emily. 2015. "The Cost of Aging in America." *Public Health Online*, January 13. Available at http://publichealthonline.gwu.edu/cost-of-aging/.

Powell, Jason L. 2013. *Globalization and Global Aging.* New York: Nova Science.

Rudawska, Iga. 2010. "Active Ageing and Labour Market." *Economics and Sociology* 3 (April): 9–24.

Samorodov, Alexander. 1999. *Ageing and Labour Markets for Older Workers: Employment and Training Papers.* Geneva: Employment and Training Department, International Labour Office Geneva.

Schleicher, Andreas. 2013. *Skilled for Life? Key Findings from the Survey of Adult Skills.* Paris: OECD.

Symonds, William C., Robert Schwartz, and Ronald F. Ferguson. 2011. "Pathways to Prosperity: Meeting the Challenge of Preparing Young Americans for the 21st Century." Available at https://dash.harvard.edu/bitstream/handle/1/4740480/Pathways_to_Prosperity_Feb2011-1.pdf?sequence=1.

Taleb, Nassim Nicholas. 2010. *The Black Swan: The Impact of the Highly Improbable.* 2nd ed. London: Penguin.

Taylor, Paul. 2014. *The Next America: Boomers, Millennials, and the Looming Generational Showdown.* New York: Public Affairs.

Tucker, Catherine. 2012. *Pennsylvania Population Projections: Fertility, Mortality and Migration.* University Park: Population Research Institute, Pennsylvania State University.

West, Loraine A., Samantha Cole, Daniel Goodkind, and Wan He. 2014. "65+ in the United States: 2010." Available at https://www.census.gov/content/dam/Census/library/publications/2014/demo/p23-212.pdf.

Discussion Questions

1. How will an increasingly older population in Pennsylvania affect the struggle for scarce government resources in the state?
2. Why do the authors argue that the changing demographics of the state are historically unique?
3. Why is an educated workforce important to funding government programs?
4. What are the major problems with Pennsylvania's workforce? Are there any solutions to these problems?
5. Why is it harder for elected representatives to address long-term problems as opposed to those that need to be immediately addressed?

Commonwealth Forum: Should Pennsylvania Tax Retirement Income?

YES

Pennsylvania is facing a structural budget deficit that will be exacerbated by an aging population. The Commonwealth is among the oldest states in the country and faces a 66.4 percent increase in residents age sixty-five and over between 2010 and 2040. More retirees equals less income tax revenue and more fiscal stress on the state through expenditures on programs that assist the elderly. The time has come to rethink our taxation scheme. Pennsylvania is one of only a handful of states that exempts all retirement plan income from taxation. This tax expenditure must be revised to promote the long-term fiscal health of the state.

Retirees have been productive members of society for decades and deserve recognition for their achievements. However, exempting public and private pension and retirement income is based on an antiquated notion that retirees cannot afford to be taxed, since they are no longer working. The facts do not support this case. The financial status of older people has gotten better over recent decades. Adjusting for inflation, the median income of married couples sixty-five and older has increased 129 percent since 1962 and 114 percent for non-married individuals in this age group. Almost 20 percent have incomes above $75,000.

The major concern about increasing taxes on retirement is how it would affect the poor. In Pennsylvania, 8.1 percent of those sixty-five and older live in poverty. However, national statistics show that the poorest quintile of Americans only relies on pensions or retirement plans for 3 percent of their income. More than 80 percent of their money comes from Social Security. Let's keep the Social Security income exemption but start to tax pensions and retirement plans like 401(k) plans. Pennsylvania will capture more revenue, while protecting its most vulnerable elderly. It will also prevent a generational shift of taxes onto younger people who are trying to raise families and buy homes.

NO

Pennsylvanians pay income tax, sales tax, property tax, local wage taxes, and a host of other taxes on top of the federal income tax. They do not need to pay more taxes when they are finally able to retire and have to live on a fixed income. Furthermore, implementing a tax on retirement income would be an administrative nightmare. Unlike the federal system, Pennsylvania does not allow the exemption of retirement contributions when paying the flat 3.07 percent income tax to the state. Taxing retirement income would then be a form of double taxation. Retirees would be forced to pay taxes twice: once when the money is put into retirement savings, and again when it is withdrawn. In addition, suddenly taxing retirement income would be an economic shock to the state's senior citizens and patently unfair. Out of the blue, they would have 3.07 percent less in their bank accounts, with little to no recourse to increase their earnings as the cost of living rises and incomes decline.

Those who support taxing retirement income have suggested the implementation of exemptions for low-income retirees in order to make the system equitable. However, when Pennsylvania first imposed an income tax, it included exemptions that were then ruled unconstitutional. It is likely the Commonwealth does not tax any form of retirement income because exemptions in this category would be ruled unconstitutional as well. Senior citizens continue to pay property taxes and sales taxes as they age while putting very little stress on public services. They deserve a break in their golden years.

For More Information

The **National Conference of State Legislatures** (http://www.ncsl.org/documents/fiscal/StateTaxOnPensions2015update.pdf) provides a report titled "State Personal Income Taxes on Pensions and Retirement Income" that provides detailed information concerning the types of tax breaks that are offered to retired people by different states.

"The Genesis of Senior Income Tax Breaks" (*National Tax Journal*, December 2012), by Karen Smith Conway and Jonathan C. Rork, gives an overview of how and why states developed tax breaks for older Americans. They show that exempting pensions from income taxes became popular starting in the 1970s.

"Revisiting State Tax Preferences for Seniors" (2006), by Elizabeth Mc-Nichol of the Center on Budget and Policy Priorities, outlines how coming demographic changes may change how states tax their older citizens. The article is available at https://www.cbpp.org/sites/default/files/atoms/files/3-6-06sfp.pdf.

The **Social Security Administration** (https://www.ssa.gov/policy/docs/chartbooks/fast_facts/2016/fast_facts16.pdf) publishes the annual "Fast Facts and Figures about Social Security." The file includes important information about what demographic groups rely most heavily on the federal program for their incomes. Sources of income are broken out across a range of sources including pensions.

Chapter 7
Health-Care Policy

The Limits of Medicaid Reform in Pennsylvania

*Thinking Regionally about Access to Insurance
and Health Care under the Affordable Care Act*

MICHELE MOSER DEEGAN
A. LANETHEA MATHEWS-SCHULTZ

States' varied decisions with respect to Medicaid expansion under the Affordable Care Act have drawn significant attention to questions about equity across states. Missing from the conversation is consideration of the varied impact that reform will have within states. This article considers how low-income Pennsylvanians will fare under Medicaid expansion. Although Medicaid reform has already expanded access to insurance to significant numbers of low-income residents in the state, improvements in access to health care are mediated by preexisting regional inequalities in social determinants of health and by Pennsylvania's system of health governance. Drawing on lessons gleaned from the literature on regionalism, and examples of success in states that have adopted regional approaches to health delivery, we offer a theoretical approach for thinking regionally in Pennsylvania by building opportunities and capacities for cross-jurisdictional approaches to health and health-care access.

The Patient Protection and Affordable Care Act (2010; ACA) is designed to make the health-care system more effective and efficient, while expanding insurance coverage and preventive care to millions of Americans. The ACA alters the existing health-care system by expanding the regulatory role of the federal and state governments and by requiring insurers and health-care providers to restructure their personnel and services to accommodate the requirements of the law. Not only is "Obamacare" the most significant health-care overhaul since 1965, when Medicaid and Medicare were instituted, but also the ACA provides a unique window for examining the politics of implementation of federal policy reform across a diverse and fragmented nation.

Extending Medicaid to uninsured low-income citizens is a key mechanism of the ACA. As originally conceived, starting in 2014, an expanded Medicaid extends coverage to all individuals under sixty-five years of age with incomes up to 138 percent of the federal poverty level (FPL) (Kenney et al. 2012).[1] The federal government is picking up 100 percent of the costs of new enrollees initially, reducing its contributions to these costs to 95 percent in 2016, and to 90 percent in 2020. The original ACA required states to expand Medicaid under threat of loss of all federal Medicaid reimbursements for existing enrollees.[2] In *National Federation of Independent Business et al. v. Sebelius, Secretary of Health and Human Services, et al.* (2012), however, the Supreme Court held that, because Congress's tax and spend powers do not extend to compel the states to enact or administer federal regulatory programs, the mandated Medicaid expansion was unconstitutional. The Court's decision, in short, made Medicaid expansion, and therefore also full implementation of the ACA, a matter of state choice.

States' varied decisions with respect to Medicaid expansion have drawn significant attention to questions about equity *across* states (see, for example, Jacobs and Callaghan 2013). To be sure, since Medicaid's inception in 1965, states have been required to comply with federal criteria—determining, for example, who receives care and what funds are provided at what costs—as a condition of receiving federal Medicaid funds. However, eligibility requirements, scope and breadth of services and benefits, and share of Medicaid funding provided by the federal government vary widely across states. As of January 2017, thirty-two states (including District of Columbia) have opted into adopting the ACA Medicaid expansion and nineteen have opted out (Kaiser Family Foundation 2017). Medicaid reform is a divisive issue; all of the states opting out are Republican led (although ten states had Republican governors when they decided to expand) and no states in the Deep South are expanding, making Medicaid reform regionally concentrated. Moreover, reducing federal reimbursements for Medicaid (both for new enrollees added through expanded eligibility requirements and traditional recipients under the pre-ACA Medicaid program) is a key goal of recent efforts to "repeal and replace" Obamacare in the 115th Congress, raising concern about the impact such efforts would have on states' ability to absorb major financial losses and on citizens' access to care. Despite uneven Medicaid expansion, by the end of 2016, Medicaid covered approximately 20 percent of the American population (Rosenbaum et. al. 2017). In this context, it is not surprising that many state governors—Democrat and Republican—

have spoken out against federal repeal-and-replace reform proposals (Sullivan 2017).

Missing from the national conversation about ACA outcomes and the political uncertainty of health-care reform is consideration of the varied impact of reform *within* states. States have diverse systems of health governance that are not inconsequential to health outcomes. This is especially true for low-income residents who face the greatest obstacles not simply to obtaining health insurance but also to accessing preventive care, clinical care, and other health services. In this context, Pennsylvania is uniquely situated for two reasons. First, it is one of only a handful of states that has a mixed, or hybrid, health governance structure, the consequences of which remain uncertain alongside ACA reforms.[3] Second, Pennsylvania's eligibility requirements for Medicaid prior to Obamacare were among the most restrictive in the nation, positioning the state to exponentially expand Medicaid enrollees and thereby significantly alter the landscape of health within its borders. The state of Pennsylvania has a vested interest in improving health for Medicaid enrollees, as they accounted for close to one-quarter of the state's population prior to Obamacare. Politically speaking, Pennsylvania is also somewhat unusual in having first opted out of the federal expansion in favor of a state-run demonstration project, only to quickly reverse course a few months later following a change in control of the governor's office.

Figure 7.1 Amish farm in Central Pennsylvania. *(Source:* Wikimedia Commons.*)*

How are low-income Pennsylvanians faring under ACA Medicaid reform? It is certain that hundreds of thousands of previously uninsured residents have gained access to health insurance, but consequences for health
care and health outcomes among the population are less clear. In this article,
we take stock of Medicaid reform in Pennsylvania with three goals in mind.
First, after a brief historical review of the political context behind the state's
labored decision to expand Medicaid, we provide a sketch of reform outcomes to date, focusing on low-income residents' access to health insurance.
Health insurance is a precursor to, not the equivalent of, health. Therefore,
our second goal is to explicate barriers to health among low-income Pennsylvanians—barriers that include geographical variation in access points to
primary health care. *Where* low-income residents can access health is determined in part by social and economic conditions of unemployment, poverty,
transportation, and housing. It is also determined by the structure of health
governance within the state, and it is this latter variable that holds our primary interest. Not only does the ACA largely sidestep these interdependent
determinants of health inequality, but also, by centralizing the administration of health, the governance structure of Pennsylvania state health may
exacerbate health inequalities. Thus, our third goal is to suggest a theoretical
framework for approaching health regionally in Pennsylvania, one that is
open to reforming administrative structures of health governance to focus
on regional, cross-jurisdictional approaches to public health and health-care
access. Absent more-comprehensive reform of the state's public health system that considers regional variation in the conditions that facilitate health,
Medicaid reform (in its current Obamacare formula) will provide access to
health insurance but, by itself, not necessarily better health outcomes for
low-income Pennsylvanians.

Political Prelude

One of the twenty-six states party to *National Federation of Independent
Businesses v. Sebelius*, Pennsylvania initially declined to participate in the
federal Medicaid expansion. Following a delayed response to the Court decision, Pennsylvania Republican governor Tom Corbett led his administration in developing a state-run alternative to the federal expansion to pay private insurers to cover the uninsured using newly available Medicaid funds.[4]
After negotiating for over a year with the Obama administration, the Centers for Medicare and Medicaid Services (CMS) granted Pennsylvania a
federal waiver in August 2014, enabling the Corbett administration to modify the state's existing Medicaid program to expand access to health insurance to adults with incomes up to 133 percent of the FPL. Corbett's plan,
Healthy Pennsylvania, was positioned to enroll up to six hundred thousand
new citizens for health-care coverage beginning January 1, 2015. Healthy

Pennsylvania had two core components. First, it modified the state's existing Medicaid program through changed benefit plans, implementation of cost-sharing premiums, and establishment of incentives to encourage healthy behaviors. Second, adults previously ineligible for Medicaid but newly eligible under the ACA's expanded requirements could gain access to health insurance through private managed health plans, or Private Coverage Option service delivery systems.[5]

Among the most controversial of these changes were cost-sharing stipulations and eligibility requirements linking health insurance access to "employment related activities." The demonstration project approved by CMS permitted the state to charge monthly premiums for individuals with incomes up to 100 percent FPL during year two, not to exceed 2 percent of household income (during the first year of the demonstration, no premiums were charged). Individuals with incomes below 100 percent FPL could also be charged copayments in some circumstances. After year one of the demonstration project, individuals could reduce their cost-sharing responsibilities by demonstrating healthy behaviors—including, for example, annual wellness exams and an established record of timely copayments.[6] In its original formulation, Healthy Pennsylvania linked health insurance eligibility for able-bodied adults, ages twenty-one to sixty-four, working fewer than twenty hours per week, to proof of engagement in "employment related activities," such as job training. Political contingencies eventually forced Corbett to weaken these conditions, such that the CMS waiver stipulated that "health coverage provided by the Medicaid program and this demonstration will not be affected by" the state's efforts to encourage employment through incentives to join training and work-related activities.[7]

Early in his administration, Corbett criticized the ACA as "federal overreach" and referred to Medicaid as a "broken system," arguing "it would be financially unsustainable for the taxpayers," to participate in the federal expansion (Beeler 2013). At the same time, however, like many governors, Corbett faced political and budgetary pressures alongside large populations of low-income residents lacking health insurance. Indeed, the Corbett administration previously eliminated adultBasic, which had provided health insurance for low-income working adults ineligible for Medicaid, generating even greater need for affordable, accessible health insurance.

Corbett's "private option" allowed the state to capitalize on additional federal funding without compromising conservative principles. One journalist referred to this approach, shared by Arkansas, Iowa, and Michigan, as "making Medicaid more Republican" (Ramsay 2015). Corbett claimed a political victory in securing "a plan that was created in Pennsylvania for Pennsylvania—a plan that would allow us to reform a financially unsustainable Medicaid program and increase access to health care for eligible individuals through the private market" (in Wenner 2014), but the political realities were more complicated. The CMS demonstration waiver imposed considerable restrictions on Healthy Pennsylvania, and ultimately the state nudged its way toward expanding Medicaid with the help of federal funds.

Corbett's Healthy Pennsylvania was criticized both within and outside of the state, and its brief life was both cause and consequence of the electoral politics of the 2014 gubernatorial elections. The second half of Corbett's first term saw declining public approval ratings (University of Virginia's Larry Sabato characterized Corbett as "the incumbent Republican governor most likely to lose in 2014" [LaRosa 2013]). Corbett's administration was flanked by seemingly endless bad news: drastic education cuts, teacher layoffs, controversial abortion legislation, poor job growth. His administration was also troubled by fallout from his own verbal gaffes and relative weak likability compared to the Democratic challenger, Tom Wolf. One of the most watched gubernatorial elections of 2014, the Corbett campaign was heavily funded by the Republican Governors Association. Wolf, the CEO of a family-owned building materials business and former state revenue secretary, donated $10 million to his own campaign and received support of major labor and teachers unions in the state. Campaigning with a promise to revoke Healthy Pennsylvania in favor of expanding the state's preexisting Medicaid program with support from ACA federal funds, Wolf secured victory with 55 percent of the vote. In what was characterized as an otherwise Republican-friendly midterm election, Corbett became the first incumbent governor in Pennsylvania not elected to a second term (Olson and Esack 2014).

Despite his loss in November 2014, Corbett's administration began implementation of Healthy Pennsylvania in January 2015. At the time of Wolf's inauguration that February, approximately 120,000 Pennsylvanians had already enrolled. True to his campaign promises, Wolf began transitioning the state away from the waiver program in early spring 2015, toward traditional ACA Medicaid. With an intended completion timeline of September 2015, Wolf announced that all individuals enrolled in Healthy Pennsylvania or eligible for Medicaid would be moved into the state's preexisting Medicaid managed-care plan, HealthChoices (Commonwealth of Pennsylvania 2015). Wolf reinstated benefit packages previously modified by the Corbett administration, while cost-sharing premiums and healthy-behavior incentives—core components in Corbett's original state demonstration project—were eliminated. Pennsylvania became the twenty-eighth state to expand Medicaid and, in 2015, the state's uninsured rate decreased by 2 percentage points to 6.5 percent (Pennsylvania Department of Human Services 2017). By the end of 2015, 21 percent of the state population was enrolled in Medicaid.

Accounting for almost 30 percent of all state general-fund spending, Medicaid remains a flashpoint of Pennsylvania politics. In July 2017, a House-passed budget bill included proposals that would require able-bodied adults to work as a condition of Medicaid eligibility and institute cost-sharing for parents of disabled children receiving Medicaid assistance. At the time of writing, a final budget package including changes to the human services code has not been reached; Democrats and Governor Wolf have opposed the proposals in the House bill and they have yet to be debated by the Pennsylvania Senate (Finnerty 2017 and Thompson 2017). Federal proposals for reform that would scale back federal payments to states for Medicaid are similar signposts of controversy. Governor Wolf has been outspoken in his opposition to Republican-backed congressional proposals to repeal and replace the ACA, including the Senate plan coauthored by Pennsylvania's Republican Senator, Pat Toomey. Governor Wolf claims the Senate plan would force the state "to either significantly scale back the health care programs we currently offer to vulnerable residents, such as seniors and individuals with disabilities, or will be forced to weigh decisions about who to cover against other critical state funding obligations, including education, infrastructure, and the environment" (Wolf 2017).

Medicaid Expansion in Pennsylvania

Perhaps the most significant anticipated effects of Medicaid reform in Pennsylvania (and elsewhere) are a result of the expansion of coverage to previously uninsured and ineligible poor adults without dependent children ("childless adults" or "other adults").[8] Medicaid reform will also enroll more working parents, previously ineligible under restrictive state requirements. According to the Kaiser Commission, before the ACA, thirty-three states limited eligibility for working parents below 100 percent FPL—in sixteen of those states, including Pennsylvania, eligibility was restricted to parents earning less than 50 percent of the FPL (Kaiser Commission on Medicaid and the Uninsured 2013). Working parents with dependent children in Pennsylvania were eligible for Medicaid with incomes up to 99 percent FPL; nondisabled adults without children were not eligible for Medicaid at all.[9] Eligibility in Pennsylvania now includes all adults, ages twenty-one to sixty-four, with incomes up to 138 percent FPL, equal to approximately $21,599 for a family of two or $32,718 for a family of four in 2017.

What does Medicaid enrollment expansion in Pennsylvania look like so far? In 2014, on the eve of its expansion, Medicaid provided coverage for approximately 2.2 million Pennsylvanians, including approximately 1.1 million adults and 1.1 million children. At the start of 2015 when Medicaid expansion took effect, state officials estimated that six hundred thousand additional residents would be eligible for health insurance under an expanded program. Within one year, the Pennsylvania Department of Health (2017) estimates that more than 7 percent of all adults statewide (ages eighteen to sixty-four) were enrolled in Medicaid. Between December 2014 and June 2017, as seen in Figure 7.2, total Medicaid enrollment increased by

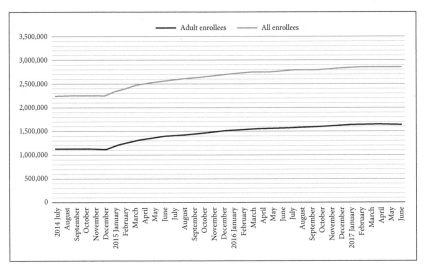

Figure 7.2 Statewide total and adult Medicaid enrollment, April 2014 to July 2017.
(Source: Pennsylvania Department of Human Services 2017.)
Note: *"Adult" refers to individuals ages twenty-one to sixty-four.*

27 percent, growing from 2,256,192 to 2,854,064 (or just under 600,000 new enrollees). A majority of these new enrollees are adults (ages twenty-one to sixty-four, now eligible with incomes up to 138 percent FPL); enrollment of these individuals increased by 46 percent, jumping from 1,122,531 in December 2014 to 1,639,619 in June 2017.

Table 7.1 and Figure 7.3 contain additional information about Medicaid enrollment both before and after the ACA expansion by county. Table 7.1 also provides the best available information about the population of each county most likely to benefit from new Medicaid requirements—adults living at or below 138 percent FPL just before the Medicaid expansion took effect.[10]

Close to 1.4 million adults ages eighteen to sixty-four were living under 138 percent FPL in 2014 across the state, and almost four hundred thousand of them were uninsured. As is to be expected, the most populous counties in the state report the highest real numbers of poor uninsured adults, including most notably Allegheny and Philadelphia Counties. But counties vary in the proportion of poor uninsured adults relative to overall county populations. For example, Pike County is a relatively small county with an overall population of 56,102 (in 2014) and a small population of poor adults, 4,910 individuals. About 36 percent of Pike County's poor adults were uninsured prior to Medicaid expansion, however, exceeding the statewide average by more than 8 percentage points.

Pennsylvania tracks and records total Medicaid enrollments by county each month, but the state does not report the numbers of enrollees newly

TABLE 7.1 POPULATION, UNINSURED, AND MEDICAID ENROLLEES PRE- AND POST-MEDICAID EXPANSION, DECEMBER 2014–JUNE 2017

	Total population (2014)*	Total population 18 to 64 under 138% FPL (2014)	Uninsured 18- to 64- year-olds under 138% FPL (2014)	Percentage uninsured 18- to 64- year-olds under 138% FPL (2014)	December 2014 adult (21–64) Medicaid enrollees	June 2017 adult (21–64) Medicaid enrollees	Change in adult enrollees December 2014–June 2017	Percentage change in adult Medicaid enrollees December 2014–June 2017
State total	*12,341,039*	*1,406,418*	*396,666*	*28.2%*	*1,122,531*	*1,639,519*	*516,988*	*46.1%*
Adams	97,107	8,130	3,226	39.7%	5,008	7,928	2,920	58.3%
Allegheny	1,195,299	133,317	33,775	25.3%	100,211	140,283	40,072	40.0%
Armstrong	67,530	7,521	2,119	28.2%	7,014	9,845	2,831	40.4%
Beaver	167,217	16,113	3,847	23.9%	15,448	21,483	6,035	39.1%
Bedford	48,570	5,593	1,847	33.0%	4,828	6,842	2,014	41.7%
Berks	399,921	45,405	13,820	30.4%	33,605	50,573	16,968	50.5%
Blair	123,524	15,539	3,730	24.0%	14,125	19,892	5,767	40.8%
Bradford	61,477	7,223	2,146	29.7%	5,594	8,091	2,497	44.6%
Bucks	617,411	32,538	9,438	29.0%	27,697	43,847	16,150	58.3%
Butler	179,754	15,192	4,004	26.4%	10,592	16,140	5,548	52.4%
Cambria	132,703	15,854	4,175	26.3%	15,001	21,298	6,297	42.0%
Cameron	4,866	525	100	19.0%	638	884	246	38.6%
Carbon	63,877	6,770	2,009	29.7%	4,889	7,844	2,955	60.4%
Centre	139,356	28,846	3,832	13.3%	6,272	9,208	2,936	46.8%
Chester	493,263	30,968	10,060	32.5%	16,745	27,165	10,420	62.2%
Clarion	37,671	6,042	1,240	20.5%	3,785	5,018	1,233	32.6%
Clearfield	76,142	10,173	2,987	29.4%	9,533	12,951	3,418	35.9%
Clinton	36,975	5,198	966	18.6%	3,883	5,434	1,551	39.9%
Columbia	62,820	9,666	2,037	21.1%	5,359	7,691	2,332	43.5%
Crawford	83,974	11,322	3,411	30.1%	8,965	12,097	3,132	34.9%
Cumberland	225,487	17,722	4,517	25.5%	11,109	17,966	6,857	61.7%
Dauphin	264,707	30,280	9,073	30.0%	22,142	36,131	13,989	63.2%
Delaware	539,364	47,378	13,929	29.4%	41,932	65,604	23,672	56.5%
Elk	31,131	2,638	587	22.3%	2,632	3,504	872	33.1%
Erie	267,763	36,737	9,246	25.2%	30,758	44,328	13,570	44.1%
Fayette	131,448	20,296	5,579	27.5%	19,771	27,315	7,544	38.2%
Forest	4,265	543	146	26.9%	569	775	206	36.2%
Franklin	148,764	13,876	5,397	38.9%	9,378	15,030	5,652	60.3%
Fulton	14,630	1,651	449	27.2%	1,298	1,867	569	43.8%
Greene	33,828	4,030	980	24.3%	4,289	6,213	1,924	44.9%
Huntingdon	40,785	4,788	1,223	25.5%	4,222	5,793	1,571	37.2%
Indiana	82,857	13,400	3,382	25.2%	7,347	11,273	3,926	53.4%
Jefferson	44,058	5,568	1,564	28.1%	5,019	6,756	1,737	34.6%

	Total population (2014)*	Total population 18 to 64 under 138% FPL (2014)	Uninsured 18- to 64- year-olds under 138% FPL (2014)	Percentage uninsured 18- to 64- year-olds under 138% FPL (2014)	December 2014 adult (21–64) Medicaid enrollees	June 2017 adult (21–64) Medicaid enrollees	Change in adult enrollees December 2014–June 2017	Percentage change in adult Medicaid enrollees December 2014–June 2017
Juniata	24,437	2,688	972	36.2%	1,805	2,413	608	33.7%
Lackawanna	205,974	24,838	6,622	26.7%	21,281	32,233	10,952	51.5%
Lancaster	512,011	46,564	14,902	32.0%	33,960	49,451	15,491	45.6%
Lawrence	87,449	10,236	2,831	27.7%	9,496	13,708	4,212	44.4%
Lebanon	131,698	11,715	3,545	30.3%	9,447	14,901	5,454	57.7%
Lehigh	345,185	37,799	13,136	34.8%	30,776	46,979	16,203	52.6%
Luzerne	308,574	38,604	11,321	29.3%	32,280	49,857	17,577	54.5%
Lycoming	111,105	13,561	3,782	27.9%	11,030	16,392	5,362	48.6%
McKean	39,824	5,717	1,330	23.3%	4,908	6,709	1,801	36.7%
Mercer	108,439	13,177	3,583	27.2%	12,354	16,828	4,474	36.2%
Mifflin	45,876	6,463	2,164	33.5%	5,150	6,803	1,653	32.1%
Monroe	165,030	18,799	6,314	33.6%	12,980	21,040	8,060	62.1%
Montgomery	789,268	44,682	13,089	29.3%	37,446	58,697	21,251	56.8%
Montour	17,764	1,610	536	33.3%	1,477	1,986	509	34.5%
Northampton	288,310	24,192	7,475	30.9%	19,947	31,087	11,140	55.8%
Northumberland	89,494	10,963	3,767	34.4%	9,495	13,620	4,125	43.4%
Perry	45,040	3,725	1,327	35.6%	2,625	4,124	1,499	57.1%
Philadelphia	1,503,569	323,469	89,620	27.7%	269,654	385,149	115,495	42.8%
Pike	56,102	4,910	1,776	36.2%	3,436	5,818	2,382	69.3%
Potter	17,144	2,169	661	30.5%	1,703	2,534	831	48.8%
Schuylkill	139,755	16,153	5,063	31.3%	14,600	20,640	6,040	41.4%
Snyder	37,598	3,609	1,285	35.6%	2,816	3,736	920	32.7%
Somerset	72,457	7,468	2,097	28.1%	6,693	9,972	3,279	49.0%
Sullivan	6,220	843	213	25.3%	613	814	201	32.8%
Susquehanna	42,207	5,029	1,633	32.5%	2,993	4,739	1,746	58.3%
Tioga	40,803	5,272	1,563	29.6%	3,550	5,818	2,268	63.9%
Union	35,709	3,781	975	25.8%	2,382	3,248	866	36.4%
Venango	53,100	6,647	1,746	26.3%	5,906	8,223	2,317	39.2%
Warren	40,211	4,543	1,356	29.8%	3,714	5,321	1,607	43.3%
Washington	203,160	19,152	5,216	27.2%	15,789	23,471	7,682	48.7%
Wayne	48,204	5,296	1,361	25.7%	4,232	6,225	1,993	47.1%
Westmoreland	354,541	32,314	7,742	24.0%	29,843	41,878	12,035	40.3%
Wyoming	27,516	2,791	697	25.0%	2,107	3,494	1,387	65.8%
York	428,721	36,797	12,125	33.0%	27,705	44,542	16,837	60.8%

Source: U.S. Census Bureau 2015; Pennsylvania Department of Human Services 2017.
*refers to the civilian, noninstitutionalized population for whom poverty status is determined. Total population in the state of Pennsylvania for 2014 was 12,787,209.

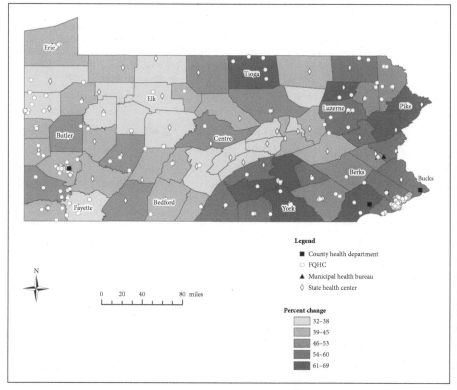

Figure 7.3 Percentage change in Medicaid enrollment, ages eighteen to sixty-four, from 2014 to 2017. *(Source: U.S. Census Bureau 2015; Pennsylvania Department of Health 2016; Pennsylvania Association of Community Health Centers 2015.)*

eligible after 2015 or new enrollees by age group or subpopulation (for example, children, childless adults, the disabled, etc.). The state Department of Human Services (2017) estimates that expansion accounted for more than 18 percent of Medicaid enrollees in 2015 (estimates after 2015 are not available). Thus, monthly enrollment figures include previously enrolled Medicaid recipients in addition to newly enrolled participants.[11] While the data reported in Table 7.1 and Figure 7.3 are not perfect, they provide a partial window into changes at the county level and statewide variation as a result of Medicaid expansion. The state as a whole experienced an almost 46 percent increase in adult Medicaid enrollment between December 2014 and June 2017. Increases within the counties range from a high of almost 70 percent in Pike County to a low of 31 percent in Mifflin County. Most of the counties with higher percentages of Medicaid enrollees are those with a higher percentage of previously uninsured people, suggesting that Medicaid expansion is having the intended effect of expanding insurance to many poor individuals. Because we say more about the Lehigh Valley region of

Pennsylvania below, it is worth noting Medicaid expansion in this region. Combined, Lehigh and Northampton Counties include about 630,000 residents, and about 61,000 of these are adults living in poverty. In 2014, 20,611 adults living in poverty in this region lacked health insurance. Lehigh County experienced a 53 percent increase in adult Medicaid enrollments since 2014; in Northampton, the increase has been about 56 percent. While these numbers are encouraging in suggesting that thousands of adults are now insured through Medicaid as a result of the ACA, as we explore further below, access to insurance is no guarantee of improved access to health *care*, particularly in a context defined by intrastate and interregional inequalities in both social determinants of health and availability of access points to care.

Thinking beyond Insurance: Health Governance and Regional Health-Care Inequality

States' pre-ACA structures and processes for administering Medicaid and other health-related programs provide a critical context for considering implementation of Medicaid reform under Obamacare, as well as for considering future health-care reform proposals. Indeed, the contours of Medicaid prior to the ACA were in many ways the result of states' interests and financial incentives, which collectively helped propel the program's evolution, decoupling it from welfare and relaxing eligibility rules in the 1980s (leading to an exponential increase in enrollment) and transitioning (in a majority of states) to managed-care plans in an effort to reduce costs in the 1990s. In 2010, Medicaid expansion was the most politically palatable option for expanding health insurance coverage, not only because it is less costly than other options but also because it is a state-administered program (Brecher and Rose 2013). The state of Pennsylvania's decision to adopt federal Medicaid reform is likely the result of both shifting political fortunes (most notably a radical ideological change in the state executive office coupled with public opinion and pressure from health providers and insurers) and financial incentives (the state Department of Health estimates that cost savings will exceed $626 million in the first year and more than $645 million in the second year alone).

The potential of Medicaid expansion to succeed in increasing access to insurance and to health care for low-income Pennsylvanians will be shaped not only by the relationship between the federal and state governments but also by the structure of health governance and the relationships between state and local governments. The state's Medicaid program, HealthChoices (previously Medical Assistance) is administered through the Office of Medical Assistance Programs, an office within the state Department of Human Services. Eligibility and program requirements are administered through county assistance offices. Medicaid recipients are enrolled in one of several managed-care organizations in the state, operating throughout five "zones" within the state.

Although the Department of Human Services administers Medicaid through its Office of Medical Assistance Programs, the Department of Health coordinates health resources in the state. Pennsylvania is one of just a handful of states in the nation characterized by a "hybrid" governmental model, that is, it contains both independent local health agencies and state-run health offices (Salinsky 2010).[12] Public health programs are overseen by the Bureau of Community Health Systems in a complex network of district offices and state health centers organized into six health districts. As shown in Figure 7.3, the state operates health centers in sixty-one of Pennsylvania's sixty-seven counties. These are directly funded by the state and managed by state employees. State health centers provide health screenings, diagnoses and clinics to prevent communicable diseases, immunizations, chronic disease prevention, health and environmental education programs, and counseling.

In addition to state-funded health centers, Pennsylvania's network of public health includes six county health departments in Erie, Allegheny, Chester, Bucks, Montgomery, and Philadelphia Counties and four local health bureaus in the municipalities of York, Wilkes-Barre, Bethlehem, and Allentown. County Health Departments and Municipal Health Bureaus are creations of Pennsylvania Act 315, the Local Health Administration Law, which allows (but does not require or incentivize) local governments to create their own localized departments in return for greater control over decisions about available services and community partner collaborations. County Health Departments and Municipal Health Bureaus are accountable for meeting state and federal public health provisions; they receive state funding but can also raise revenues through local taxation, service fees, and external grants. Staffed by local government employees, County Health Departments and Municipal Health Bureaus typically offer expanded public health services and work closely with community health providers. Prior to Obamacare, County Health Departments and Municipal Health Bureaus proved especially important for providing preventive services and primary care to individuals ineligible for Medicaid, and for providing services insufficiently covered by private providers. For example, the Bethlehem Health Bureau provides free individual and group counseling on weight loss, diabetes, hypertension, high cholesterol, and smoking cessation for residents of Bethlehem. Similarly, the Allentown Health Bureau is part of a community-wide effort, Healthy Kids Healthy Allentown, which promotes good nutrition and physical activity programs for children under eighteen years of age.

Of course, government organizations are not the only entities in public health. Private and nonprofit organizations are critical partners in the delivery of health care and the extension of services to low-income populations. Most significant for our purposes, community health centers, including those designated as Federally Qualified Health Centers (FQHCs) and Rural Health Clinics (RHCs), are a primary source of care and preventive services for Medicaid enrollees and the uninsured and, with increased federal funding provided through the ACA, will continue to serve as a significant source of primary care for low-income populations. The FQHCs and RHCs are non-profit organizations, supported by federal and state funds, that provide preventive primary health services under section 330 of the Public Health Service Act. They may provide services such as primary medical, dental, and behavioral health care regardless of a patient's ability to pay. As shown in Figure 7.3, there are currently over 260 sites in Pennsylvania located in forty-five of Pennsylvania's sixty-seven counties, serving approximately seven hundred thousand individuals (Pennsylvania Association of Community Health Centers 2015). In addition to these organizations, there has been an increase in the number of private care centers, such as Patient First, as well as drop-in care centers run by area hospitals. While the apparent influx of new entities is encouraging, in most cases this patchwork health-care delivery system continues to lack comprehensive coverage for hospitalization, long-term care, and emergency care as well as dental care, eye and vision care, and mental health services. Likewise, little is known about the extent to which private-sector health clinics are helping to fill delivery gaps, especially for the Medicaid population.

In the best-case scenario, Pennsylvanians still lacking health insurance or without easy access to primary care through a private provider can receive primary care through FQHCs or a similar organization, reducing the risk and prevalence of preventable diseases, which in turn will reduce the cost of care, as individuals will be treated earlier and require less hospitalization. However, this assumes that FQHCs, or their equivalent, are located in areas accessible to these individuals. Returning to Figure 7.3, most FQHCs and RHCs are concentrated in the urban core of Philadelphia and in far western Pennsylvania, even though there have been larger increases in Medicaid enrollment in south-central and northeastern counties. Figure 7.4 provides complementary information about the geographic distribution of the ratio of the population to primary-care physicians using the Robert Wood Johnson Foundation's County Health Rankings and Roadmaps data. These data include primary-care physicians specializing in medicine, family medicine, internal medicine, or pediatrics and provide a measure of the availability of health care and access to providers. As shown, many counties with higher ratios of population to primary-care physicians (those shaded darker on Figure 7.4) also have few if any FQHCs or RHCs, potentially forcing residents to forgo preventive care, or to seek out hospital emergency rooms for nonemergency care. Comparing Figures 7.3 and 7.4 further emphasizes the need to consider more access to

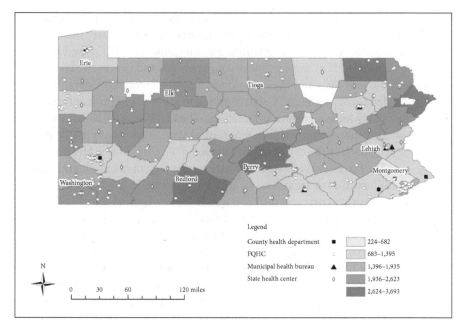

Figure 7.4 Primary care physician ratio by county. *(Source: Robert Wood Johnson Foundation 2013; Pennsylvania Department of Health 2016; Pennsylvania Association of Community Health Centers 2015.)*

preventive health care for low-income residents. For example, counties such as Pike, Perry, Monroe, and Bedford, which lack a sufficient number of physicians to serve the overall county population, *also lack* federally assisted health centers for low-income residents *and* have seen higher increases in Medicaid enrollment. Clearly, there is a need to consider a better way to organize health services for low-income individuals living in these regions.

While these figures suggest that the state's hybrid system of health governance promotes horizontal equity in some respects—nearly every county has a state-run health center, for example—it is clear that there is considerable variation in the extent of need among low-income residents across counties and in structural and environmental factors across the state. In short, low-income Pennsylvanians faced varied access to primary health care. As suggested above, the increase in insured adults as a result of Medicaid expansion could lead to *greater* health inequality, as those lacking access to health services, because of a limited number of physicians or facilities, maintain their current level of health while those living in areas with more options for health care have greater access. Additionally, previously insured individuals may face difficulties scheduling health-care visits because of the increase in demand and limited supply of health-care workers. In light of these pressures, the Commonwealth has taken steps to improve access to quality care starting with the Health Innovation in Pennsylvania plan in

2016 (Pennsylvania Department of Health 2016). Funding from a Center for Medicare and Medicaid Innovation grant is helping the state develop and implement a new Medicaid-provider payment plan and focus more attention on access to primary health care in rural regions. The plan is currently in its first year of implementation, with the targets to achieve these objectives by the end of 2019. This plan calls for a top-down approach to address future health-care demands. In lieu of the current approach, the remainder of our article suggests a theoretical way of thinking regionally to derive the greatest benefit from the ACA's twin promise of improving health *insurance* and health *care* for low-income Americans.

Seeking Regional Solutions to Health Challenges in Pennsylvania

The ultimate success of the ACA will depend in large part on the willingness and ability of states, health insurers, and health-care providers to transform the existing health-care system. Because federally designed Medicaid reform relies on states to run and implement the expansion, it is inherently linked to a preexisting landscape of health inequalities, socioeconomic disparities, inequalities in the social determinants of health, and varied obstacles to care. In this context, location matters, as health is shaped by many factors that lie outside the boundaries of health care, including access to employment opportunities, adequate transportation, environmental issues such as air and water quality, and racial equity. Literature in the field of regionalism, for example, suggests that neighborhood access to healthy food, concentrations of poverty within geographic regions, and resource disparities within larger regional contexts are all factors that affect health outcomes at both individual and community levels (e.g., Hutson et al. 2012; Lynch et al. 1998). Moreover, individuals rely on their local communities for health care; therefore, measurement of the ACA's success must include consideration of the equity, accessibility, and affordability of services within more localized areas.

A regional boundary is defined by where people reside, travel, work, shop, and play (Hamilton 2014; Miller 2002). The recognition that municipalities within a region are interdependent is now commonplace within research and practitioner communities (Dreier, Mollenkopf, and Swanstrom 2004; Hamilton 2014; Ledebur and Barnes, 1993; Orfield 2002; Pastor et al. 2000; Rusk 2003; Savitch et al. 1993; Savitch and Vogel 2000; Swanstrom, Dreier, and Mollenkopf 2002). While there is debate about the extent and direction of this interdependency, a regional perspective is critical for understanding social disparities and economic growth at the local-government level. Regions present unique governing challenges because they typically include multiple local governments and often lack static legal boundaries.

The subject of health equity itself is well traversed—scholars and practitioners have long drawn attention to issues related to population health: racial and ethnic disparities in health and health care, state and local policy efforts to alleviate health disparities, the interconnectedness of residential segregation, lack of access to health care, environmental stressors (such as violence), and community infrastructure (e.g., Institute of Medicine 2011; Kirby and Kaneda 2005; Lynch et al. 1998; Schulz et al. 2002). These findings are increasingly considered in the context of regionalism; indeed, a recent PolicyLink report says, "Much of the innovative work around health and regional equity is occurring at the intersection between health and other areas such as transportation, housing, and economic opportunity" (2002, 23). Past research has linked race-based residential segregation and socioeconomic status to the social and material resources that promote health and limit disease (Schulz et al. 2002).

Most critically for our purposes, studies of health-care utilization suggest that an individual's decision to access primary health-care services depends on spatial considerations, including regional availability and regional accessibility, and aspatial factors, such as income, race, ethnicity, education level, or sex (Wang and Luo 2005). Of particular importance, researchers estimate that individuals are more likely to access services within a fifteen-mile radius or not exceeding a thirty-minute barrier (e.g., Luo 2004; Wang and Minor 2002).

While Medicaid expansion has already significantly expanded access to health insurance for more than five hundred thousand low-income Pennsylvanians, far surpassing the numbers of individuals who have enrolled in individual insurance plans through the federal marketplace, our concern is the next step, how to ensure access to preventive and primary care for low-income individuals with or without health insurance. Translating gains in health insurance into healthier residents and greater health equity across the state will require coordinated regional strategies. These strategies include changing state health governance structures to establish a more decentralized public health system, one that allows for regionalized implementation and state support for new collaborative regional health-care systems.

For example, recent research suggests that centralized, state-run health governance systems—such as the system characterizing health governance in Pennsylvania—are associated with the lowest health outcome measures on several dimensions of health, including adult smoking, low birth weight, teen births, and preventive screenings for breast cancer and diabetes (Hays et al. 2014). One of the benefits of the U.S. system of federalism is the ability to learn from state-level variation in public-health delivery systems. Here, we briefly draw on Minnesota and Massachusetts, two states consistently ranked among the healthiest in the nation by the United Health Foundation and the Association of State and Territorial Health Officials. Like Pennsylvania, both states have histories rooted in strong local governance. Unlike Pennsylvania, both Minnesota and Massachusetts have integrated regional approaches to public health through statewide planning that emphasizes devolving accountability and health-delivery planning to local governments with state-level oversight and support.

Regional Public Health in Minnesota

In Minnesota, the Community Health Services system has been in place since 1976, when the state passed the Community Health Services Act (Minn. Stat. §145A), now called the Local Public Health Act. Unlike Pennsylvania's Act 315, which permits, but does not require, counties and municipalities to create health departments, the state of Minnesota designates Community Health Boards (CHBs) as the legal governing authorities for local public health. These CHBs can be multi-county, single county, or city based but must serve a minimum population equal to thirty thousand people (Minnesota Department of Health, n.d.). The CHBs are better positioned to tailor health services to fit the needs of a smaller population than is possible with a state-governed structure. Funding for CHBs is provided through a mix of federal, state, and local funding as well as fees and reimbursements. Noncategorical state funding provides the base funding for the CHBs in addition to targeted funding to address state-level public and community health priorities (Mays and Frauendienst 2014). A recent report measuring performance indicators on CHBs suggests that many work with local partners to increase health education programming, particularly in school settings. Also, most engage in activities to promote healthy behaviors, particularly nutrition and physical activity (Minnesota Department of Health 2014). Other program areas include maternal and child health, infectious disease prevention, and promotion of environmental health, such as radon testing.

One of the challenges faced by Minnesota CHBs is funding. Even though the state provides significant governmental transfers, many CHBs struggle to provide sufficient local tax and nontax revenue (Minnesota Department of Health 2015). Changes in population demographics, including the decline of rural populations, are another concern. In spite of these challenges, evidence suggests that there is increasing ability for CHBs to meet state performance standards, and the state is encouraging all CHBs to apply for Public Health Department Accreditation, which would provide additional technical support and research to improve service delivery. Minnesota's CHBs provide decentralized health centers with strong support from the state, providing residents with more-targeted services and programming to meet the unique needs of each region.

Regional Public Health in Massachusetts

If states such as Minnesota provide empirical support that legislative and administrative decentralization may help improve community health, Massachusetts provides an example of the benefits of engaging providers of public and private services in regionalizing public health. Massachusetts is both one of the healthiest states in the nation and characterized by one of the most decentralized systems of health. Historically, each municipality was responsible for providing public health services and acted as the primary funder for these services. In fact, until 2006, state law did not provide for the opportunity for any direct funding for public health. With over three hundred communities and varying degrees of financial capacity, state leaders recognized that the existing system was no longer sustainable and that a more centralized approach, with greater state-level engagement, was needed to ensure equitable access to care for all citizens.

Following on the heels of the landmark Massachusetts health reform that was the precursor to the ACA, local health department and state officials prepared a report recommending several improvements to the public health system (Hyde and Tovar 2006). These recommendations, along with further study of the problems by public health leaders, led to the creation of several additional policy changes. First, in December 2006 the state launched the Massachusetts Public Health Regionalization Project with the goal of establishing consortiums of local health departments across multijurisdictional boundaries to provide a "consistent standard of care and equal level of services" (Boston University, n.d.). Six regional consortiums received Public Health District Incentive Grants from the state, supported by a grant from the U.S. Centers for Disease Control and Prevention. These consortiums bring together local health boards and community health-care providers to create regional health improvement plans and coordinate services. For example, the Central Massachusetts Regional Health Public Alliance, comprising seven local health boards and over ninety community organizations and hospitals, developed a strategic plan that includes a focus on health equity and health disparities (Central Massachusetts Regional Public Health Alliance 2014). Second, to further enable and encourage regionalization, in 2008 state policy makers revised Chapter 529, an Act Relative to Public Health Reorganization, which removed barriers to regionalization. This law provides the legal basis for state funding for public health but retains legislative prerogative for development of the funding formula and subsequent annual funding. Third, in 2013, Massachusetts created the Office of Local and Regional Health, the hub for partnerships between the state Department of Health and Human Services and regional consortiums.

This office is similar in scope to Pennsylvania's Bureau of Community Health Systems. The evolution of the expansion of state efforts to support the new regional collaborative and local health boards is still relatively new. However, research by the Institute of Community Health points to early positive outcomes in the District Incentive Grant Program and regional health consortium (Hays et al. 2014).

Opportunities for Regionalizing Public Health in Pennsylvania

Our goal here is not to suggest a one-size-fits-all approach; to be sure, Massachusetts and Minnesota are significantly different both from each other and from Pennsylvania culturally, politically, geographically, and economically. Rather, our goal is to draw attention to the experiences in Minnesota and Massachusetts, and to emergent research on public health governance, to suggest that thinking regionally offers innovative routes for improving health care and population health outcomes. Pennsylvania is well positioned to encourage greater decentralization of public health by revising existing legislation to encourage a regionally driven public health system. For example, policy makers could consider revising Act 315 to provide greater incentives for counties and municipalities to create local health departments and multijurisdictional health departments that include two or more counties as a regional economic entity.

Regional health departments are beneficial for several reasons. First, by design, they would be attuned and responsive to residents within identified geographies, including at-risk populations in cities and suburbs. Currently operating Health Bureaus offer more-expanded clinical services, environmental health, and targeted community education opportunities to residents than do state-run health centers and are more adaptable to local community issues. Regional health departments, we expect, would provide the same attention to community needs. Second, regional health departments would increase community engagement in public health. Act 315 requires that county commissioners appoint five residents within a health department's geographic boundary to serve on a Board of Health, ensuring greater localized autonomy over public health provisions than is current practice in most counties in the state. Third, localized health departments would provide opportunities for greater coordination of regional health services including, for example, county departments of human services in the areas of mental health, aging, and children and youth services. Regional health departments would also have greater ability to coordinate services directly with nonprofit and private providers to improve regional health, as shown through the examples of CHBs and Regional Health Departments in Massachusetts.

If regionalizing Pennsylvania's approach to health is a good idea, and we think it is, there are important funding, cost, and political considerations (more on this below). A large question, in light of current state budget woes, is funding. Deeper consideration of the cost of implementation is necessary;

however, one assumption is that expenditures for state health centers would be shifted from the current state health centers, which would no longer be needed, to the new regional entities. Further funding would be raised through local sources, federal grants, and service provision.

An even more politically feasible and practical step toward thinking regionally is to encourage growth and proliferation of FQHCs and RHCs and similar organizations providing community-level primary care. FQHCs and RHCs receive funding from the Health Resources and Services Administration of the U.S. Department of Health and Human Services. Maximizing the potential for federal funding by providing additional state funds to organizations operating within high-need locations would serve those most in need of affordable health services.

Combined, these efforts would provide a better foundation for reducing health disparities by recognizing the importance of regional health planning that includes collaboration with neighboring government entities as well as nonprofit and private-sector providers.

Regional Case Study of the Lehigh Valley

Figure 7.5 provides an example for thinking regionally in the way that we imagine by examining the spatial relationships of public health offices and FQHCs in the Lehigh Valley region of Pennsylvania. The Lehigh Valley region comprises Lehigh and Northampton Counties, sixty-two municipalities, and seventeen school districts. The Valley is home to approximately six hundred thousand residents, with median income ranging from $54,923 to $60,097. Approximately 14 percent of Lehigh County lives at 100 percent FPL; in Northampton, the poverty rate is just under 10 percent FPL. Lehigh County is home to Allentown, the third-largest city in the Commonwealth, with a poverty rate of 28 percent. As shown in Figure 7.5, the state operates a health center in each county, while the cities of Allentown and Bethlehem have their own Health Bureaus. There is also an FQHC located in Allentown.

Given Allentown's relatively high poverty rate, it is an obvious place to locate services designed to provide affordable health care. Nonetheless, closer examination of U.S. Census tracts in the Lehigh Valley as a whole suggests there are other places in the region that would benefit from more-accessible health care. Following Governor Wolf's expansion of traditional Medicaid, we would expect most areas on Figure 7.5 to show fewer uninsured people over time, as more individuals register for HealthChoices in the coming years. Indeed, recall our discussion above and Table 7.1, which shows that Lehigh and Northampton Counties exceed the statewide average rate of change in Medicaid enrollments in the years stretching from December 2014 to June 2017.

We expect that some of these individuals will now seek more-frequent primary and preventive care. However, like many regions in the state, the

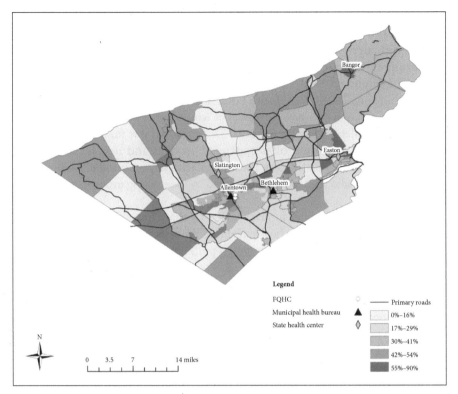

Figure 7.5 Percentage uninsured up to 138 FPL by census tract, Lehigh and Northampton Counties. *(Source: U.S. Census Bureau 2015; Pennsylvania Department of Health 2016; Pennsylvania Association of Community Health Centers 2015.)*

Lehigh Valley is characterized by barriers to health care and improved health outcomes that cannot be overcome simply through the extension of health insurance. Community-health needs assessments in the region conducted in compliance with the requirements of the Affordable Care Act have demonstrated, for example, that transportation, housing, employment, and cultural and language barriers are important factors explaining disparities in health outcomes and access to preventive health services (Mathews 2012; Mathews-Schultz and Brill 2015). Further, the needs of residents living in the urban core areas of the Lehigh Valley differ from those living in the suburban and rural outskirts of the region; access (particularly for residents lacking transportation) is particularly significant in the rural areas. Communities in the northern and southern tiers of the Lehigh Valley, for example, lack access to the region's bus system, the only form of public transportation.

Interestingly, policy and county leaders in the Lehigh Valley previously took steps toward creating a bicounty health department in the region.

Lessons from this experience reveal both the appeal of thinking regionally about health and the practical and political barriers to implementing regionalism without clear incentives and support from state (and possible) federal institutions. In 2010, several organizations within the health-care community in Lehigh and Northampton Counties, including the two municipal health bureaus, Two Rivers Health Foundation, and the local hospitals, proposed the creation of a new bureau that would replace the existing Allentown and Bethlehem Health Bureaus. That proposal was for a larger multicounty entity that would offer expanded services and new locations in Easton, Bangor, and Slatington, three areas with a large number of low-income residents who tend to be underserved by the existing urban-core health bureaus.

Unfortunately, despite empirical evidence that a bicounty health department would better serve the health needs of the region's low-income population, these efforts failed to gain enough political support among either Lehigh or Northampton County political elites and elected leaders who had to approve its creation. The main sticking point for the county commissioners and opponents of the regional health department stemmed from the proposed expectation that each county and the three cities would contribute resources to operate the new bureau. In the midst of the recession, and with Tea Party Republicans on both the Lehigh and Northampton county councils opposed to increasing the size of government, this requirement was not politically viable. It is likely that opposition to regional health bureaus will continue without state-level reforms to decentralize public health similar to those in Minnesota and Massachusetts and incentives to make it easier for regions to expand autonomy and accountability.

Moving Forward after Obamacare: Tentative Conclusions and New Questions

It is certain that large numbers of low-income, previously uninsured Pennsylvanians will gain health insurance as a result of the state's Medicaid expansion. Early indications suggest that a far greater number of residents enrolled in HealthChoices—the newly designed and named state-run Medicaid program—than enrolled in the private health marketplace created under Obamacare. It is difficult to overstate the significance of Medicaid in extending health insurance to low-income residents in the state. More than five hundred thousand Pennsylvania residents are newly insured as a result of the Medicaid expansion.

With this backdrop, our primary goal in this article is to suggest that the preexisting landscape of health inequalities in access to care across different regions of the state, coupled with the centralized hybrid structure of health governance, will mediate and potentially limit health outcomes among the newly insured population. Better and more health insurance will not necessarily lead to better health care or improved health outcomes. Access to preventive health services and primary-care physicians is not distributed equitably across the state; those newly insured and those who remain uninsured will have differential access to health care depending to a large degree on where they live.

Emergent literature on regionalism and public health, coupled with experiences of innovative regional approaches in states such as Minnesota and Massachusetts, suggest that there are tangible ways Pennsylvania (and other states) can think regionally about how to best address inequalities in access to health. Many academics, research institutions (see, for example, the Institute for Public Policy and Economic Development), and practitioners advocate statewide regionalization for many policy areas beyond health. For example, these areas include police, fire, public education, water and wastewater, economic development, transportation, and planning.

Statewide obstacles similar to those found in the Lehigh Valley have frustrated these efforts to regionalize while, ironically, the fragmentation of Pennsylvania's local governments further contributes to service delivery challenges and fiscal stress. Nonetheless, there has been limited success in regionalization that gives us reason for optimism. Since 1971, for instance, twenty-nine regional Intermediate Units (IUs), multijurisdictional entities, have provided educational services and instruction. The IUs operate as a statewide network to provide services to school districts and other educational entities that would not be provided if each district were expected to provide its own services; while IUs cannot raise their own tax revenues, they do charge fees for service and receive state and local funding (Joint State Government Commission 1997). There are other examples of successful regionalization in the state; there are at least 35 regional police departments across 125 municipalities, and interstate and intrastate regional planning commissions are now commonplace throughout the Northeast.

As we show, Pennsylvania's health system requires an overhaul. Pennsylvania continues to rank below national averages on measures of state population health. The Kaiser Commission recently reported that individuals living in rural areas of the state are most likely to face the greatest obstacles in accessing health care and in obtaining improved health outcomes. A State Health Care Innovation Plan awarded to Pennsylvania in 2013 has begun the development of telemedicine initiatives to help address some of these disparities (Kaiser Family Foundation 2016). While a worthy goal, the above suggests that without a more regionalized strategic focus on services and service-access barriers, many low-income Pennsylvanians will continue to lack access to health care and improved health, even if newly insured as a result of the ACA Medicaid expansion.

NOTES

This article was previously published as Michele Moser Deegan and A. Lanethea Mathews-Schultz, "The Limits of Medicaid Reform in Pennsylvania: Thinking Regionally about Access to Insurance and Health Care under the Affordable Care Act," *Commonwealth* 18, no. 2 (2016). © 2016 The Pennsylvania Political Science Association. ISSN 2469-7672 (online). http://dx.doi.org/10.15367/cjppp.v18i2.112. All rights reserved.

1. The ACA extends Medicaid coverage to individuals living at 133 percent FPL, but requires states to apply a 5 percent income disregard in determining eligibility, effectively bringing minimum eligibility requirements to 138 percent FPL.

2. In response to mandated Medicaid expansion and to the "individual Mandate" provisions of the ACA requiring individuals to obtain health insurance or face a tax penalty, twenty-six states and the National Association of Independent Businesses sued the federal government. The states were Alabama, Alaska, Arizona, Colorado, Florida, Georgia, Idaho, Indiana, Iowa, Kansas, Louisiana, Maine, Michigan, Mississippi, Nebraska, Nevada, North Dakota, Pennsylvania, Ohio, South Carolina, South Dakota, Texas, Utah, Washington, Wisconsin, and Wyoming.

3. Others include Arkansas, Maine, Oklahoma, Tennessee, and Wyoming. Of these, only Arkansas is reforming Medicaid and it is doing so through a Section 1115 Waiver, rather than the ACA expansion. Pennsylvania is the only mixed or hybrid state to have adopted the ACA Medicaid expansion.

4. A handful of additional states pursued similar state-run privatized alternatives for expanding Medicaid, including Arkansas, Iowa, Michigan, and Tennessee.

5. These individuals are referred to as PCO beneficiaries because they receive care through private managed plans. Eligibility under Corbett's Private Coverage Program was limited to individuals ages twenty-one to sixty-four with incomes up to 133 percent FPL, including childless adults and those with incomes greater than 33 percent FPL, which was previously the income cap for Medicaid in Pennsylvania. Existing Medicaid recipients were funneled into one of two new managed plans: a high-risk pool enrolling pregnant women, Social Security beneficiaries, and those eligible for Medicare and Medicaid; and a low-risk pool offering more-limited medical services. Newly eligible adults not determined to be "medically frail" were enrolled in the Private Coverage option.

6. The CMS project stipulated that cost sharing and premium contributions could not exceed 5 percent of family income.

7. Marilyn Tavenner, Secretary, U.S. Department of Health and Human Services, to Beverly Mackereth, Secretary of the Pennsylvania Department of Public Welfare, August 28, 2014. Pennsylvania was one of four states, along with Arizona, Indiana, and Kentucky, to have submitted a request that would have required work as a condition of Medicaid eligibility. Although these requests were denied by CMS, the agency changed course in March 2017, noting that it could use its authority to approve state options making Medicaid contingent on work requirements (Musumeci 2017). A Senate health-care bill, under consideration at the time of writing, similarly permits states to impose work requirements on Medicaid beneficiaries.

8. Prior to the ACA, states were already required to provide coverage at higher levels to children and pregnant women.

9. Some nineteen- and twenty-year-old adults without children with incomes up to 33 percent FPL previously were eligible for coverage.

10. One limitation is that for the purposes of Medicaid eligibility in the state of Pennsylvania, adults are considered individuals ages twenty-one to sixty-four. The U.S. Census data on poverty and the uninsured, however, defines adults as those ages eighteen to sixty-four. The Pennsylvania Department of State provides additional estimates about county-

wide Medicaid enrollment using enrollment and utilization data, but, unlike our approach, it does not use the population living at or below 138 percent FPL as a point of reference.

11. We do not estimate it here, but it is important not to underappreciate the effects of Obamacare and Medicaid expansion on individuals previously eligible for but nonetheless unenrolled in Medicaid. Likewise, our analysis does not examine increased Medicaid enrollment among children, which has fueled overall increases in some counties.

12. Prior to implementation of the ACA, county and municipal health departments could provide primary-care services not available through state district offices, such as immunizations, mammograms, and dental services.

REFERENCES

Beeler, Carolyn. 2013. "Corbett Rejects Obamacare Medicaid Expansion for Pennsylvania." *WHYY*, February 5. Available at https://whyy.org/articles/corbett-rejects-obamacare-medicaid-expansion-for-pennsylvania.

Boston University. n.d. "MA Public Health Regionalization Project." Available at http://www.bu.edu/regionalization/ (accessed January 18, 2018).

Brecher, Charles, and Shanna Rose. 2013. "Medicaid's Next Metamorphosis." *Public Administration Review* 73 (s1): s60–s68.

Central Massachusetts Regional Public Health Alliance. 2014. "Greater Worcester Community Health Improvement Plan: 2014 Annual Report." Available at http://healthycentralma.com/wp-content/uploads/2015/02/CHIP-annual-report-FINAL-for-web.pdf.

Commonwealth of Pennsylvania. 2015. "150,000 Additional Pennsylvanians Enrolled in Governor Wolf's Medicaid Expansion Plan." July 22. Available at https://www.governor.pa.gov/150000-additional-pennsylvanians-enrolled-in-governor-wolfs-medicaid-expansion-plan.

Dreier, Peter, John Mollenkopf, and Todd Swanstrom. 2004. *Place Matters: Metropolitics for the Twenty-First Century*. 2nd ed. Lawrence: University Press of Kansas.

Finnerty, John. 2017. "Legislature May Add Medicaid Changes to State Budget Bills." *Daily Item*, July 23. Available at http://www.dailyitem.com/news/local_news/legislature-may-add-medicaid-changes-to-state-budget-bills/article_6543b3e7-42ff-5504-a519-fb8647183125.html.

Hamilton, David K. 2014. *Governing Metropolitan Areas: Growth and Change in a Networked Age*. 2nd ed. Florence, KY: Routledge.

Hays, Justeen, Naxmim Bhuiya, Maeve Conlin, Michael Coughlin, and Geoffrey Wilkinson. 2014. "Impact of a District Incentive Grant Program on Regional Cross-Jurisdictional Public Health Services in Massachusetts." Paper presented at the Keeneland Conference, Lexington, KY.

Hutson, Malo Andre, George A. Kaplan, Nalini Ranjit, and Mahasin S. Muhahid. 2012. "Metropolitan Fragmentation and Health Disparities: Is There a Link?" *Milbank Quarterly* 90 (March): 187–207.

Hyde, Justeen, and Alison Tovar. 2006. "Strengthening Local Public Health in Massachusetts: A Call to Action." Available at http://www.bu.edu/regionalization/files/2013/05/Strengthening-Local-Public-Health-in-Massachusetts.pdf.

Institute of Medicine. 2011. *State and Local Policy Initiatives to Reduce Health Disparities: Workshop Summary*. Washington, DC: National Academies Press.

Jacobs, Lawrence R., and Timothy Callaghan. 2013. "Why States Expand Medicaid: Party, Resources, and History." *Journal of Health Policy and Law* 38 (October): 1023–1050.

Joint State Government Commission. 1997. "Intermediate Units in Pennsylvania: The Role of Educational Service Agencies in Promoting Equity in Basic Education." Available at http://jsg.legis.state.pa.us/resources/documents/ftp/publications/1997 -89-iureport.pdf.

Kaiser Commission on Medicaid and the Uninsured. 2013. "Where Are States Today? Medicaid and CHIP Eligibility Levels for Children and Non-disabled Adults." March. Available at https://kaiserfamilyfoundation.files.wordpress.com/2013/04/ 7993-03.pdf.

Kaiser Family Foundation. 2016. "The Pennsylvania Health Care Landscape." Available at https://kff.org/health-reform/fact-sheet/the-pennsylvania-health-care-landscape.

———. 2017. "Status of State Action on the Medicaid Expansion Decision." Available at https://www.kff.org/health-reform/state-indicator/state-activity-around-expanding -medicaid-under-the-affordable-care-act.

Kenney, Genevieve, Lisa Dubay, Stephen Zuckerman, and Michael Huntress. 2012. "Opting Out of the Medicaid Expansion under the ACA: How Many Uninsured Adults Would Not Be Eligible for Medicaid?" Urban Institute, July 5. Available at http://www.urban.org/research/publication/opting-out-medicaid-expansion-under -aca-how-many-uninsured-adults-would-not-be-eligible-medicaid.

Kirby, James B., and Toshiko Kaneda. 2005. "Neighborhood Socioeconomic Disadvantage and Access to Health Care." *Journal of Health and Social Behavior* 46 (March): 15–31.

LaRosa, Michael. 2013. "Corbett Could Be First Governor to Lose Re-election in Pa. History." *MSNBC*, September 13. Available at http://www.msnbc.com/hardball/ corbett-could-be-first-governor-lose-re-el.

Ledebur, Larry C., and William R. Barnes. 1993. *All in It Together: Cities, Suburbs, and Local Economic Regions.* Washington, DC: National League of Cities.

Luo, Wei. 2004. "Using a GIS-Based Floating Catchment Method to Assess Areas with Shortage of Physicians." *Health and Place* 10 (March): 1–11.

Lynch, John W., Richard D. Cohen, Katherine E. Heck, Jennifer L. Balfour, and Irene H. Yen. 1998. "Income Inequality and Mortality in Metropolitan Areas of the United States." *American Journal of Public Health* 88 (July): 1074–1080.

Massachusetts Public Health Regionalization Project. 2009. "Status Report." Available at http://www.ct.gov/dph/lib/dph/government_relations/local_health_council/ma _regionalization_status_report_9-1-09.pdf.

Mathews, Lanethea. 2012. "St. Luke's Community Health Needs Study: Survey Findings." Available at http://quakertown.slhn.org/Community-Health-Needs-Assessment.

Mathews-Schultz, Lanethea, and Robert Brill. 2015. "The Lehigh Valley Disability Community: Re-examining Community Needs and Opportunities." Available at https:// www.goodshepherdrehab.org/sites/goodshepherdrehab.org/files/images/Needs%20 Assessment%202015%20Report.Final%20from%20LVRC.01.04.16.pdf.

Mays, Glenn, and Renee Frauendienst. 2014. "Making the Case for Public Health." Available at http://www.health.state.mn.us/divs/opi/pm/ran/docs/1406ran_makingthecase .pdf.

Miller, David Y. 2002. *The Regional Governing of Metropolitan America.* Boulder, CO: Westview.

Minnesota Department of Health. n.d. "Minnesota's Public Health System." Available at http://www.health.state.mn.us/divs/opi/gov/context.html (accessed January 23, 2018).

———. 2014. "Measures Matter: Using Performance Measures to Understand and Improve Local Public Health Capacity and Services." Available at http://www.health
.state.mn.us/ppmrs/library/docs/2013_systemsummary.pdf.

———. 2015. "Building a Solid Foundation for Health: 2015 Report to the Minnesota
Legislature on Public Health System Development." Available at http://www.health
.state.mn.us/divs/opi/resources/docs/1501legreport.pdf.

Musumeci, MaryBeth. 2017. "Medicaid and Work Requirements." *Kaiser Family Foundation Issue Brief*, March. Available at http://files.kff.org/attachment/Issue-Brief
-Medicaid-and-Work-Requirements.

National Federation of Independent Business et al. v. Sebelius, Secretary of Health and
Human Services, et al. 2012. 567 U.S. 519.

Olson, Laura, and David Esack. 2014. "Tom Wolf Elected Pennsylvania Governor in
Landslide." *Morning Call*, January 24. Available at http://www.mcall.com/news/
local/elections/mc-pa-governor-election-wolf-corbett-20141104-story.html.

Orfield, Myron. 2002. *American Metropolitics: The New Suburban Reality*. Washington,
DC: Brookings Institution.

Pastor, Manuel, Jr., Peter Dreier, J. Eugene Grigsby III, and Marta Lopez-Garza. 2000.
Regions That Work: How Cities and Suburbs Can Grow Together. Minneapolis:
University of Minnesota Press.

Patient Protection and Affordable Care Act. 2010. Public Law 111–148, 124 Stat. 1029.

Pennsylvania Association of Community Health Centers. 2015. "Community Health
Centers Pennsylvania Directory." Previously available at http://pachc.com/health
_center.html.

Pennsylvania Department of Health. 2016. "Health Innovation in Pennsylvania Plan."
Available at http://www.health.pa.gov/your-department-of-health/innovation/
documents/health%20innovation%20in%20pa%20plan%2020160630%20for%20
cmmi.pdf.

Pennsylvania Department of Human Services. 2017. "Medicaid Expansion Report."
Available at http://www.dhs.pa.gov/cs/groups/webcontent/documents/document/
c_257436.pdf.

PolicyLink. 2002. "Promoting Regional Equity: A Framing Paper." Available at http://
www.policylink.org/sites/default/files/RegionalEquityFramingPaper_final.pdf.

Ramsay, David. 2015. "Red States Are Reinventing Medicaid to Make It More Expensive
and Bureaucratic." *New Republic*, January 18. Available at https://newrepublic.com/
article/120781/republican-governors-accept-medicaid-expansion-make-it-costlier.

Robert Wood Johnson Foundation. 2013. "County Health Rankings and Roadmaps:
Pennsylvania." Available at http://www.countyhealthrankings.org/app/pennsyl
vania/2013/rankings/outcomes/overall.

Rosenbaum, Sara, Sara Rotheberg, Sara Schmucker, Rachel Gunsalus, and Zoe Becker-
man. 2017. "How Will Repealing the ACA Affect Medicaid? Impact on Health Care
Coverage, Delivery, and Payments." *Commonwealth Fund Issue Brief*, March 22,
pp. 1–10.

Rusk, David R. 2003. *Cities without Suburbs: A 2000 Census Update*. 3rd ed. Washington,
DC: Woodrow Wilson Center.

Salinsky, Eileen. 2010. "Governmental Public Health: An Overview of State and Local
Public Health Agencies." National Health Policy Forum Background Paper No. 77.
Available at https://www.nhpf.org/library/background-papers/BP77_GovPublic
Health_08-18-2010.pdf.

Savitch, H. V., David Collins, Daniel Sanders, and John P. Markha. 1993. "Ties That Bind: Central Cities, Suburbs and the New Metropolitan Region." *Economic Development Quarterly* 7 (November): 341–357.

Savitch, H. V., and Ronald K. Vogel. 2000. "Paths to New Regionalism." *State and Local Government Review* 32 (Autumn): 158–168.

Schulz, Amy J., David R. Williams, Barbara A. Israel, and Lora Bex Lempert. 2002. "Racial and Spatial Relations as Fundamental Determinants of Health in Detroit." *Milbank Quarterly* 80 (December): 677–707.

Sullivan, Peter. 2017. "Governors from Both Parties Slam House Healthcare Bill, Call for Bipartisan Senate Approach." *The Hill*, June 16. Available at http://thehill.com/policy/healthcare/338157-governors-of-both-parties-call-for-bipartisan-senate-approach-on-healthcare.

Swanstrom, Todd, Peter Dreier, and John Mollenkopf. 2002. "Economic Inequality and Public Policy: The Power of Place." *City and Community* 1 (December): 349–373.

Thompson, Charles. 2017. "Medicaid Politics Comes to Harrisburg via Pennsylvania's State Budget Debate." *PennLive*, July 15. Available at http://www.pennlive.com/politics/index.ssf/2017/07/medicaid_politics_comes_to_har.html.

U.S. Census Bureau. 2015. "2010–2014 ACS 5-Year Data Profiles." Available at https://www.census.gov/acs/www/data/data-tables-and-tools/data-profiles/2014/.

Wang, Fahui, and Wei Luo. 2005. "Assessing Spatial and Nonspatial Factors for Health-Care Access: Towards an Integrated Approach to Defining Health Professional Shortage Areas." *Health and Place* 11 (June): 131–146.

Wang, Fahui, and W. William Minor. 2002. "Where the Jobs Are: Employment Access and Crime Patterns in Cleveland." *Annals of the Association of American Geographers* 92 (September): 435–450.

Wenner, David. 2014. "Corbett Claims 'Historic' Achievement in Pa. Plan to Use Obamacare Expansion Funds." *PennLive*, August 28. Available at http://www.pennlive.com/midstate/index.ssf/2014/08/pennsylvania_corbett_obamacare.html.

Wolf, Tom. 2017. Letter to Pat Toomey. June 21. Available at https://www.governor.pa.gov/governor-wolf-asks-senator-toomey-to-consider-bipartisan-concern-over-medicaid-cuts/.

Discussion Questions

1. What effect did the Supreme Court's decision in the *National Federation of Independent Businesses v. Sebelius* have on Medicaid expansion under the Affordable Care Act?
2. Why did Governor Corbett oppose Medicaid expansion? What was the "private option" plan he created for Pennsylvania? What effects did the 2014 gubernatorial election have on Medicaid expansion in the Commonwealth?
3. Who has benefited the most from Medicaid expansion in Pennsylvania?
4. Why does the expansion of Medicaid not necessarily ensure that lower-income people will have access to better care and healthier lives?

5. What lessons can be learned from the Minnesota and Massachusetts case studies concerning regional health-care provision?

Commonwealth Forum: Should the State Provide Support to Rural Hospitals?

YES

Health care is a human right. In a nation as wealthy as the United States, not
providing basic health care to every citizen is immoral. There are fifteen
hospitals in the state of Pennsylvania considered "critical access," a designa-
tion given by the Centers for Medicare and Medicaid to some rural hospitals
in response to closures in the late twentieth century. This means these hospitals provide care when the next-closest option might be more than forty
miles away. In the event of a heart attack or another acute-care issue, access
means the difference between life and death. Rural Pennsylvanians deserve
the same ability to attend to their health needs as any other urban or suburban citizen.

In recent years, rural hospitals across the United States have been facing
increasing closures. First, the lack of health insurance means hospitals provide care but are uncompensated for it. People simply cannot pay the bills.
Second, rural hospitals serve small populations, an often shrinking market,
who are not as wealthy as their counterparts in other regions. Thankfully,
the passage of Medicaid expansion has enabled more rural citizens to have
health insurance and has financially stabilized some of the most vulnerable
rural hospitals. Those rural hospitals in nonexpansion states provide more
uncompensated care, putting them at risk of closure. During the budget im-
passe of Governor Wolf's first year, rural hospitals in the Commonwealth
were operating on the brink of closure because of delayed Medicaid payments from the state. When lives are on the line, state government needs to
fulfill its responsibilities to the people. Politicians should not play politics
with the basic needs of the people they are supposed to represent.

NO

There are nearly seven hundred rural hospitals on the brink of financial collapse in the United States. They stay open because of huge injections of taxpayer money into an unsustainable system. The numbers simply do not add
up. Rural populations are shrinking, yet residents of these areas believe they
have a right to a hospital. Rural areas have plenty of other amenities. For
example, they are much less polluted with car exhaust and concentrated

heavy industry than their suburban and urban counterparts. They have open vistas, and peace and quiet. Residents do not have to sit in traffic for hours simply to get to work. However, what rural areas do lack is easy access to a hospital. But why should the residents of a state or the citizens of the rest of the country fund what comes down to a personal decision about where to live?

Rural hospitals are falling apart because of the realities of our market economy, and it is no place for government to continue to waste public money sustaining them. Rural areas often have trouble attracting enough doctors and medical personnel to staff a hospital. Rural residents tend to lack good health insurance or have no insurance at all, and so the hospital is forced to function while providing services for free or at far under market value. In addition, in many areas, there simply are not enough people requesting services at the hospital to justify keeping the doors open. Should rural residents be provided with medical care? Of course. But a general physician or small clinic could suffice, and patients could travel for more-severe conditions. Sustaining failing rural hospitals is just another reason the cost of health care in the United States continues its exponential climb.

For More Information

The **Pennsylvania Office of Rural Health** (http://www.porh.psu.edu/) at Pennsylvania State University is a partnership among the federal government, the Commonwealth, and the university. There are fifty state offices funded by the Federal Office of Rural Health Policy in the U.S. Department of Health and Human Services and Pennsylvania Department of Health.

The **U.S. Department of Health and Human Services Federal Office of Rural Health Policy** (https://www.hrsa.gov/rural-health/index.html) was created in 1987 to address rural access to health care, study the market stability of rural hospitals, and the role of Medicaid and Medicare in financing rural hospitals.

The **National Organization of State Offices of Rural Health** (https://nosorh.org/) provides news, studies, and discussion of best practices related to rural health issues across the country.

Chapter 8
Alcohol Policy

The Issue That Will Not Go Away

*Models of Public Policy Making and Four Decades of Republican
Efforts to Privatize Pennsylvania's State Liquor Monopoly*

GEORGE E. HALE

After Prohibition's repeal, Pennsylvania adopted one of the nation's strongest governmental monopolies for the sale of wine and spirits. Since 1980, three Republican governors—Dick Thornburgh, Tom Ridge, and Tom Corbett—have tried to privatize the state's monopoly. More recently, Republican lawmakers seized the initiative to do so. Despite support from over 60 percent of the public, all four of these efforts failed. James Q. Wilson's work on client politics, where costs are widely distributed and benefits are narrowly concentrated, partly explains why the state's liquor policy is difficult to change. The unionized workers in the state-owned liquor stores, the primary beneficiaries of the current policy, mobilized support for the current state monopoly while the potential beneficiaries of privatization remained unorganized and on the sidelines. In recent years this changed, and the issue moved into the arena of interest-group politics where a variety of interests are now pushing for modification. In the 1980s and 1990s, Republican governors received support on privatization from only about half the Republican lawmakers, as the lawmakers from rural areas generally opposed privatization. However, since 2012, Republican unity increased on the issue of liquor privatization. While client politics and morality politics blocked major reforms in the past, under the last two governors privatization is now on the legislative agenda every year. The issue will not go away.

For decades, Pennsylvania was one of only two states operating a governmental monopoly of the selling of wine and spirits at both the wholesale and retail levels. This policy dates from the repeal of Prohibition in 1933 (Schell 2006, 77), but it is supported by only a third of the state's residents (George 1997; Yost et al. 2013). Nonetheless, three Republican governors—Dick Thornburgh, Tom Ridge, and Tom Corbett—tried but failed to privatize the state liquor monopoly (Hale 2013). More recently, Republican lawmakers began pushing for reform.

Privatization of the sale of alcoholic beverages periodically surfaces as an issue for several reasons. First, many people view the monopoly system as expensive and inefficient. Others consider the sale of alcoholic beverages to be a matter best left to the private sector. Furthermore, the sale of state liquor stores ("state stores") and the auction of private licenses can provide significant one-time revenue to the state. Conversely, supporters of the system argue that it provides well-paid jobs with good benefits. Religious groups and groups like Mothers Against Drunk Driving (MADD) oppose the private sale of alcoholic beverages because it could increase consumption and related social problems. Finally, opponents believe the state would lose ongoing revenues associated with the profits generated by state stores.

Research findings are mixed and support some claims on each side of the debate. Economists Seim and Waldfogel (2013, 835) contend that states with private liquor retailing have lower labor costs. They find that unionized state-store workers averaged $43,680 in pay and benefits in 2007 compared with $21,000 for private employees in other states. Additionally, state stores employ an average of 7.9 employees compared with 4.6 employees in privately owned stores. Seim and Waldfogel (2013, 850) also claim that the system inconveniences consumers who must drive longer distances to shop. While the state operates only six hundred stores, a licensing system for private stores would probably grow to at least fifteen hundred stores. Nonetheless, some rural areas benefit from the monopoly with better coverage than would be likely under a free-market approach.

While Seim and Waldfogel (2013) uncover no systematic evidence that prices are higher in Pennsylvania than in neighboring states, many consumers believe otherwise. Public Financial Management (PFM) estimates that 10–30 percent of total sales are lost to neighboring states through what is termed "border bleed" (Public Financial Management 2011, 9). The system also appears to result in approximately 15 percent lower alcohol consumption than in neighboring states (Seim and Waldfogel 2013, 852). Yet when PFM compared Pennsylvania with surrounding states, it found no clear relationship between a public or a private system for selling alcohol and the rate of alcohol-related motor vehicle fatalities or rate of underage drinking (Public Financial Management 2011, 11).

On balance, the evidence suggests that unionized employees are major beneficiaries of current policy and that the public is inconvenienced. Pennsylvanians travel longer distances to purchase alcoholic beverages. Conversely, others view reduced consumption as a social benefit. Finally, state stores are less efficient and less profitable than private stores, but the Pennsylvania Liquor Control Board (PLCB) does transfer approximately $90 million to the state's General Fund annually.

Creating the Governmental Monopoly

Prohibition was an effort by Protestant, middle class, and rural Americans to reassert their values over a growing Catholic, immigrant, and urban population (Gusfeld 1963). The repeal of Prohibition came swiftly in 1933 when the Democratic landslide of 1932 was interpreted as a referendum on the issue. The Twenty-First Amendment, repealing Prohibition, granted states power to control the sale of alcoholic beverages. States could remain "dry," and eight southern and plains states chose to do so. Many states, including Pennsylvania, also gave their local governments the option to remain "dry." For states allowing the sale of alcoholic beverages, the major options were a licensing system or a monopoly system with government stores selling directly to the public. The monopoly option was promoted to address problems thought to be associated with private enterprise, including favoritism in licensing, political corruption, and overconsumption. Initially, fifteen states adopted the monopoly model and twenty-five established a licensing system (Meier 1994, 161).

In Pennsylvania, Republican Governor Gifford Pinchot, a Progressive and a "dry," pushed to establish the nation's first governmental monopoly for the sale of wine and spirits. According to one observer at the time, Pinchot "is an out-and-out dry. He is just as dry in a wet city when he is campaigning as he is in a dry country district. There is not a drop of moisture in any of his speeches" (Beers 1980, 74). Establishing the monopoly was a remarkable accomplishment, given that the state had voted to repeal Prohibition by better than a three-to-one margin. Lawmakers from rural areas were overrepresented in the General Assembly and they gave Pinchot the necessary support, making Pennsylvania the largest and "wettest" state to adopt a liquor monopoly (Schell 2006).

Public Policy Making

To understand why the state liquor monopoly has proved so resistant to change, it is instructive to consider several models of the policy-making process. Agenda building is central to making policy. Downs (2005) depicts an "issue attention cycle," in which triggering events spark public interest in an issue, thereby creating conditions for nonincremental policy making. Nonetheless, opportunities for policy change become limited when public interest in the issue declines and new issues displace them on the agenda. Cobb and Elder (2005) focus on triggering events but note that authoritative decision makers can place items on the agenda. Using a more sophisticated model that incorporates both external events and the actions of policy makers, Kingdon (2003) argues that policies change when three streams—problems, solutions, and politics—come together at critical times. As he notes, "A problem is recognized, a solution is available, the political climate makes the time right for change, and the constraints do not prohibit action" (Kingdon 2003, 88). "Policy windows open infrequently," he adds, "and they do not stay open long" (166).

For James Q. Wilson (2012), the policy-making process is shaped by the structure of an issue. He considers public policies in terms of a four-cell typology that reflects whether the perceived costs and benefits are widely or narrowly distributed. This typology also explains why some policies are harder to change than others. For example, the state monopoly on the sale of wine and spirits features aspects of what Wilson calls "client" politics, or "policy under which some small group receives the benefits and the public at large endures the costs" (2012, 344). Wilson suggests that client policies are difficult to change because the costs are small, and "payers have very little incentive to organize" (346).

Eric Patashnik builds on Wilson's typology by asking what happens after enactment of "general interest reforms" (2008, 16). To enact reforms, policy advocates must overcome entrenched opposition by placing reforms on the agenda, neutralizing opponents, mobilizing supporters, and building winning coalitions. Patashnik (2008, 20) contends that adoption of general interest reforms also requires advocates to link reforms to salient issues. Often it is necessary as well to employ strategies that shift the venue for making policy to new arenas where self-interested economic groups lose their customary advantages. Finally, tactics such as compensation, side payments, and transition measures are needed to neutralize the opposition of beneficiaries or clients of the policy. To make reforms last, says Patashnik, it is essential to accomplish a "recasting of interests, institutions, and ideas" (2008, 19). He notes that "reforms may persist for reasons other than those which prompted the reforms' original adoption" (161). When specific groups receive economic benefits from a policy, groups can grow up around a particular policy and shield it from change.

Aside from generic models of policy making, studies of policies regulating the sale of alcoholic beverages reveal a persistent role for "morality" politics. Since the 1930s, fundamentalist Protestant groups have helped shape policy regarding the selling of wine and spirits. David Schell (2006) attributes the Pennsylvania monopoly system to the "politics of provincial- ism." Kenneth Meier and Cathy Johnson (1990) find that "dry" religious groups opposing alcohol consumption have a significant impact on the reg- ulation of alcoholic beverage sales in many states. John Frendreis and Ray- mond Tatalovich identify a "strong linkage between Evangelical Protestant population and the decisions of U. S. counties to elect to be 'dry' counties, demonstrating the persistence of religion as a vital factor in some public policy debates, especially those falling into the realm of morality politics" (2010, 315). Similarly, Pennsylvania allows municipalities to remain dry and to ban the sale of malt beverages and distilled liquor. The dry municipalities are heavily concentrated in the state's rural central and northern regions. According to Wilbur Zelinsky, the "pattern of partial and complete prohibi- tion seems to be related, to a significant degree, to ethnic and religious fac- tors and to even more fundamental social attitudes, which do vary consider- ably among various Pennsylvania localities" (1995, 148–149).

Significant regional differences within Pennsylvania are reflected in par- tisan identification, political ideology, and views about moral issues. Penn- sylvania is a highly diverse state with two major urban centers and a vast rural area in its central and northern regions (Kennedy 1999, 8–11). Renee Lamis (2009, 230) uses five regions of the state to analyze public opinion. Republican identification and conservatism is strongest in the central and northern tier (see Table 8.1). Regional differences also exist on political and cultural issues. In a 2004 survey, 25 percent of central and northern tier re- spondents identified moral issues as their top concern. This region also is the one most likely to have "dry" municipalities. Furthermore, an August 2012 poll found support for "selling the state-owned liquor stores to private com- panies as a way for the state of Pennsylvania to balance its budget" to be weakest in the northern and central regions of the state (Yost et al. 2013).

Policies involving the sale of alcoholic beverages thus involve aspects of morality politics as an overlay to what might otherwise be a straightforward contest over the role of government and private enterprise or a struggle

TABLE 8.1 PARTY AND POLITICAL PHILOSOPHY IN PENNSYLVANIA BY REGION

Region	Party identification: Republican (%)	Political philosophy: Liberal (%)	Top 2004 issues: Moral values (%)
Philadelphia	14	35	7
Philadelphia suburbs	45	23	11
Northeast	37	27	15
Pittsburgh and west	34	20	19
Central and northern tier	54	16	25

Source: Lamis 2009, 232–233, 237.

among competing private interests. Schell (2006, 313) argues that religious and social conservatism not only explain the formation of the state monopoly but also are among the factors—along with union power—that insulate the policy from change.

Efforts to Reform Public Policy in Pennsylvania

Governor Dick Thornburgh (1979–1987)

Several Pennsylvania governors have entertained notions of abolishing the state-store system. In 1934, Democrat George Earle complained that prices in state stores were too high. In 1968, Governor Raymond Shafer's Liquor Code Advisory Committee reviewed problems with the state liquor system. In the 1970s, Governor Milton Shapp unsuccessfully proposed privatization of the state-store system (Beers 1980, 369). Republican Richard "Dick" Thornburgh's 1978 platform included privatization of state liquor stores, but his campaign focused instead on "corruption and mismanagement in state government" and the need to "clean up Harrisburg" (Thornburgh 2003, 74).

Thornburgh initially addressed improving PLCB management by trying to secure confirmation of his nominees as commissioners. According to Thornburgh's former chief of staff, when Democrats blocked the governor's efforts to name a majority of the PLCB commissioners, Thornburgh "turned into a champion of privatization" (Richard Stafford, personal communication, August 2011). A Democrat also observed that if Thornburgh could not gain political control of the board, "he would join forces with those advocating abolition of the liquor control system" (Carocci 2005, 191). Thornburgh acknowledged, "I had stated its transformation to a private, consumer-oriented system as a goal in our 1978 campaign, but our efforts were largely rhetorical until, early in my second term, I then presented a detailed plan to accomplish that goal." For the governor, privatization was a matter of reform: "The much-derided state store system had become a monument to inefficiency, inhospitality and occasional corruption" (Thornburgh 2003, 167). A 1983 report by Touche Ross and Co. identified needed improvements in PLCB operations and predicted falling operating profits resulting from inefficient pricing, merchandising, inventory, and distribution practices. According to Thornburgh, "Poor service was driving many customers out of state for their purchases, causing a loss of revenue, while expenses continued to rise. I hoped declining profits, if nothing else, would sound the death knell for this dinosaur" (167).

Recognizing that the issue was a "hard sell," Thornburgh's advisers developed a "back-up plan." While working on legislation for the sunset review of state agencies, which required the periodic legislative reauthorization or termination of agencies, gubernatorial aides saw to it that the PLCB was scheduled for sunset review. This gave Thornburgh "an opportunity to block reauthorization in one legislative chamber or to sustain a veto of reauthorizing legislation" (Stafford, personal communication, August 2011).

In the interim, Thornburgh had no success in pushing privatization. The House of Representatives refused to vote on his plan. The Republican Senate also took no action on S.B. 597, introduced in 1981 by Republican Senator Stewart Greenleaf, providing for a private-license system. At Thornburgh's request, Greenleaf sponsored S.B. 92 for a statewide referendum in 1983, but it went nowhere. Other Senate bills failed to reach the floor. Thornburgh concluded that his plan "was stymied by a strong, if somewhat odd, coalition of organized labor, especially the powerful state Store employees' union; Bible Belt 'drys,' opposed to liquor in general and fearful of more convenience to consumers; and organizations like MADD" (2003, 167). Democrats were solidly arrayed against Thornburgh's plans. For Democrats, one insider noted:

It was largely a jobs issue for them; the LCB's three-thousand-plus employees enjoyed some sort of job protection either through unionized collective bargaining or by civil service status. . . . A considerable number of Republicans also were opposed, though for entirely different reasons, having largely to do with unfettered access to the purchase and consumption of booze. (Carocci 2005, 213)

With time, Thornburgh grew more passionate about the issue. During a goodwill mission to the Democratic Republic of the Congo, Thornburgh bought a bottle of wine at a privately owned store. "That was the last nail in the coffin, the straw that broke the Camel's back," he said. "That Marxist-Leninist state has privatized liquor sales," he exclaimed, "but Pennsylvania, this bastion of free enterprise, has a state-run socialist monopoly" (Gruson 1986). In 1986, the backup plan took center stage. The PLCB was to be terminated through the sunset process unless reauthorized by the General Assembly. This maneuver transferred the advantage to Thornburgh, who needed only one chamber's support to block reauthorization. While the representatives voted 158–40 to extend the PLCB for ten years, Republican leaders in the Senate kept the reauthorization off the agenda. In a 27–22 party-line vote after midnight on the last legislative day of 1986, Democrats failed to get the PLCB extension issue onto the agenda. In December 1986, one month before leaving office, Thornburgh issued an executive order to terminate the PLCB, to auction off 705 state stores, and to phase out the agency by July 1, 1987. Thornburgh recalled, "With undisguised glee, I affixed huge symbolic 'For Sale' signs to retail outlets. Predictably, our opponents sought redress in the courts" (2003, 168). Thornburgh's directive was challenged, and Commonwealth Court overturned the executive order but also ruled that without legislative action by June 30, 1987, the PLCB would expire (Munshi 1997).

Nonetheless, Thornburgh's leverage was limited because his lieutenant governor, William Scranton III, lost the 1986 race for governor to Democrat Bob Casey. Casey had pledged to continue liquor control, conditioned on passage of reforms to make the agency more responsive to consumers. Casey promoted H.B. 1000, which contained reforms: placing enforcement powers with the state police, creating administrative law judges, and permitting consumer-oriented reforms such as discounts, variable hours, and credit card payment for purchases. A Republican amendment in the House of Representatives to privatize wholesale and retail sale of wine failed by a vote of 163–34, and H.B. 1000 passed the House on April 29, 1987, by almost the same margin of support. On June 17, 1987, the Senate by 39–10 defeated an amendment to allow the sale of liquor and wine in private retail stores. Only one Democrat supported the amendment, as did barely a third of the Republicans (see Table 8.2). A majority of Republicans from the Philadelphia and Pittsburgh suburbs backed the privatization measure, but only a single Republican among the thirteen from central and northern tier counties did so. On June 29, 1987, H.B. 1000 passed the Senate on an identical 39–10 vote. The PLCB was back in business.

On the same day, the House of Representatives approved H.B. 1000 as amended 155–45. Democrats supported the bill 99–2, and Republicans supported it 56–43. Republicans from suburban Philadelphia and Pittsburgh opposed PLCB reauthorization. In the central and northern regions, just sixteen of forty-three Republican lawmakers voted against reauthorization (see Table 8.3). These votes illustrate why Governor Thornburgh failed. Republicans were divided on the issue, with majority support coming only from those lawmakers from suburban Pittsburgh and Philadelphia.

TABLE 8.2 VOTE ON GREENLEAF AMENDMENT TO H.B. 1000
ALLOWING PRIVATIZATION BY PARTY AND REGION (JUNE 17, 1987)

Regions	Senate Democrats		Senate Republicans	
	Yes	No	Yes	No
Philadelphia	0	6	0	1
Philadelphia suburbs	0	2	6	1
Northeast	0	5	0	2
Pittsburgh and west	1	6	2	2
Central and northern tier	0	2	1	12
Total	*1*	*21*	*9*	*18*

Source: Roll call data from *Pennsylvania Legislative Journal*, June 17, 1987, p. 739, available at http://www.legis.state.pa.us/WU01/LI/SJ/1987/0/Sj19870617.pdf; regions based on Lamis 2009.

The 1992 Vote

During Governor Casey's tenure, privatization got to a floor vote in the House of Representatives one more time. In February 1992, a Republican amendment to a liquor-licensing bill proposed selling the 681 state stores to the highest bidders subject to several restrictions designed to mollify opponents concerned about any expansion of liquor sales. No licensee could hold more than 10 percent of the statewide licenses or more than 20 percent in an individual county. Proponents claimed the auction of stores and inventory would yield over $600 million for school district property-tax relief. The amendment failed 47–149 (see Table 8.4). Only a pair of the Democrats supported it. Republicans narrowly favored the amendment by only 45–40. Again, Republicans representing suburban Philadelphia backed privatization. Elsewhere fewer than half the Republicans supported privatization.

TABLE 8.3 FINAL LEGISLATIVE VOTE ON H.B. 1000 REESTABLISHING THE LIQUOR CONTROL BOARD BY PARTY AND REGION (JUNE 29, 1987)

Region	House Democrats Yes	No	House Republicans Yes	No
Philadelphia	21	0	5	0
Philadelphia suburbs	4	0	10	20
Northeast	17	1	9	2
Pittsburgh and west	42	1	5	5
Central and northern tier	15	0	27	16
Total	*99*	*2*	*56*	*43*

Source: Roll call data from *Pennsylvania Legislative Journal*, June 29, 1987, pp. 1193–1194, available at http://www.legis.state.pa.us/WU01/LI/HJ/1987/0/19870629.pdf; regions based on Lamis 2009.

TABLE 8.4 VOTE ON AMENDMENT NO. AO 417 TO H.B. 695 TO AUCTION OFF 681 STATE STORES (FEBRUARY 5, 1992)

Region	House Democrats Yes	No	House Republicans Yes	No
Philadelphia	0	24	1	3
Philadelphia suburbs	1	3	18	9
Northeast	0	17	4	8
Pittsburgh and west	1	42	6	4
Central and northern tier	0	23	16	16
Total	*2*	*109*	*45*	*40*

Source: Roll call data from *Pennsylvania Legislative Journal*, February 5, 1992, p. 267, available at http://www.legis.state.pa.us/WU01/LI/HJ/1992/0/19920205.pdf; regions based on Lamis 2009.

Governor Tom Ridge (1995–2001)

In his 1994 campaign, Republican Tom Ridge, a former congressman, supported privatizing the liquor monopoly, claiming the state did not need to provide the service. Like Thornburgh, however, Ridge waited before presenting a plan. According to John Jones, Ridge's point man as PLCB chair and now a federal district judge, Ridge got to the issue "ahead of schedule in 1996 when he was grappling with how to provide state funding for new sports stadiums in Philadelphia and Pittsburgh." After hiring Price Waterhouse to study the issue, Ridge's team developed a privatization proposal. According to Jones, Ridge was "all in" on the issue: "The numbers made sense, and it was not a core function of state government" (John Jones, personal communication, November 2011).

In early 1997, Ridge proposed to sell the state stores and use the estimated $650 million in proceeds to fund the construction of stadiums and other projects. Neither Ridge nor Jones appreciated "how tough it would be" (Jones, personal communication, November 2011). Once more, the United Food and Commercial Workers and its labor allies, religious groups such as the Pennsylvania Council of Churches, and MADD, dominated the debate (Schell 2006, 307–308).

A poll conducted by Mansfield University found 60 percent of voters in favor of selling state stores (George 1997, 52). Notwithstanding its support among the public, the proposal remained lodged in the Senate's Law and Justice Committee. Ridge could not muster support for his proposal before the summer recess. Democratic legislators then held hearings around the state highlighting opposition from state-store employees and other groups. After receiving multiple death threats, Jones was given a security detail. He later recalled the long hearings on the subject: "It was brutal. I had the stuffing kicked out of me. It was blood sport" (Couloumbis 2010). Jones later recalled, "I felt like George Custer at the Battle of the Little Bighorn" (Jones, personal communication, November 2011).

While Ridge's proposal sparked pitched opposition from employee unions and their allies, Republican lawmakers looked for ways to duck the issue after PLCB employees fanned out over the summer recess to tell lawmakers about the jobs to be lost in their districts. As PLCB Chairman, Jones fielded calls throughout the summer of 1997 from Republicans who "didn't want to have to vote on Ridge's plan." He recalled, "The jobs issue was the key one," and "Nobody wanted to vote to put thousands of people out of work. As a result, lawmakers never got to making decisions based on the numbers" (Jones, personal communication, November 2011).

Ridge's plan also lacked support from business. As Jones remarked, "The proponents were few and the objectors were many." He also reflected, "What that taught me from a political standpoint is that there is no overarching passion within the General Assembly, or in the public at large, for privatization. Unless and until there is a general hue and cry, it is very unlikely there will be a privatization initiative that succeeds" (Twedt 2008). The leader of the state-store employees union agreed: "There isn't this critical mass screaming for change" (Couloumbis 2010). As Jones concluded, "Major initiatives do better when there are private entities pushing them. You need not just a governor, you also need lobbyists." That fall, Ridge abandoned the proposal when legislative leaders told him "this dog isn't going to hunt" (Jones, personal communication, November 2011). It did not resurface after his 1998 reelection or during the remainder of his tenure.

Governor Tom Corbett (2011–2015)

The issue of what to do with the state's monopoly over the sale of alcoholic beverages receded until the 2010 gubernatorial election. From 2003 to 2011, Democratic Governor Ed Rendell took modest steps to make the PLCB more businesslike and consumer friendly. New legislation allowed a few discount state stores in several locations near state borders, permitted selected stores to open on Sundays, and authorized a few stores within grocery stores. In 2010, the Republican Attorney General Tom Corbett supported privatization during his successful campaign for governor. The new governor's support for liquor privatization fit into a broader framework for promoting free-market solutions, such as privatizing the state lottery. Republicans also won control of the General Assembly with a 30–20 and 111–90 majorities. Moreover, public opinion supported the sale of state stores. Newspaper articles predicted action on phasing out the state stores.

Initially Corbett wrestled with the impact of the Great Recession, a state budget with a potential $4 billion deficit, and his own no-tax pledge. With the governor preoccupied by budget issues, House Majority Leader Mike Turzai took the lead on privatization. The governor's contribution was commissioning PFM to study privatizing the wholesale and retail operations of the PLCB.

Supporters of the state monopoly also prepared for battle. In 2010, only $1,000 of the $216,550 contributed by the United Food and Commercial Workers to state candidates went to a Republican. The PLCB also proposed its own legislative package to undercut charges of being unresponsive to consumers. It sought authorization to ship wine directly to residents, to remove restrictions on Sunday sales, to allow state stores to be retailers for the lottery, and to expand market-based pricing. During the spring of 2011, the House Democrats' Policy Committee held hearings attacking Turzai's proposal.

Nothing happened until PFM issued its report in October 2011. It documented a negative ten-year trend in which PLCB revenues increased at a

3.5 percent compounded annual growth rate, while expenses climbed at 5.5 percent annually. PFM also found that most PLCB stores were unprofitable, with high operating costs, personnel costs, and full-time staffing levels compared to other control states. They also determined that Pennsylvania's apparently low levels of alcohol consumption partly resulted from high markups and taxes that encouraged "cross-border" purchasing. PFM concluded that the number of retail licensees could be increased to approximately 1,500 to better serve the public. They also estimated that the range of revenues to be gained from a potential auction of retail and wholesale licenses to be between $1.1 billion and $1.6 billion (Public Financial Management 2011).

Two months later, the House Liquor Committee gutted Turzai's H.B.11. On a 15–10 party-line vote, the Republican majority torpedoed the majority leader's proposal for full privatization by amending it to allow existing beer distributors to sell wine. The amendment also retained the state-store system. Committee Democrats opposed this partial privatization measure, since it would have undermined the PLCB's revenue stream. Moreover, many beer distributors opposed the amended bill out of fear that only the largest beer distributors could afford the enhanced license.

In June 2012, floor debate over privatization took place for the first time since 1992. Turzai offered a proposal to replace the more than six hundred state stores with sixteen hundred private outlets while also giving the approximately one thousand beer distributors a chance to buy retail wine and liquor licenses. After three hours, debate was suspended at 10:00 P.M. on June 11 with over three hundred amendments still pending when Republican leaders failed to corral the necessary votes. Despite Turzai's efforts to find allies by giving beer distributors a chance to buy retail licenses, the Pennsylvania Malt Beverage Distribution Association opposed the measure. They complained that allowing big retail chains to obtain multiple licenses would damage the competitive position of the mom-and-pop distributors holding single licenses.

Despite supportive statements from the governor, some Republicans complained he was not sufficiently involved in securing votes for the measure. The very groups that might benefit from privatization—beer distributors, big box stores, convenience stores, and grocery chains—also feared the potential harm they would suffer if their competitors dominated the bidding for licenses. These rivalries complicated the process of building a coalition supporting privatization. Republican John Taylor, chair of the House Liquor Committee, compared putting together the votes for privatization to solving a Rubik's Cube: "As soon as you twist one color, another color gets out of joint" (Krebs 2012).

When the General Assembly adjourned its two-year session in 2012, Turzai expressed optimism about the future chances for privatization but stated that next time the proposal needed to come from the governor (Couloumbis 2012). Nonetheless, the prospects for change were not promising in the 2013–2014 legislative session. The Republican Senate was not enthusiastic about the issue, and the 2012 election narrowed their edge over Democrats to 27–23.

In 2013, Governor Corbett was ready to push the issue in preparation for the 2014 election. Representative Turzai introduced H.B. 790, the governor's proposal, to auction off the state stores and use the expected $1 billion proceeds to fund education. It did not take long for Republicans on the House Liquor Committee to water down the proposal. They amended the bill to give beer distributors the first opportunity to purchase the new wine and spirits licenses, and they protected the distributors by insisting that grocery stores applying for a license to sell beer could do so only in a restaurant-style seating area within their stores. Additionally, state stores would not be sold immediately. They would be phased out over time and possibly remain open permanently in the some rural areas. Word went out that Corbett badly needed a legislative win. On March 21, 2013, following heavy lobbying by the governor's office, Republicans gave Corbett a victory by passing the weakened measure 105–90, with only five Republicans in opposition.

When the bill moved to the Senate, things slowed down. No Senate leader championed privatization. Instead several spoke of a desire to "modernize" the PLCB. The Law and Justice Committee waited over a month before holding hearings. In addition to opposition from the employee unions, the beer distributors worried that privatization might increase competition from supermarkets and convenience stores. The Republicans in the Senate were less enthusiastic about a major reworking of the system, and no consensus emerged on large-scale change. The Senate developed its own bill to begin moving the state out of the retail business and to set the stage for eventually leasing the wholesale operations if it proved to be financially feasible. The Senate bill was never called up for a vote. Reflecting on the 2013 experience, the next year the Senate Majority Leader Dominic Pileggi stated, "I don't see the auction idea—auctioning off the wholesale and retail licenses—as something we have 26 votes for in this body this year. Knowing the vote count from the last time we went into this in detail, there wasn't support for that level of change. There was support for change. The question is can we line up what we have support for here with what they have in the House" (Frantz 2014).

The stalemate between Republicans in the House of Representatives and the Senate continued in 2014. Several situational factors explained why the Republicans failed to convert their control of the governorship and both legislative chambers into a big win. First, there was no consensus in the Senate for transformational as opposed to incremental change. Related to this, action on privatization was delayed throughout 2013 as the Senate held the liquor issue hostage as they tried to leverage Republicans in the lower chamber into supporting a major increase in transportation funding by raising the gas tax. The two bills were uncoupled only after passage of Act 89 providing for major gasoline tax increases in November 2013.

Second, the legislative session saw big increases in lobbying on all sides of the privatization issue. The issue was no longer a binary yes-or-no issue. Lobbying now focused on how to divide the potential gains from privatization. Ironically, the increase in pro-privatization lobbying often resulted in various economic interests competing against each other. In addition to employee unions spending over $500,000 lobbying to oppose change, the biggest spenders were supermarkets that wanted to make sure privatization would allow them to sell wine and spirits. Wegmans supermarkets spent over $300,000 on alcohol-related lobbying. Giant Eagle supermarkets allocated $286,000. Walmart spent $156,000. Gas station and convenience store chains also lobbied heavily. The Sheetz chain spent $203,000 and Wawa invested $65,000 on lobbying. The Malt Beverage Distributors Association spent $91,000 on lobbying out of concern that the larger retail chains could win a "David-and-Goliath" fight against the smaller family-owned beer distributors. These fears were reinforced by the fact that major brewers Anheuser-Busch and MillerCoors invested over $300,000 to make sure that if grocery stores or other retailers were allowed to sell wine or spirits, they also would be allowed to sell beer (Giammarise 2014).

Third, weak gubernatorial leadership also contributed to lost opportunities. Corbett's relationship with legislative leaders was never strong. As attorney general he indicted several leaders of both parties on charges of corruption, and the grand jury he empaneled issued a report highly critical of a legislative culture of corruption. Paula Holoviak and Thomas Baldino conclude, "He thus began his term of governor with a legislature that, although controlled by his party, regarded him as hostile to the institution. His relationships with legislators of both parties remained strained throughout his term" (2016, 41). Additionally, Corbett's reserved personality and his distaste for public speaking compromised his effectiveness across the board. In addition to liquor privatization, Corbett also came up short on his priorities of pension reform, property tax reform or reduction, and the sale of the state lottery (Holoviak and Baldino 2016). Perhaps the best testimony on his weakness is the governor's own words. When discussing his difficulty of getting Republican support for his agenda, Corbett stated, "Getting them all on the same page, and working in the same direction, is probably the most difficult job I've ever had to do" (Levy 2012). After four years, the Republicans failed to capitalize on their united control of the executive and legislative branches because of lackluster Senate support for privatization, complex interest-group activity, and weak gubernatorial leadership.

Republican Legislative Activism and Governor
Tom Wolf (2015–present)

When Corbett lost to Democrat Tom Wolf in 2014, state government returned to a divided model of governance. In the past, the privatization issue would have disappeared from the legislative agenda under a Democratic governor. This would not be the case during Wolf's first term. By 2014, substantial party unity on the issue developed in the House of Representatives. Additionally, the strongest privatization advocate, Majority Leader Turzai, was elevated to speaker. Increasingly sharp partisan politics virtually guaranteed that Republican lawmakers kept the issue alive under Governor Wolf. Moreover, the issue was no longer a matter of client politics, that is, a simple choice between the interests of highly concentrated beneficiaries, such as the state-store workers, versus unorganized interests that might theoretically gain by ending the monopoly. Grocery stores, big box retailers, gas stations and convenience stores, national breweries, family-owned beer distributors, and restaurants now kept the issue alive.

Soon after Governor Wolf's election, he engaged in a lengthy battle with Republicans over the budget. The new governor pushed for large tax increases to restore the Corbett-era budget cuts. The large Republican majorities resisted. The resulting standoff extended from February 2015 until March 2016, when a budget that included none of Wolf's proposed tax increases became law without the governor's signature. Wolf was off to a bad start. Holoviak and Baldino note, "In addition to failing to enact a budget for nearly a year, the governor was also unsuccessful on other important issues" (2016, 36). In late 2015, only 30 percent of the public rated Wolf's performance as "excellent" or "good." Republicans saw the 2014 election as a rejection of Corbett rather than as an embrace of Wolf's liberal ideology. They successfully challenged the new governor and tarnished his image. The issue of liquor privatization played out as part of this highly partisan struggle.

In 2015, Republicans pushed liquor privatization forward as a potential short-term solution to the state's budget issues by suggesting that a $1 billion windfall from the sale of new licenses could offset a big portion of the $2 billion budget gap. In June 2015, the General Assembly on party-line votes enacted a privatization bill—House Bill 466—and a state budget, even though it was clear that Wolf would veto both bills since the budget did not reflect his spending priorities or proposed tax increases. House Bill 466 ended up as the product of negotiations between House and Senate Republicans. The bill created permits allowing beer distributors and holders of restaurant licenses, including some grocery stores, to sell wine and liquor. As private licensees opened in an area, the PLCB was to close the nearby state liquor stores. The bill also provided for the PLCB to lease and eventually sell its wholesale operations (Langley 2015).

The linkage between the privatization bill and the Republican budget was clear when Governor Wolf vetoed the entire package on July 2, 2015. Regarding House Bill 466, the governor stated, "The legislation falls short of a responsible means to reform the state liquor system and to maximize revenues to benefit our citizens." He cautioned, "It makes bad business sense for the Commonwealth and consumers to sell off an asset especially before maximizing its value." Additionally, the governor signaled that he was open to some changes or "modernization" of the state liquor system: "I am open to options for expanding the availability of wine and beer in more locations, including supermarkets." The same day he vetoed the Republican budget because it was too dependent on one-time revenues and fund transfers rather than on tax increases. As a result, the budget deadlock continued for another nine months and Republican lawmakers soon resumed their efforts to overturn the state's liquor monopoly (Langley 2015).

In June 2016, a second major liquor bill arrived on Governor Wolf's desk. The House passed a privatization bill in the fall of 2015 and the Senate amended the measure by substituting a series of provisions to "modernize" the liquor code along lines Wolf could support. The Senate version allowed grocery stores that were selling beer to also sell limited quantities of wine, permitted direct shipments of wine from producers to consumers, eliminated restrictions on state-store Sunday hours, and provided for 24/7 service at casinos in the state. The bill also allowed the PLCB to auction and reissue restaurant licenses that had been revoked or not renewed. Restaurants could also sell limited quantities of wine on a takeout basis. While the measure was trumpeted as a major reform, in practice its impact was limited. For instance, the provision allowing grocery stores approved to sell beer to also sell wine affected only about 350 stores statewide, and consumers were unable to buy more than four bottles at a time. Republicans in the House of Representatives were not happy with the watered-down Senate revisions. Nonetheless, in late June Speaker Turzai allowed the compromise measure to come to a vote. It passed with bipartisan support 157–31 (McKelvey 2016).

The modernization bill's most popular feature was expanding wine sales in grocery stores with restaurant licenses. When signing Act 39 of 2016, Governor Wolf hailed the measure "truly historic" by allowing consumers to buy wine in grocery stores and restaurants. He also hoped it would undermine efforts to privatize the system. Speaker Turzai, meanwhile, claimed the new law "will accelerate public demand for full privatization." While others hailed the measure as a productive compromise, the president of the state-store employees union predicted the beginning of the end of the PLCB system because it would erode state-store revenues and profits: "I think it will lead to liquor store closings and eventually the end of the LCB" (Langley 2016). Other groups expressed dissatisfaction for different reasons. For example, the Distilled Spirits Council called for expanded access to liquor in those grocery stores that now could sell wine and beer.

Thus Wolf's first two years in office saw major liquor legislation twice land on his desk. First, legislation to privatize the state's monopoly was vetoed in the middle of the yearlong budget battle. Second, the governor signed a major compromise modernization bill that allowed for some grocery stores to sell wine and for restaurants to sell wine to take home. While the governor hoped the modernization bill would short-circuit future calls for privatization, clearly by the spring of 2017 the issue was not going away. On Tuesday, April 25, 2017, the House of Representatives passed four bills to move the state toward privatization. The package included measures to "free the wine" by allowing all grocery stores, not just those with restaurant seating capacity, to obtain permits to sell wine and to purchase wine from private-sector wholesalers instead of the PLCB. Another bill would create a new class of wine and spirit retail store licenses. A third proposal allowed holders of restaurant and hotel licenses already selling up to four bottles of wine to also sell limited quantities of takeout spirits. Finally, House Bill 1075, sponsored by Speaker Turzai, provided for the complete privatization and divestiture of the PLCB's wholesale system for wine and spirits. The short-term prospect for these measures is not promising. Governor Wolf has made it clear that he wants to wait and see the impact of the modernization. Additionally Senate Majority Leader Corman stated that he did not see any significant liquor expansion in the near term.

Nonetheless, it is possible that Republicans may revive the issue before the end of the legislative session in order to differentiate the Republican candidate from Governor Wolf in the 2018 election, or try to leverage budget negotiations. Furthermore, in the 2016 election, the Republican majorities also grew by three in both the Senate and the House of Representatives to 34–16 and 122–81. Additionally, if Republicans recapture the governorship in 2018, they would be well positioned to try again. By mid-2017, clearly the House of Representatives seized the initiative by taking action that very year (see Table 8.5).

Conclusion

Three times in thirty years Pennsylvania governors failed to dismantle the state's liquor monopoly and replace it with a free-market system. All three governors encountered unified opposition from Democrats, and were stymied by a divided Republican party. The opposing coalition skillfully mobilized its members—the United Food and Commercial Workers Union, the AFL-CIO, MADD, the Pennsylvania Council of Churches, and beer distributors. Representative Dante Santoni, formerly the ranking minority

TABLE 8.5 INCREASING ACTIVITY ON LIQUOR PRIVATIZATION ISSUE

Governor	Proposal	House vote	Senate vote	Notes
Thornburgh (R)	1983–1987: governor proposes privatization	None	None	No action taken on Thornburgh's proposals
	Thornburgh blocks PLCB reauthorization	No	Yes	Senate Republicans block vote reauthorizing PLCB
Casey (D)	1987: reestablishing PLCB after sunset	Yes	Yes	Democrats and majority of Republicans support reestablishing the PLCB
	1992: Republican amendment for privatization	No	No	Democrats oppose, as do 40 of 85 Republicans
Ridge (R)	1997: governor proposes privatization	None	None	No action taken on Ridge's proposals
Rendell (D)	None	—	—	No proposed privatization
Corbett (R)	2011–2012: majority leader's proposal	None	None	Majority leader's proposal fails to receive floor vote
	2013–2014: governor's proposal	Yes	None	Governor's proposal amended and passed by House; not voted on by Senate
Wolf (D)	2015–2016: House proposes privatization	Yes	Yes	Senate amends bill to provide for partial privatization; Governor Wolf vetoes bill in 2015
	House proposes privatization	Yes	Yes	Senate amends bill to provide "modernization," including sale of wine in selected grocery stores; Governor Wolf signs bill in 2016
	2017–2018: House proposes privatization	Yes	?	House passes privatization legislation in April 2017

member of the House Liquor Committee, described the coalition as "strange bedfellows" not accustomed to working together. "While many members feared the loss of union jobs," he noted, "other more conservative lawmakers worried about the negative impact of increased consumption" (Dante Santoni, personal communication, September 2011). The formidable alliance of unions and social and religious groups encountered little opposition.

From the perspective of Kingdon's model, it appears that favorable conditions did not exist in the problem, solution, and political streams. The governors unsuccessfully tried to mobilize support by linking privatization to other issues. Thornburgh tried "reform" and "inefficiency." Ridge tried connecting it to financing for sports stadiums. Corbett linked it to relief for the state's fiscal problems. None of these issues caught fire. Despite Thornburgh's and Ridge's success on a wide range of issues, they failed on this one, and Corbett also failed to break up the state liquor monopoly.

One problem with Kingdon's model is that it does not explain why the timing may never be right on some issues. For example, all three governors encountered opposition within their party from the same areas of the state that supported Prohibition in the 1930s. Frank Sorauf (1963) and John Kennedy (1999) may offer an explanation. They examined the classic issue of "delegate" versus "trustee" by asking Pennsylvania lawmakers whether their voting is guided more by their constituency's views, by their own judgment, or by a combination of the two. Both scholars found Republican lawmakers to be more likely than Democrats to cite constituency as their decision-making guide. Writes Kennedy, "In the tightly knit rural and small-town communities, perhaps a closer, more personal relationship develops between legislator and constituents. These areas tend to be represented by Republicans" (1999, 77). Rural Republican legislators and those from metropolitan districts may simply be reflecting different constituencies, and constituency may trump party on this issue.

Wilson's typology of public policies provides a partial explanation of the outcomes. His model focuses exclusively on the distribution of economic costs and benefits. His description of client politics as resistant to change is convincing: "Client politics seems like an irresistible force, but sometimes it gets changed" (Wilson 2012, 146). Client politics rarely changes unless the public decides the beneficiaries are illegitimate or the costs of the policy become too high. During the Thornburgh and Ridge years, the debate took place in the arena of client politics. The beneficiaries of the current policy—the state-store workers, beer distributors, and their allies—were well organized. The groups that might have benefited from privatization stood on the sidelines. As Jones noted, "Governors alone can't do the job" (Jones, personal communication, November 2011). However, today the issue has changed from "client" politics to "interest group" politics, with the potential winners and losers from privatization actively engaged on the issue. Grocery stores, convenience stores and gas stations, restaurants, national brewers, and beer distributors all want a piece of the action.

Patashnik (2008) argues that reformers often need to change the venue or the rules for making decisions so that the economic beneficiaries of current policy no longer have the advantage. Thornburgh recognized this idea by proposing a referendum and by maneuvering so that the sunset legislation might allow him to prevail. Patashnik (2008) also suggests that side payments may promote reform by providing benefits to others to buy their support. While Governor Thornburgh did not try this strategy, Ridge's and Corbett's proposals for using the proceeds from the sale of the state stores did not enlist powerful allies. Now side payments and economic benefits in the form of licenses are available to the large organized interests pushing to break the state's liquor monopoly.

Several factors will keep the issue of liquor privatization alive. First, Republican legislative majorities have swelled to 122–81 and 34–16, and Republicans in the House of Representatives have supported far-reaching privatization three different times during Governor Wolf's tenure. Second, while Senate Republicans favor more-modest changes, they seem willing to respond to private interests one step at a time. Third, the issue has matured and is no longer an issue of client politics. It is now in the interest-group arena. Numerous parties are looking for a piece of the action. Finally, as Republican unity has grown, the regional cleavages associated with "morality" politics, so important in the 1980s and 1990s, have become less important. One key question is: Can Democrats hold back the tide moving in the direction of ending the state liquor monopoly? Another question is: Will Republicans enact a transformational reform that ends the PLCB monopoly in one bold stroke, or will the PLCB slowly collapse as its revenue stream is diverted by incremental legislative initiatives? This is the issue that will not go away!

REFERENCES

Beers, Paul B. 1980. *Pennsylvania Politics Today and Yesterday*. University Park: Pennsylvania State University Press.

Carocci, Vincent P. 2005. *A Capitol Journey: Reflections on the Press, Politics and the Making of Public Policy in Pennsylvania*. University Park: Pennsylvania State University Press.

Cobb, Roger D., and Charles D. Elder. 2005. "The Dynamics of Agenda Building." In *Classics of Public Policy*, edited by Jay M. Shafritz, Karen S. Layne, and Christopher P. Borick, 128–136. New York: Pearson Longman.

Couloumbis, Angela. 2010. "LCB's Epic Run Might Be Near End." *Philadelphia Inquirer*, December 19. Available at http://www.philly.com/philly/hp/news_update/20101219 _LCB_s_epic_run_might_be_near_end.html.

———. 2012. "Inquirer Poll Finds Wide Backing for Privatizing Liquor Sales." *Philadelphia Inquirer*, October 31. Available at http://www.philly.com/philly/news/politics/poll/ 20121031_Inquirer_Poll_finds_wide_backing_for_privatizing_liquor_sales.html.

Downs, Anthony. 2005. "Up and Down with Ecology." In *Classics of Public Policy*, edited by Jay M. Shafritz, Karen S. Layne, and Christopher P. Borick, 137–147. New York: Pearson Longman.

Frantz, Jeff. 2014. "Could 2014 Be the Year Pennsylvania's Liquor Privatization Movement Reaches Full Proof?" *PennLive*, January 7. Available at http://www.pennlive .com/midstate/index.ssf/2014/01/pennsylvania_alcohol_sales_pri.html.

Frendreis, John, and Raymond Tatalovich. 2010. "A Hundred Miles of Dry: Religion and the Persistence of Prohibition in the U.S. States." *State Politics and Policy Quarterly* 10 (November): 302–319.

George, Mary Selene. 1997. "Privatization of Pennsylvania Liquor Stores." Master's thesis, East Stroudsburg University.

Giammarise, Kate. 2014. "Pennsylvania Liquor Overhaul Brews Bid Spending." *Pittsburgh Post-Gazette*, May 26. Available at http://www.post-gazette.com/news/

politics-state/2014/05/26/Pa-liquor-overhaul-brews-big-spending/stories/
201405260074.

Gruson, Lindsey. 1986. "Liquor Sales Divide Pennsylvanians." *New York Times,* December 21. Available at http://www.nytimes.com/1986/12/21/us/liquor-sales-divide-pennsylvanians.html.

Gusfeld, Joseph R. 1963. *Symbolic Crusade: Status Politics and the American Temperance Movement.* Urbana: University of Illinois Press.

Hale, George E. 2013. "Three Strikes and You're Out? Why Three Republican Governors Failed to Privatize Pennsylvania's Liquor Monopoly." *Commonwealth: A Journal of Political Science* 16 (1): 63–80.

Holoviak, Paula A. Duda and Thomas J. Baldino. 2016. "Governor Wolf's First Year: A Comparative Analysis." *Commonwealth: A Journal of Pennsylvania Politics and Policy* 18 (2): 32–45.

Kennedy, John J. 1999. *The Contemporary Pennsylvania Legislature.* Lanham, MD: University Press of America.

Kingdon, John W. 2003. *Agendas, Alternatives, and Public Policies.* New York: Longman.

Krebs, Jeanette. 2012. "Pennsylvanians Keep Their Spirits Up despite Another Liquor Privatization Stall." *PennLive,* June 23. Available at http://www.pennlive.com/editorials/index.ssf/2012/06/pennsylvanians_keep_their_spir.html.

Lamis, Renee M. 2009. *The Realignment of Pennsylvania Politics since 1960: Two-Party Competition in a Battleground State.* University Park: Pennsylvania State University Press.

Langley, Karen. 2015. "Wolf Vetoes GOP Liquor Privatization Bill for Pennsylvania." *Pittsburgh Post-Gazette,* July 2. Available at http://www.post-gazette.com/news/politics-state/2015/07/02/Wolf-vetoes-GOP-liquor-privatization-bill-pennsylvania/stories/201507020196.

———. 2016. "Governor Signs Bill Expanding Wine Sales." *Pittsburgh Post-Gazette,* June 8. Available at http://www.post-gazette.com/news/state/2016/06/08/Gov-Wolf-signs-into-law-a-bill-allowing-Pennsylvania-grocery-stores-sell-wine/stories/201606080201.

Levy, Marc. 2012. "Persuading GOP Legislators Is a Difficult Job, Governor Says." *Morning Call,* November 27. Available at https://www.newspapers.com/newspage/273241620.

McKelvey, Wallace. 2016. "Pennsylvania's First Major Liquor Reform Bill since Prohibition Becomes Law." *PennLive,* June 8. Available at http://www.pennlive.com/politics/index.ssf/2016/06/liquor_reform_pa_wolf.html.

Meier, Kenneth J. 1994. *The Politics of Sin: Drugs, Alcohol, and Public Policy.* Armonk, NY: M. E. Sharpe.

Meier, Kenneth J., and Cathy M. Johnson. 1990. "The Politics of Demon Rum: Regulating Alcohol and Its Deleterious Consequences." *American Politics Quarterly* 18 (October): 404–429.

Munshi, Mihir A. 1997. "Share the Wine—Liquor Control in Pennsylvania: A Time for Reform." *University of Pittsburgh Law Review* 58 (Winter): 507–547.

Patashnik, Eric M. 2008. *Reforms at Risk: What Happens after Major Policy Changes Are Enacted.* Princeton, NJ: Princeton University Press.

Public Financial Management. 2011. "Liquor Privatization Analysis: Final Report." Available at http://www.pabudget.com/Display/SiteFiles/154/Documents/Resources%20and%20Publications/Liquor%20Privatization/PLCB_Report_FINAL_10.20.11.pdf.

Schell, David A. 2006. "Keeping Control: Gifford Pinchot and the Establishment of the Pennsylvania Liquor Control Board." Ph.D. diss., Temple University.

Seim, Katja, and Joel Waldfogel. 2013. "Public Monopoly and Economic Efficiency: Evidence from the Pennsylvania Liquor Control Board's Entry Decisions." *American Economic Review* 103 (2): 831–862.

Sorauf, Frank. 1963. *Party and Representation*. New York: Atherton Press.

Thornburgh, Dick. 2003. *Where the Evidence Leads: An Autobiography*. Pittsburgh: University of Pittsburgh Press.

Twedt, Steve. 2008. "Pa.'s Liquor Control System Lets State Keep a Tight Grip on the Bottle." *Pittsburgh Post-Gazette*, January 27. Available at http://www.post-gazette .com/life/libations/2008/01/27/Pa-s-liquor-control-system-lets-state-keep-a-tight -grip-on-the-bottle/stories/200801270192.

Wilson, James Q. 2012. *American Government: Brief Version*. 10th ed. Boston: Wadsworth.

Yost, Berwood A., G. Terry Madonna, Angela N. Knittle, and Kay K. Huebner. 2013. "Franklin and Marshall College Poll: Survey of Pennsylvanians; Summary of Findings." Available at https://www.fandm.edu/uploads/files/182574997702288562 -keyfeb13.pdf.

Zelinsky, Wilbur. 1995. "Cultural Geography." In *A Geography of Pennsylvania*, edited by E. Willard Miller, 132–153. University Park: Pennsylvania State University Press.

Discussion Questions

1. How are liquor and wine sales different in Pennsylvania from other states? How long has this system been in place?
2. Why have attempts to privatize the liquor monopoly failed even though the public supports them? Why have the interests that have allied against privatization been called "strange bedfellows"?
3. How have the approaches of Democratic and Republican governors been different on the issue of liquor privatization? Why?
4. Republicans have traditionally opposed government intrusion into the marketplace. Why have they not been able to stick together as a party and privatize liquor stores in Pennsylvania?
5. How does Hale use the policy literature to explain the history of liquor policy in Pennsylvania?

Commonwealth Forum: Should Pennsylvania Rely on Sin Taxes for Revenue?

YES

The health of Americans is a serious public policy concern. In Pennsylvania 30.2 percent of residents are obese, 17.7 percent engage in excessive drinking, and 18.1 percent smoke. Smoking alone is responsible for 27.9 percent of all cancer deaths in the Commonwealth and accounts for $6.38 billion in health-care costs each year ($2.07 billion of which comes from publicly funded Medicaid). A single program, Medicaid, accounts for 37 percent of Pennsylvania's budget. The quality of life for millions of Pennsylvanians is compromised by bad health. Resources that could be devoted to education or income tax cuts are being diverted to address poor health.

Policy makers have the ability to address health concerns by increasing taxes on products that promote our increasingly unhealthy lifestyles. So called "sin taxes" are placed on items such as cigarettes and alcohol to raise prices and thus discourage their consumption. These taxes should be expanded beyond the traditional products to increase the costs of unhealthy behaviors. For example, Philadelphia began collecting a tax on "sugary drinks" in 2017. The objective was to nudge people to drink noncaloric beverages in an effort to combat obesity. Pennsylvania could expand the use of sin taxes to a wide range of food products that promote bad health. This would have the twofold benefit of discouraging poor eating choices while at the same time raising revenue that could be used for public health programs promoting healthy consumption habits and exercise. This win-win situation would positively affect the lives of Pennsylvanians while at the same time cutting back on the amount the Commonwealth spends on health-care services.

NO

Two of the most popular sandwiches in Pennsylvania are the Pitts-burger and Cheese from Primanti Bros. in Pittsburgh and a cheesesteak from Pat's King of Steaks in Philadelphia. If your mouth is watering at the thought of these two culinary delights, take note of these statistics: the Pitts-burger contains 775 calories (39 percent of the recommended daily intake) and 51 percent of the recommended daily allotment of fat. A cheesesteak has about the same amount of calories but 59.6 grams of fat—a whopping 92 percent of the recommended daily intake. No one would argue that eating these sandwiches on a daily basis is a good idea. However, if people occasionally stop to grab one on the way home from a Phillies or Pirates game, who has the right to discourage them? What we eat is a matter of preference, and we each suffer the consequences of our dietary choices.

Not so fast. There's a group of people who believe they know what's best for us and want to change our consumption habits. They want to levy "sin taxes" on products they think people should avoid. It started with cigarette and alcohol taxes and has moved on to the current fight over taxes on soda. There are two major problems with the expansion of these taxes. First, the process for determining which product is subject to extra taxes is arbitrary.

For example, Philadelphia taxes "sugary drinks." A twenty-ounce bottled Coke from a convenience store gets taxed, but a White Chocolate Mocha with whole milk from Starbucks does not. This is true even though the latter, with 580 calories, 67 grams of sugar, and 85 percent of the daily recommended amount of saturated fat, is worse for you than a Coke's 240 calories, 65 grams of sugar, and 0 percent saturated fat. Second, sin taxes are often less about changing behavior and more about finding easy sources of revenue by taxing products that are deemed to be against the public interest. It is always easier to bridge budget gaps by taxing cigarettes than it is to raise income taxes. At the end of the day, sin taxes are just a way for the government to tell us what it thinks is good for us rather than letting us make our own decisions. They are a bad idea.

For More Information

The **Fiscal Survey of the States** (https://www.nasbo.org/reports-data/fiscal -survey-of-states) is published in the spring and fall by the National Association of State Budget Officers. The survey contains data on tax increases in the states, with specific sections on sin taxes levied on products such as alcohol and tobacco.

"Do 'Sin Taxes' Really Change Consumer Behavior?" (February 10, 2017) is a podcast featuring University of Pennsylvania Professor Benjamin Lockwood discussing his research on the economics of sin taxes. Visit http://knowledge.wharton.upenn.edu/article/do-sin-taxes-really-change -consumer-behavior for a transcript and audio of the podcast.

The **Tax Foundation** (https://taxfoundation.org/state-tax/excise-taxes/) provides original research on excise taxes in the states from a small-government perspective. Many of its pieces are devoted to studying the effects of sin taxes.

"The Pros and Cons of Taxing Sweetened Beverages Based on Sugar Content" (http://www.taxpolicycenter.org/sites/default/files/publication/ 136861/pros_and_cons_of_taxing_sweetened_beverages_based_on _sugar_content.pdf) was funded by the American Heart Association and written by scholars at the Urban Institute. The 2016 study examines the feasibility and desirability of collecting beverage taxes at the national, state, and local levels.

Chapter 9
Social Policy

FMLA in Pennsylvania

Analysis of Family and Medical Leave Policy in the State

JENNIE SWEET-CUSHMAN

This chapter details the impact of the federal FMLA, as well as the complex web of additional protections many states have. Not all Americans enjoy the same rights to family and medical leave, because 40 percent of them do not live in states that have written additional protections into state law. Pennsylvania is one such state. This chapter offers a case study of the policy impact on citizens—particularly women, minorities, and the poor—in Pennsylvania, one of twenty-one states where lawmakers have not expanded their coverage beyond that of federal law.

S ince its enactment more than twenty years ago, the Family and Medical Leave Act (FMLA) has allowed millions of Americans to maintain
job security while they tend to the important needs of their families.
However, there are limits to the breadth of the federal law, and many states
have either subsequently passed their own leave protections that expand coverage in many ways or had preexisting laws that went farther than the federal law. This article details the impact of the federal FMLA, as well as the
complex web of additional protections many states have. Critically, not all
Americans enjoy the same rights to family and medical leave, because
40 percent of them do not live in states that have written additional protections into state law. Thus, this article also offers a case study of the policy
impact on citizens—particularly women—in Pennsylvania, one of twenty-
one states where lawmakers have not expanded their coverage beyond that
of federal law.

Family Medical Leave Laws

Signed into law in 1993, the FMLA guarantees eligible employees up to twelve weeks of unpaid leave per year for health conditions, a new child, or military service. At the conclusion of the approved leave, eligible employees are guaranteed that their job (or one of comparable position) will have been held for their return. Employees that work in a business with more than fifty workers are eligible if they have worked for the company for at least a year, they have worked at least 1,250 hours during the previous year, and if they work at a location with at least fifty employees within a seventy-five-mile radius. This generally means that part-time and self-employed individuals are not likely to be eligible. While these protections are for both men and women, the law was celebrated as being the first national effort to acknowledge maternity leave (albeit unpaid) for women.

Prior to passage, thirty-four states had some version of law that governed family and/or medical leave, though eleven of them applied only to state employees (Commission on Family and Medical Leave 1996). Only twelve states and the District of Columbia had laws that required employers to offer maternity leave (Irwin and Silberman 1993; Waldfogel 1994; Women's Legal Defense Fund 1993). However, it should be noted that both large and/or unionized workplaces oftentimes had maternity and medical leave policies that were, in some cases, more generous than state law required (Waldfogel 1999). This continues to be the case.

Impact of FMLA

Following the passage of the FMLA, a series of government and academic studies aimed to determine whether the objectives of the law had been achieved. Three major conclusions were drawn about the effectiveness of the law in allowing workers greater access to job-protected leave.

The first conclusion pertained to the number of Americans who became eligible for leave protections under the new law. The Commission on Family and Medical Leave reported that as many as two-thirds of employees were employed by FMLA-covered employers (1996), but this statistic is misleading. Of this number, some employees did not work the required one-year total of 1,250 hours and still others had not been employed for the required one year. Ultimately, perhaps only as few as one-half of workers were eligible (Ruhm 1997).

Mothers fared even worse, as far fewer were eligible for maternity leave under the FMLA. It was estimated that 31 percent of working women of childbearing age had been with their employer the one year required for eligibility and a mere 19 percent of new mothers met eligibility requirements (Klerman and Leibowitz 1994). Considering the spattering of state laws and private employer policies that granted leave for one reason or another, in some form prior to implementation of the FMLA, it is unlikely that a significant percentage of the workforce suddenly experienced a dramatic new access to protected leave. In fact, only 7 percent of workers who took a type of leave covered by the FMLA in 1994–1995 reported that they were able to do so by exercising FMLA benefits (Ruhm 1997); the remainder had other benefits they were able to utilize.

Additional findings were discussed following adoption of the law. The second conclusion was that as employers adjusted their benefit packages to bring them in line with the new law, which two-thirds report having done (Waldfogel 2001), they faced little hardship in having done so. The Commission on Family and Medical Leave stated that 90 percent of covered employers reported that the changes "had no noticeable effect on business performance or growth" (Ruhm 1997, 181). These positive reviews were also reflected in a survey of employers done in 2000 as well (Waldfogel 2001). Jane Waldfogel estimated in 1999 that it cost an employer only about $250 per year for each employee who took leave.

Third, the law increased the frequency of leave-taking. This was most pronounced for new mothers and at medium-sized firms that would have been less likely to have had preexisting policies (Waldfogel 1999). An important consequence of the law is that it also institutionalized rights to parental leave, not just maternal leave; under the law, men now have the same rights to paternity leave as women do to maternity leave. Another possible positive externality is the effect on women's employment. Since the 1960s, there has been a steady increase of women who return to the workplace after they have a child. Fifty-five percent of new mothers are back in the workforce within a year of their child's birth (U.S. Census Bureau 2010, table 6).

In summation, while the FMLA offered a modest expansion of rights for workers, it did provide both more coverage and more usage for working women while imposing negligible costs to employers. Much of the reflection on the law's early impact argues that this does not amount to a tremendous impact. However, it should be noted that most scholars observe (see Ruhm 1997; Waldfogel 1997, 1999), as did the legislation's supporters in the 1990s, that the law was not designed to be far-reaching. The limited scope and strength of the law is a major contributor to its limited impact. Where the law had holes or inadequacies in coverage to meet the needs of the contemporary workforces, it was left up to states to compensate in the form of more-expansive laws.

More-Comprehensive State Laws

Today, many of the original state laws that governed workers' family and medical leave needs before passage of the FMLA are superseded by the more comprehensive federal law. Other states have passed laws that add to or expand the protections in the federal law. In addition to the federal FMLA, twenty-nine states have taken steps to expand the coverage for their own workers by adding additional benefits and/or expanding which employees are eligible for protections in their states.

Table 9.1 identifies the additional benefits states have enacted and in which states these more-expansive laws apply.

While each state that has enacted more-comprehensive legislation has a different formula for what is covered and for whom, there are some general categories in which state laws have become more comprehensive than federal law. These categories are discussed below.

Definition of Family

In some states, what constitutes a family is redefined by including domestic partnerships, children of domestic partnerships, grandparents, or in-laws. In Washington, D.C., which has the most inclusive definition, "family members include parents, spouses, children, domestic partners, parents-in-law, grandchildren, children's spouses, siblings, siblings' spouses, children with whom the employee lives and whom the employee has responsibility for, and a person with whom the employee shares a residence and committed relationship" (District of Columbia 2010). In New Jersey, which also passed a FMLA in

TABLE 9.1 ADDITIONAL LEAVE PROTECTIONS IN CURRENT STATE LAW, BY TYPE AND STATE

Type of expansion	Expansion states
Paid leave	CA, NJ, NY, RI
Application to smaller employers (fewer than 50 employees)	DC, ME, OR, VT (family leave) CA, IL, ME, NE, NY, OR, RI (military leave) CA, CT, IA, LA, NH, WA (maternity leave) CA, MN, NC, VT (small necessities leave)
Broader, more-inclusive definition of "family"	CA, CT, DC, HI, ME, NJ, OR, RI, TN, VT, WA, WI
Additional military protections	CA, CT, IL, IN, ME, MN, NE, NY, OH, OR, RI, WA
Pregnancy as specific disability	CA, CT, HI, IA, LA, MT, NH, WA
"Small necessities" allowances	CA, CO, DC, IL, LA, MA, MN, NV, NC, RI, VT
Domestic violence coverage	CA, CO, DC,* FL, HI, IL, ME, NM, NC, OR, WA
Temporary disabilities	CA, HI, NJ, NY, RI
Paid sick leave	AZ, CT, CA, DC, MA, OR, VT
Adoptive parents	CO, KY, MD, MA, MN, NE, NY, VT, WI

Source: Compiled from Nolo, n.d.; National Conference of State Legislatures 2016.
* Washington, D.C., requires that this leave be paid.

1993 (NJFLA), the definition of eligible immediate family coincides with the federal definition, but extends it slightly to include a spouse's parents (New Jersey Department of the Treasury 2016). These states also have more-flexible options when it comes to company size and leave availability.

Additional Military Benefits

Leave in the case of having a loved one on active duty is only available in twelve states. The most inclusive is Minnesota's policy, wherein an employee is entitled to limited leave if a grandparent, parent, legal guardian, sibling, child, grandchild, spouse, or fiancé is deployed, returning from deployment, or injured while deployed. Other states, such as Maine, entitle domestic partners to leave. Some set limits on how many days of leave are permitted depending on the length of the deployment (it usually has to be over ninety days) (Nolo, n.d.).

Pregnancy as Specific Disability

Legislation regarding disability due to pregnancy is generally vague. States such as Connecticut, Hawaii, and Montana give "reasonable" leave for pregnancy, while other states put a time limit on length of leave, commonly at least three weeks. Recognizing pregnancy in itself as a disability has been a contentious issue since 1976, when the Supreme Court ruled in *General Electric Co. v. Gilbert* that discrimination on the basis of pregnancy alone did not equate to discrimination based on sex and was, therefore, not necessarily illegal. Congress responded in 1978 with the Pregnancy Discrimination Act (PDA), but the law has limitations when it comes to accommodations pregnant workers may need to continue working. National Public Radio recently reported that the Equal Employment Opportunity Commission (EEOC) has received 46 percent more pregnancy-related complaints over the last fourteen years (Chappell 2014). The Philadelphia EEOC district office (which includes coverage of the entire state of Pennsylvania) registered more than three hundred complaints in that period—second only to the Miami district office. As a result of the increased claims, the commission issued a detailed clarification of how the PDA should be applied in cases of disability and other issues of leave in July 2014 (U.S. Equal Employment Opportunity Commission 2014).

Small Necessities

Some states offer their employees with children a few hours per year of unpaid leave for parent-teacher conferences or even for involvement in their children's schools. These protections range from forty hours per year

(California) to four hours per year (North Carolina), while Nevada has a statute that makes it illegal to terminate an employee who leaves to attend to their children's needs (National Conference of State Legislatures 2016).

Domestic Violence Coverage

Employees of certain states are allowed some unpaid leave to get social, family, and medical services, such as medical or legal assistance, or to enhance the security of their homes, after a violent assault. Maine and Washington employers are required to grant leave to employees who have a family member who has been attacked (Nolo, n.d.).

Temporary Disability

California, Hawaii, New Jersey, New York, and Rhode Island have Temporary Disability Insurance and Paid Family Leave that entitles employees to a percentage of their wages, previously withheld from their paychecks through payroll deduction, much like unemployment insurance.

Paid Sick Leave

A number of states and the District of Columbia offer paid sick leave depending on how many employees a company has and how many hours the employee has worked. In D.C., this leave also includes domestic violence or family leave. Most of these laws have been enacted in just the last few years, several by statewide ballot measures approved by voters.

Leave for Adoptive Parents

While recent interpretations of federal law recognize adoptive and other caretaking scenarios as parenting relationships covered by the FMLA (U.S. Department of Labor 2010), these protections are not extended to employers who are not required to offer protections or private companies that offer their own set of benefits that go above and beyond. However, some states award adoptive parents the same rights to leave as birth parents in all cases, as long as the company offers parental leave to biological parents. Some states— namely, New York and Nebraska—make provisions regarding the child's age. No state extends these additional benefits to stepparents or foster parents.

Family Medical Leave in Pennsylvania

Twenty-one states offer no additional family leave protections. Pennsylvania is one of the more populous of these states. Because there are currently no additional rights other than those afforded by the federal law, many of the state's working women and their families have fewer protections than their peers in many other states.

Paid Leave

The largest disadvantage Pennsylvanians have is that state law does not mandate that private employers provide paid leave for its employees. While many private employers and municipalities do offer paid sick, family, and/or parental[1] leave (Van Giezen 2013), they are not required to do so by federal or state law. So, while workers may be eligible for leave under the FMLA, exercising it may be limited by financial considerations. Indeed, research shows that leave is much less exercised by women with lower levels of education or women who are single parents (Han, Ruhm, and Waldfogel 2009).

Take into consideration the 24 percent of Pennsylvania families with household income that is below 200 percent of the federal poverty level (FPL) (Pathways PA 2009).[2] Many of these families (21 percent) have at least one parent with a low level of education, making it difficult for them to secure jobs with wages high enough to make ends meet. Lower-income jobs, such as health-care aides, retail or fast-food workers, and childcare providers, are disproportionately held by women. In fact, the Corporation for Enterprise Development recently reported that 21 percent of Pennsylvanians face "asset poverty," meaning they would not have the resources to survive for up to three months of sustained loss of income. Single women are 40 percent more likely than single men to be asset poor in Pennsylvania—which is a greater disparity than in most states (Brooks et al. 2014). For these individuals and families who are living paycheck to paycheck, any reduction in household income caused by an unpaid leave can seriously affect already precarious household budgets. Taking an unpaid leave simply is not a viable financial option.

In recent years, there have been numerous pieces of legislation (introduced and cosponsored almost exclusively by Democrats) in the General Assembly that attempt to institute various versions of paid leave in Pennsylvania. The latest version, H.B. 1634, introduced in June of 2017 by Representative Tim Briggs, mirrors the federal FMLA but requires eligible employees be paid for their protected twelve weeks of leave (Pennsylvania General Assembly 2017). Legislators are not hopeful about the bill's success.

In the absence of federal or state guarantees of paid leave, the city of Philadelphia passed a law in 2011 that required city contractors to allow their workers to accrue paid sick leave. A more expansive law took effect in 2015 requiring all employers in the city with more than ten employees to allow their employees to earn sick leave beginning in May 2015 (City of Philadelphia, n.d.).

As local efforts to require leave within their jurisdictions continue, members of the Pennsylvania General Assembly introduced House Bill

1807, the Leave Policy Act, which would prohibit "political subunits" in the state from enacting legislation requiring private employers to offer paid leave of any kind (Pennsylvania General Assembly 2014c). Similar legislation was introduced in 2017 but—likely because it faces a strong veto threat from Governor Tom Wolf—has made little progress.

Adult Caregivers

For many working women, it is not only their own health or the birth of a child that requires them to weigh their options for being off work. Increasingly, adult children are faced with providing care for aging parents. According to the Pennsylvania Department of Aging (2013), there are 1.3 million "informal caregivers" in the state who invest 1.4 billion hours of unpaid time in caring for the elderly in the state. Historically, this burden has fallen on the adult daughters (and presumably daughters-in-law) of the aging individual who needs care (Smith 2004), many of whom are still in the process of caring for their own children's needs. According to Dr. Lynn Martire and her colleagues of the University of Pittsburgh's Department of Psychiatry (2000), this burden is not just financial but psychological as well. This dual demand on working women exacerbates stress-related depression, especially as it complicates their other roles as employee, wife, and mother.

The state offers some help with the financial burden with a means-tested program—the Pennsylvania Caregiver Support Program—that reimburses qualified applicants for some of the expenses associated with caretaking. Eligibility for the program is income based and uses a sliding-scale cost-sharing approach that may reimburse caretakers up to $500 a month for expenses such as uncovered medical costs or up to $2,000 for home renovations (Pennsylvania Department of Aging 2014).

Governor Corbett's 2014–2015 budget proposal unsuccessfully requested over $40 million in additional funds for programs for the state's elderly (Pennsylvania Department of Aging 2014), but regardless, it is not clear how much, if any, of those funds would have been directed into the Caregiver Support Program. Presently, the program is only aiding around seven thousand caretakers, and not all of them are eligible for financial support; some qualify for only counseling or referral services. A decision, then, to take unpaid time off under the FMLA to care for an aging parent can mean financial hardship in precisely the same way faced by new parents or those with personal or immediate family medical needs.

Small Necessities

Not all the demands on working mothers are long term or overly significant. Several states recognize that working parents have smaller needs that require their attention during work hours, like parent-teacher conferences and regular trips to the pediatrician. Often referred to as a "small necessities" law, a bill that would have protected a worker's right to a handful of hours' leave time to attend to these things was recently introduced in Pennsylvania. House Bill 1673, the Parental Involvement Leave Act, was introduced in 2013 to "[provide] statewide uniformity regarding vacation and other forms of leave mandated by political subdivisions, for parental involvement leave and for civil remedies." The legislation was referred to the House Labor and Industry Committee but has not come up for any votes. The legislation's original prime sponsor, Dan Miller (D-Allegheny), has since withdrawn his original sponsorship, but in August 2013 he wrote to his colleagues to encourage them to support the legislation's goal of enhancing parental involvement in their children's school by requiring Pennsylvania employers to guarantee parents paid leave time to attend parent-teacher conferences and other related functions (Pennsylvania General Assembly 2014a). Miller reintroduced the legislation in the 2015–2016 term as H.B. 849, picking up nineteen cosponsors, but with no Republicans among them, the bill did not succeed in the Republican-controlled legislature (Pennsylvania General Assembly 2015). The bill had not been reintroduced as of mid-2017.

This type of legislation generally only provides a few hours per year for workers to access protected leave, and it is exclusively unpaid. It does allow parents to participate in important events in their children's lives.

Definition of Family

Many Pennsylvanians are also limited in their access to the FMLA protections by the law's narrow definition of "family." The Obama administration expanded the interpretation of the law to include coverage for same-sex parents of children who lack a biological relationship with the child (U.S. Department of Labor 2010). This extension of the law serves to allow for job-protected parental leave for parents in Pennsylvania's estimated 31,412 same-sex households (U.S. Census Bureau 2015). The Supreme Court struck down the Defense of Marriage Act (1996) in their 2013 ruling on *United States v. Windsor*, which had—in part—prevented the extension of federal benefits to individuals in same-sex marriages. Initially, this meant that the FMLA protections were extended to couples with marriages that were legally recognized in the state in which they work (U.S. Department of Labor 2015), and are now—in theory—extended to all legally married couples regardless of their state of residence or work. There is some continued ambiguity about how these benefits will be extended to Pennsylvanians in same-sex unions since the May 2014 legal decisions[3] that made same-sex marriage legal in the state, given the absence of workplace discrimination protections in the Commonwealth.

What is less clear is how the limited definition of family will apply to same-sex couples as the interpretation of the law expands, because there is no state law prohibiting workplace discrimination. Void of a more inclusive state law, committed couples or couples with marriages performed in other states will fail to have protections that extend to family members other than a spouse or children (e.g., in-laws, grandchildren, siblings).

Military

Some states' laws recognize a family member's military deployment as a "condition" sufficient for granting leave, known as a "qualifying exigency." A member of the Armed Forces' (including National Guard and Reserves) spouse, parents, or children (of any age) would be entitled to this leave under certain conditions requiring their absence from work (e.g., child or parent care, postdeployment activities) (U.S. Department of Labor 2015). Pennsylvania's more than fifty-six thousand military personnel (U.S. Department of Defense 2017) were only given this recognition by a federal expansion of the FMLA that took effect in early 2013 (U.S. Department of Labor, n.d.). The state's thousands of veterans from the Iraq and Afghan wars would not have been covered under this expansion. Also, despite the Obama administration's 2010 repeal of the Don't Ask, Don't Tell policy, same-sex spouses or partners as well as extended family of deploying military personnel continue to have no guaranteed right to leave.

Some Pennsylvania military families who fall through this particular crack might be helped by a state program run through the state's Department of Military and Veterans Affairs. Using both public funds and private donations, the Military Family Relief Assistance Program (MFRAP) offers grants of up to $3,500 to qualifying service members or family members to help with costs associated with hardships due to deployment—including childcare and other loss of employment income (Pennsylvania Department of Military and Veterans Affairs, n.d.).[4] However, the MFRAP is a small program and awarded only $41,000 to twelve approved applications in 2016, very few of which described circumstances that would have been governed by an expanded FMLA (Pennsylvania Department of Military and Veterans Affairs 2017). Veteran support groups in the nonprofit sector also offer services that presumably could help families struggling with leave-related issues.

Domestic Violence and Sexual Assault

According to the National Network to End Domestic Violence, an average of more than 2,400 adults and children receive services for domestic violence (e.g., shelter, counseling) in Pennsylvania each day and there are, on average, thirty-two calls to hotlines every hour (National Network to End Domestic Violence 2016). These statistics represent only a portion of individuals coping with domestic violence, as they do not reflect victims who do not seek outside help. In 2012, thirty thousand Pennsylvanians sought help as victims of sexual violence (Pennsylvania Coalition against Rape 2013). Again, many of these crimes go unreported and/or victims do not actively seek support in their recovery. In their lifetimes, one in four women will experience domestic violence (Pennsylvania Coalition against Domestic Violence, n.d., "Educators").

These victims of both domestic violence and sexual assault face discrimination and problems in obtaining needed time off in their jobs (Swanberg, Ojha, and Macke 2012; Brownmiller 2013). Pennsylvania's employers are required to provide potentially critical workplace safety under the Occupational Safety and Health Act of 1970, and employees would qualify for leave under the FMLA if their absence would be to seek medical treatment for or to recuperate from injuries due to an incidence of domestic violence or sexual assault. State statutes also provide work leave for a related subpoena or court appearance (Swanberg, Ojha, and Macke 2012).

However, victims of both domestic and sexual violence face far more than the physical wounds they may have received in these attacks. Scholars who study the aftermath for victims of these crimes describe a long list of psychological concerns, as well—including post-traumatic stress disorder, anxiety, insomnia, anger, self-harm, and high rates of depression (Armour et al. 2014; Humphreys and Thiara 2003). There are also more-practical considerations, like victims needing to find a new place to live and, in some cases, establishing credit in their own names. These scenarios and others demonstrate how crucial the need to maintain employment can be to future empowerment of the victim. According to the Pennsylvania Coalition against Domestic Violence (n.d., "Pending"), while the state legislature is considering several pieces of legislation that support victims in other ways (e.g., laws to strengthen protection for children in environments of abuse), there is currently no legislation being considered in the state that would offer greater or more-expansive employment protection for victims of either domestic or sexual violence.

As a result, the vast majority of Pennsylvanians have no leave protections under these dire circumstances. However, employees within the city of Philadelphia do have additional protections that were passed by the City Council and took effect in 2009. The ordinance provides up to eight weeks of unpaid leave to workers of any Philadelphia employer who are victims of not only domestic or sexual violence but also stalking.[5] The ordinance allows an employee to take time off to tend to physical or psychological injuries, seek help from a domestic or sexual violence organization, receive counseling, relocate, or seek legal assistance for themselves or a member of their immediate family (Philadelphia Commission on Human Relations 2009). However, there is some concern that this ordinance will be overturned by legislation passed by the state House of Representatives in March 2014 (H.B. 1796) that would prohibit municipalities from requiring certain benefit mandates from private employers (Pennsylvania General Assembly 2014b) similar to the Leave Policy Act mentioned above. To date, versions of this bill have been reintroduced, but have not received full consideration by either the House or the Senate.

Temporary Disability and Pregnancy

The Social Security Administration provides income replacement to workers who become disabled or ill and are not able to work for twelve months or more (Social Security Administration 2012). Shorter-term leave needs would be (for those covered) governed by the FMLA, but would be unpaid unless the employer offers additional benefits or the absence is covered under a state or municipal statute that offers paid time off for short-term needs. Many employers do offer short-term disability insurance programs that serve this function. The important distinction is, however, that while these insurance programs will provide compensation, they do not offer job protection. While most states have statutes that extend the FMLA job protection to short-term disabilities, Pennsylvania does not (John A. Gallagher, personal communication, May 5, 2014).[6] Theoretically, employees in Pennsylvania could be approved for short-term disability payments through the insurance program they participate in, but lose their jobs while on leave.

A few states (e.g., California, New York) have incorporated a paid leave component into their state leave laws that require employee contributions to a short-term disability program, effectively removing any additional burden from employers because the funds come from employees not employers. Examples from the handful of states that have implemented these programs indicate that employees take the leave they need more often and for longer duration because they are receiving compensation when they do. In California, for example, single mothers are among the biggest beneficiaries of this program (Koss 2003).

Short-term disability issues are particularly complex in the context of a pregnancy, and the issue remains unresolved in states, like Pennsylvania, that have not made clear statutes defining pregnancy as a disability. According to legal scholar Jeanette Cox, recent expansions of the Americans with Disabilities Act (ADA) have allowed for more conditions that may be concomitant with pregnancy—like shortness of breath or back pain—to be protected under the law (and thus recognized by the FMLA, as well). However, courts continue to bar extension of FMLA protection to pregnant workers suffering from ADA-recognized disabilities because pregnancy is not recognized as being a condition from which disabilities can stem. As Cox states, "The primary remaining justification for concluding that pregnant workers may not obtain ADA accommodations is that pregnancy is a physically healthy condition rather than a physiological defect" (2012, 443).

Pennsylvania has been named one of the ten worst states in the country for pregnancy discrimination (National Partnership for Women and Families 2008). Without specific state law that defines pregnancy as a disability, expectant mothers in Pennsylvania who are in some way limited from performing their job responsibilities by side effects of normal pregnancies cannot receive reasonable accommodation under the ADA or exercise FMLA rights. Without either of these protections, these women face potential repercussions by their employers when their job performances are affected. As a result, the National Women's Law Center reports that many women are forced to take a reduction in hours without pay, forced to quit, or fired from their jobs when employers refuse to make even small accommodations that are extended to disabled workers.[7] Even when nondisability conditions associated with pregnancy are recognized, employers may insist that employees take the FMLA leave intermittently. Considering the law allows for only twelve weeks of protected leave, leaves during pregnancy can erode the amount of time available to a new mother once her baby is born (National Women's Law Center 2013).

In 2014, the Philadelphia City Council voted to amend the Philadelphia Fair Practices Ordinance of 2013 to include protections for pregnant workers in the city that require city employers to make reasonable accommodations (Council of the City of Philadelphia 2013). Testimony in support of the amendment drew attention to the fact that 53 percent of Philadelphia children were being raised by single working mothers, women who could not afford to suffer job and income loss because of pregnancy (Council of the City of Philadelphia 2013).

Representative Mark Painter (D-Montgomery) introduced H.B. 1892, the Pennsylvania Pregnant Workers Fairness Act, in February 2014. The legislation is designed to eliminate discrimination and ensure reasonable workplace accommodations for workers whose ability to perform the functions of a job are limited by pregnancy. The bill was referred to the Labor and Industry Committee, but no further action has been taken (Pennsylvania General Assembly 2014d). It has not been subsequently reintroduced.

Conclusion and Policy Prescriptions

Pennsylvania's leave laws and supporting statutes provide some of the nation's most meager protections for workers. In the twenty years since the passage of the federal FMLA, a majority of states and municipalities around the country have expanded the law's scope with statutes of their own.

However, in nearly every way other that states have chosen to expand the FMLA to offer additional rights and protections for their citizens, Pennsylvania has not.

In recent years, the state's political climate has not been conducive to action. The Democratic minority in the General Assembly continues to introduce legislation that would expand leave, but such legislation has received very little Republican support. To this point, increased partisan polarization makes compromise unlikely on even modest expansions, let alone more-dramatic proposals such as a paid leave policy for the state.

However, one need only look to neighboring New Jersey to identify a dramatically different trend. Two large cities in the state—Newark and Jersey City—passed municipal laws mandating that employers allow employees to accrue paid days off. East Orange is considering a similar measure, and five municipalities passed citizen-initiated ballot measures in fall 2014 that require employers to facilitate paid time off in their communities, joining several other municipalities. The Associated Press reports that, as a result, New Jersey lawmakers are seriously considering legislation that would make the requirement apply to the entire state and there appears to be enough support in the legislature to accomplish it (Associated Press 2014). The state's governor, Chris Christie, however, has expressed his reluctance to require businesses to provide paid time off to employees in the state, despite opinion polls that show more than 80 percent of citizens support government-mandated paid sick time (Dawsey 2015). Christie recently vetoed an attempt to expand the state's 2009 paid family leave insurance program, but the partial veto allowed a longer coverage period and extended coverage benefits to more family members (Marcus 2017).

Meanwhile, Pennsylvania has taken no action. This inaction has created a work environment in the state that is less protective of workers than those in many other states. Most significantly, these gaps in protection and rights have the biggest impact for the state's most vulnerable citizens. For example, as identified above, low-income families, single parents, and individuals living on meager budgets cannot afford to take unpaid leave. Employees straining under the burden of caring for elderly loved ones (and perhaps children concurrently) have far too many limitations in their leave options. Victims of domestic or sexual violence face further hardships in trying to manage serious needs that arise out of their victimization when it puts their jobs in jeopardy. Pregnant women can still be discriminated against when their pregnancy affects their job performance.

Advocates of family and medical leave in Pennsylvania could push on the following four fronts to encourage greater coverage: action by municipalities, leadership from the private sector, support from the nonprofit community, and expansion of state laws.

Municipal Opportunity

One way expansions of leave laws have taken place in Pennsylvania, despite inaction by the state legislature, is the enactment of local policies. Philadelphia and Pittsburgh, the state's most populous cities (as well as Allegheny County), have recently instituted numerous policies that give workers who are employed within the city more access to and more-expansive leave rights.[8] While there are political forces at work against continuing to allow municipalities to enact these types of locally applied ordinances, it remains an option for other communities that want to improve leave options in their jurisdiction.

In municipalities where significant political support for progressive protections for workers exist, an effort to address these types of issues on their governing councils could certainly be tackled. Even smaller municipalities may see prudence in protecting the quality of their local government workforces by improving benefits that local government employees and/or contractors receive—a move that would be entirely within a local governing body's authority. Of course, a community-by-community expansion of leave offers no comprehensive solution for workers who continue to fall through the cracks in the federal law, but developments in population-dense areas where a majority of jobs are could greatly expand the number of Pennsylvanians who could enjoy the same protections as those who live in states with more-comprehensive laws.

Role for Private Sector

A frequent argument made by conservatives regarding state regulation of employment policies is that telling private businesses how to run their businesses can limit economic growth and is not an appropriate role for state legislators. Where state laws fall short, then, private companies are left to make decisions on what type of leave policies they will offer their employees. Responsible employers should and often do recognize that offering their employees access to the leave they need has the potential to decrease employee turnover and resources needed for training new employees, as well as a happy, healthy, and loyal workforce (Grover and Crooker 1995; Batt and Valcour 2003). As Steven Grover and Karen Crooker found, "Employees who had access to family-responsive policies showed significantly greater organizational commitment and expressed significantly lower intention to quit their jobs" (1995, 271).

Studies following the implementation of the federal FMLA also indicated that the cost of implementing (and employees exercising) leave policies is small. Because it can make good business sense, employers, from small to

large and regardless of industry, should feel compelled to revisit their existing leave policies and consider expanding their benefits in perhaps small but
significant ways that could improve the lives of their employees and create a
culture of greater work-life balance in their industry. Even a slightly expanded leave policy could mean a great deal to workers faced with a personal
need that prompts a tough choice about how to juggle their employment and
the health and safety of themselves and their loved ones.

Need for Nonprofit Advocacy and Support

In reality, political will and corporate motivation to expand workers' access
to leave may require significant social pressure and targeted advocacy. A
coordinated effort among organizations with missions that recognize the
needs of workers, women, parents, families, children, the working poor, victims of domestic and sexual violence, and others could draw heretofore un-
seen attention to the implications of the minimal protections Pennsylvanian
workers have compared to workers in other states. A campaign that united
these diverse but influential advocacy sectors to expand state or local leave
laws could be more effective than individual organizations that have merely
touched on some of these needs in their reform priorities. A larger, more
expansive effort could draw attention to the vast opportunities lawmakers
and employers have to improve working conditions in the state.

Absent expanded laws, nonprofit organizations may also need to examine how they might develop programs that meet the needs of workers who
have legal, personal, or financial hardships when managing their leave needs.
The nonprofit community is uniquely skilled at developing education and
service programs that address many of the problems created by inadequate
leave laws, as well as partnering with private corporations to meet many of
these needs. There are many considerations the nonprofit community could
begin to make if there was an effort to more specifically address issues of
leave in the state.

Action by State Legislature

Finally and most significantly, without changes in state law and even with ad
hoc policy changes at other levels, many Pennsylvanians will continue to
face protection under federal laws that is inadequate for their needs. As outlined above, this disproportionately disadvantages many of the state's most
vulnerable populations (see Table 9.2). Lawmakers should examine prudent
means of comprehensively extending additional protections to the state's
workers—with a specific examination of viable legislative options in the
state. The bicameral, and bipartisan Women's Health Caucus in the General
Assembly seems a likely starting point for this endeavor.

TABLE 9.2 IMPLICATIONS FOR UNDERCOVERED GROUPS UNDER
PENNSYLVANIA LAW

Undercovered groups	Under Pennsylvania law
Low-income families	Leave requires financial hardship
Parents	No leave for nonmedical needs; narrow options for adult caregiving leave
The disabled	Private insurance programs do not protect jobs
Military families	Families of recently deployed veterans had few leave options
LGBT families	State law has limited recognition of nontraditional families in application of existing law
Pregnant women	Employers can force leave or terminate instead of making reasonable accommodations
Victims of domestic/sexual abuse	Justification for leave may not meet needs of victims
All Pennsylvanians	Scope, availability, justifications for, and ease of taking leave more limited than in other states

The caucus revealed the Pennsylvania Agenda for Women's Health in December 2013 and has since introduced bipartisan legislation that addresses women's health, safety, and financial security in the state. One of the group's initiatives is H.B. 1892, the Pennsylvania Pregnant Workers Fairness Act, discussed above, which addresses issues of pregnancy discrimination and accommodation. None of the other agenda items directly deal with issues of family or medical leave, but these issues are distinctly in the spirit of the caucus's mission.

In particular, the legislature and the governor should consider options for extending paid leave to millions of Pennsylvanians who have none whatsoever through their employers. One possibility that could bring diverse political views together is creating a paid leave insurance program in the Commonwealth. Driven by competition in the private sector, this system could function much like private market short-term disability programs.

Many states have recognized the limitations of the federal law and have acted in important ways through state statute to strengthen the options available to workers. Doing so in Pennsylvania would give working women and their families, as well as working men, greater flexibility to manage their health, the health of their families, and unforeseen emergencies. With this flexibility, quality of life and work environment could be improved for all workers in the state, regardless of their economic or family status or gender. This has been successfully done in many other states as the modest federal FMLA law provoked state legislatures to fill in the gaps. Thus, it seems reasonable to expect that with the right political attention, some moderate expansion of leave laws in Pennsylvania could be possible.

NOTES

1. Many offer only maternity leave, but employers are increasingly offering new parents—regardless of gender—some form of paid leave.

2. In 2009, the FPL was under $40,000 for a family of four (Pathways PA 2009).

3. The decisions were *Whitewood v. Wolf* and *Palladino v. Corbett*.

4. The grants are also awarded for several circumstances other than deployment, which would not be covered by family leave laws.

5. Employers with more than fifty employees must provide up to eight weeks of leave, while those with fewer than fifty are required to provide up to four weeks. This applies regardless of whether the employer is subject to the FMLA.

6. John Gallagher is a Pennsylvania disability attorney.

7. In March 2015, the U.S. Supreme Court set an important precedent that pregnant women have some right to pregnancy-related accommodation in *Young v. United Parcel Service*. Presumably if pregnant workers are more easily able to get accommodations from their employers, fewer will need to take leave during their pregnancy.

8. According to Pittsburgh city councilwoman Natalia Rudiak (personal communication, March 17, 2015), the city could offer paid leave only to city employees because legal precedent prevents the council from requiring that it be offered by employers within the city.

REFERENCES

Armour, Cherie, Ask Elklit, Dean Lauterbach, and Jon D. Elhai. 2014. "The DSM-5 Dissociative-PTSD Subtype: Can Levels of Depression, Anxiety, Hostility, and Sleeping Difficulties Differentiate between Dissociative-PTSD and PTSD in Rape Victims?" *Journal of Anxiety Disorders* 28 (May): 418–426.

Associated Press. 2014. "New Jersey Assembly Speaker Backs Paid Sick Leave." *Press of Atlantic City*, August 6. Available at http://www.pressofatlanticcity.com/news/new -jersey-assembly-speaker-backs-paid-sick-leave/article_667b3822-1d84-11e4-9b3a -0019bb2963f4.html.

Batt, Rosemary, and P. Monique Valcour. 2003. "Human Resources Practices as Predictors of Work-Family Outcomes and Employee Turnover." *Industrial Relations: A Journal of Economy and Society* 42 (April): 189–220.

Brooks, Jennifer, Kasey Wiedrich, Lebaron Sims Jr., and Jennifer Medina. 2014. "Treading Water in the Deep End: Findings from the 2014 Assets and Opportunity Scorecard." Available at https://prosperitynow.org/files/PDFs/2014_Scorecard_Report.pdf.

Brownmiller, Susan. 2013. *Against Our Will: Men, Women and Rape*. New York: Open Road Media.

Chappell, Bill. 2014. "EEOC Announces Tougher Rules Protecting Pregnant Workers." *NPR*, July 16. Available at http://www.National Public Radio.org/blogs/thetwo -way/2014/07/16/331945772/eeoc-announces-tougher-rules-protecting-pregnant -workers.

City of Philadelphia. n.d. "Paid Sick Leave." Available at http://www.phila.gov/MDO/ Pages/PaidSickLeave.aspx (accessed January 19, 2018).

Commission on Family and Medical Leave. 1996. *A Workable Balance: Report to Congress on Family and Medical Leave Policies*. Washington, DC: U.S. Department of Labor.

Council of the City of Philadelphia. 2013. "Bills 130002, 130687, and 130701; Resolution 130023 and 130715." November 22. Available at http://legislation.phila.gov/ transcripts/Public%20Hearings/lawngov/2013/lg112213.pdf.

Cox, Jeanette. 2012. "Pregnancy as 'Disability' and the Amended Americans with Disabilities Act." *Boston College Law Review* 53 (2): 443–489.

Dawsey, Josh 2015. "N.J. Cities Pass Paid-Sick-Leave Laws despite Opposition from Christie." *Wall Street Journal*, April 15. Available at http://www.wsj.com/articles/n -j-cities-pass-paid-sick-leave-laws-despite-opposition-from-christie-1429134120.

District of Columbia Office of Human Rights. 2010. "Amendments to Title 4, Chapter 16—District of Columbia Family and Medical Leave Act." Available at https://www .dcregs.dc.gov/Common/NoticeDetail.aspx?NoticeId=N0005056.

Grover, Steven L., and Karen J. Crooker. 1995. "Who Appreciates Family-Responsive Human Resource Policies: The Impact of Family-Friendly Policies on the Organizational Attachment of Parents and Non-parents." *Personnel Psychology* 48 (June): 271–288.

Han, Wen-Jui, Christopher Ruhm, and Jane Waldfogel. 2009. "Parental Leave Policies and Parents' Employment and Leave-Taking." *Journal of Policy Analysis and Management* 28 (Winter): 29–54.

Humphreys, Cathy, and Ravi Thiara. 2003. "Mental Health and Domestic Violence: 'I Call It Symptoms of Abuse.'" *British Journal of Social Work* 33 (March): 209–226.

Irwin, Helen, and Ralph Silberman. 1993. *Family and Medical Leaves: The New Federal Statute and State Laws.* New York: Warren, Gorham, Lamont.

Klerman, Jacob A., and Arleen Leibowitz. 1994. "The Work-Employment Decision among New Mothers." *Journal of Human Resources* 29 (2): 277–303.

Koss, Natalie. 2003. "California Family Temporary Disability Insurance Program." *American University Journal of Gender Social Policy and Law* 11 (2): 1079–1088.

Marcus, Samantha. 2017. "Christie Vetoes Paid Family Leave Expansion." *NJ.com*, July 23. Available at http://www.nj.com/politics/index.ssf/2017/07/christie_vetoes _paid_family_leave_expansion.html.

Martire, Lynn M., Mary Ann P. Stephens, and Aloen L. Townsend. 2000. "Centrality of Women's Multiple Roles: Beneficial and Detrimental Consequences for Psychological Well-Being." *Psychology and Aging* 15 (March): 148–156.

National Conference of State Legislatures. 2016. "State Family and Medical Leave Laws." July 19. Available at http://www.ncsl.org/research/labor-and-employment/state -family-and-medical-leave-laws.aspx.

National Network to End Domestic Violence. 2016. "Pennsylvania Summary." *Domestic Violence Counts* 11. Available at https://nnedv.org/mdocs-posts/census_2016 _handout_state-summary_pennsylvania.

National Partnership for Women and Families. 2008. "The Pregnancy Discrimination Act: Where We Stand 30 Years Later." Available at http://go.nationalpartnership .org/site/DocServer/Pregnancy_Discrimination_Act_-_Where_We_Stand_30 _Years_L.pdf.

National Women's Law Center. 2013. "It Shouldn't Be a Heavy Lift: Fair Treatment for Pregnant Workers." Available at http://www.nwlc.org/sites/default/files/pdfs/ pregnant_workers.pdf.

New Jersey Department of the Treasury. 2016. "NJ Family Leave Act and Family and Medical Leave Act of 1993: Frequently Asked Questions and Answers." In *Employers'*

Pensions and Benefits Administration Manual. Trenton: New Jersey Department of the Treasury. Available at http://www.state.nj.us/treasury/pensions/epbam/additional/fmla-qa.htm.

Nolo. n.d. "State and Family Medical Leave Laws." Available at http://www.nolo.com/legal-encyclopedia/state-family-medical-leave-laws (accessed January 19, 2018).

Pathways PA. 2009. "Pennsylvania at a Glance: A Follow-up to *Investing in Pennsylvania's Families* (2007)." Available at http://www.workingpoorfamilies.org/pdfs/pennsylvania_at_a_glance042709.pdf.

Pennsylvania Coalition against Domestic Violence. n.d. "Educators." Available at http://www.pcadv.org/Learn-More/Professional-Resources/Educators (accessed February 7, 2018).

———. n.d. "Pending Legislation." Available at http://www.pcadv.org/Public-Policy/Pending-Legislation/ (accessed January 24, 2018).

Pennsylvania Coalition against Rape. 2013. "PA Says No More." *The Horizon*, November. Available at http://www.pcar.org/sites/default/files/resource-pdfs/horizon_fall_2013_for_web_final.pdf.

Pennsylvania Department of Aging. 2013. "PA Department of Aging Marks November as Caregiver Support Month." *PR Newswire*, November 5. Available at https://www.prnewswire.com/news-releases/pa-department-of-aging-marks-november-as-caregiver-support-month-230688921.html.

Pennsylvania Department of Military and Veterans Affairs. n.d. "Military Family Relief Assistance Program (MFRAP)." Available at http://www.dmva.pa.gov/veteransaffairs/Pages/Programs%20and%20Services/Military-Family-Relief-Assistance-Program.aspx.

———. 2017. "Military Family Relief Assistance Program Annual Report for FY 2016." Available at http://www.dmva.pa.gov/veteransaffairs/Documents/MFRAP/MFRAP%20Annual%20Report%20FY2016.pdf.

Pennsylvania General Assembly. 2014a. "Regular Session 2013–2014: House Bill 1673." January 30. Available at http://www.legis.state.pa.us/cfdocs/billinfo/billinfo.cfm?syear=2013&sind=0&body=H&type=B&bn=1673.

———. 2014b. "Regular Session 2013–2104: House Bill 1796." Available at http://www.legis.state.pa.us/cfdocs/billinfo/BillInfo.cfm?syear=2013&sind=0&body=H&type=B&bn=1796.

———. 2014c. "Regular Session 2013–2014: House Bill 1807." February 10. Available at http://www.legis.state.pa.us/cfdocs/billInfo/billInfo.cfm?sYear=2013&sInd=0&body=H&type=B&bn=1807.

———. 2014d. "Regular Session 2013–2014: House Bill 1892." February 19. Available at http://www.legis.state.pa.us/cfdocs/billInfo/billInfo.cfm?sYear=2013&sInd=0&body=H&type=B&bn=1892.

———. 2015. House Bill 849; Regular Session 2015–2016." Available at http://www.legis.state.pa.us/cfdocs/billinfo/bill_history.cfm?syear=2015&sind=0&body=H&type=B&bn=849.

———. 2017. "House Bill No. 1634: Session of 2017." Available at http://www.legis.state.pa.us/CFDOCS/Legis/PN/Public/btCheck.cfm?txtType=PDF&sessYr=2017&sessInd=0&billBody=H&billTyp=B&billNbr=1634&pn=2180.

Pennsylvania Office of the Governor. 2014. "Governor Corbett's 2014–15 Executive Budget Drives Strategic Investment for Stronger Pennsylvania." *PR Newswire*, February 4. Available at https://www.prnewswire.com/news-releases/governor-corbetts

-2014-15-executive-budget-drives-strategic-investment-for-stronger-pennsylvania
-243516431.html.
Philadelphia Commission on Human Relations. 2009. "Your Rights to Unpaid Leave
due to Domestic or Sexual Violence." Available at http://www.phila.gov/Human
Relations/Documents/Unpaid Leave Domestic Violence poster2.pdf.
Ruhm, Christopher J. 1997. "Policy Watch: The Family and Medical Leave Act." *Journal
of Economic Perspectives* 11 (Summer): 175–186.
Social Security Administration. 2012. "Disability Benefits." Available at http://www.ssa
.gov/pubs/EN-05-10029.pdf.
Smith, Peggie R. 2004. "Elder Care, Gender, and Work: The Work-Family Issue of the
21st Century." *Berkley Journal of Employment and Labor Law* 25 (2): 351–399.
Swanberg, Jennifer E., Mamta U. Ojha, and Caroline Macke. 2012. "State Employment
Protection Statutes for Victims of Domestic Violence: Public Policy's Response to
Domestic Violence as an Employment Matter." *Journal of Interpersonal Violence* 27
(February): 587–619.
U.S. Census Bureau. 2010. "Fertility of American Women: 2010." Available at https://
www.census.gov/data/tables/2010/demo/fertility/women-fertility.html#par_list_46.
———. 2015. "Characteristics of Same-Sex Couple Households: 2005 to Present." Avail-
able at https://www.census.gov/data/tables/time-series/demo/same-sex-couples/ssc
-house-characteristics.html.
U.S. Department of Defense. 2017. "DoD Personnel, Workforce Reports and Publications." Available at https://www.dmdc.osd.mil/appj/dwp/dwp_reports.jsp.
U.S. Department of Labor. n.d. "Fact Sheet: Final Rule to Implement Statutory Amendments to the Family and Medical Leave Act Military Family Leave Provisions."
Available at http://www.dol.gov/whd/fmla/2013rule/fs-military.htm (accessed January 19, 2018).
———. 2010. "Administrator's Interpretation No. 2010-3." June 22. Available at http://
www.dol.gov/WHD/opinion/adminIntrprtn/FMLA/2010/FMLAAI2010_3.htm.
———. 2015. "Fact Sheet #28F: Qualifying Reasons for Leave under the Family and
Medical Leave Act." July. Available at http://www.dol.gov/whd/regs/compliance/
whdfs28f.htm.
U.S. Equal Employment Opportunity Commission. 2014. "EEOC Issues Updated Enforcement Guidance on Pregnancy Discrimination and Related Issues." July 14.
Available at http://www.eeoc.gov/eeoc/newsroom/release/7-14-14.cfm.
Van Giezen, Robert W. 2013. "Paid Leave in Private Industry over the Past 20 Years."
Beyond the Numbers, August. Available at http://www.bls.gov/opub/btn/volume-2/
paid-leave-in-private-industry-over-the-past-20-years.htm.
Waldfogel, Jane. 1994. "Women Working for Less: Family Status and Women's Pay in
the US and UK." Ph.D. diss., Harvard University.
———. 1997. "The Effect of Children on Women's Wages." *American Sociological Review*
62 (April): 209–217.
———. 1999. "The Impact of the Family and Medical Leave Act." *Journal of Policy
Analysis and Management* 18 (Spring): 281–302.
———. 2001. "Family and Medical Leave: Evidence from the 2000 Surveys." *Monthly
Labor Review*, September, pp. 17–23.
Women's Legal Defense Fund. 1993. *State Laws and Regulations Guaranteeing Employees Their Jobs after Family and Medical Leaves*. Washington, DC: Women's Legal
Defense Fund.

Discussion Questions

1. What is the purpose of the federal Family and Medical Leave Act (FMLA)? What benefits does it provide?
2. What impact has the FMLA had on the lives of people it covers?
3. Other states have expanded the benefits beyond those provided by the FMLA. How does policy in Pennsylvania compare to leave policies in other states?
4. What makes family medical leave a partisan issue? Given Pennsylvania's current partisan divisions, is it likely that policies related to family medical leave will be expanded in the Commonwealth in the near future?
5. Is this an issue that should be handled primarily by the federal government so that there is one uniform policy across the country? Or is it best left to the states so they can experiment with different types of medical leave policies?

Commonwealth Forum: Would Mandated Paid Leave Be a Competitive Disadvantage for Pennsylvania?

YES

Businesses in Pennsylvania do not need more regulations from the state dictating what benefits they give their employees. Currently, the state's unemployment rate is 0.7 percentage points above the national average. In 2016, Pennsylvania ranked fourteenth from the bottom in terms of job creation. Forcing businesses to spend more on employee benefits will not attract more firms to Pennsylvania or encourage citizens to start up their own businesses with prohibitive employee costs. Implementing another layer of cost on employers when nearby states do not do so will likely cost the state jobs and revenue as businesses flee across the border.

One of the ways firms attract top talent is through offering the benefits such talent desires. While not every business in Pennsylvania offers paid family and medical leave, some do. Not everyone desires paid family and medical leave as a benefit, yet such a program would mandate that businesses offer such a program. Maybe some employees would prefer to have these benefits offered in wages? For example, what about late-middle-age employees whose children are raised and parents deceased? What benefit is mandated paid leave to them? Employers and employees should have the option to implement the type and amount of benefits they would prefer as part of free and open labor contract negotiations. If some people are working for businesses that do not offer such benefits at all, yet the employee would like to have that benefit, it can only serve as an incentive to work harder toward a career within a more competitive labor market.

NO

Federal government statistics show that a majority of Americans with children under age six are employed. As of 2016, both parents were employed in 56.3 percent of married households, while 66.8 percent of women and 83.8 percent of men in single-parent households had jobs. These families rely on their earnings to put a roof over their heads and provide food and clothing to their children. Changes in social mores and the transition to a postindustrial economy have made the prospect of a parent staying at home to raise children an antiquated concept for most families.

Paid family medical leave in Pennsylvania would encourage one or both parents to stay home with their children in the early months of their lives. Adopting paid family medical leave would not harm business fortunes in the Commonwealth. In fact, it would actually benefit business competitiveness and the bottom line while helping families. After California adopted a paid leave law, 90 percent of employers surveyed reported that they suffered either no financial losses or actually increased profitability as a consequence of the law. Paid family leave reduces turnover, meaning that firms spend less on recruiting, hiring, and training new employees. It also results in more women returning to their jobs after childbirth, which is a plus, because they have the skill sets and institutional knowledge to hit the ground running after leave. Among firms that adopt paid family leave, morale and worker productivity has been shown to increase. All of these things lead to a better-trained workforce without any negative side effects for business. Adopting paid family medical leave is a perfect way to attract good talent to Pennsylvania and increase the strength of the Commonwealth's workforce.

For More Information

The **Wage and Hour Division of the U.S. Department of Labor** (https://www.dol.gov/whd/fmla/) provides guides and fact sheets for employees and employers explaining the details of the federal Family and Medical Leave Act.

The **National Conference of State Legislatures** (www.ncsl.org/research/labor-and-employment/employee-leave.aspx) keeps track of the states' family and medical leave laws including coverage and eligibility, the provisions (paid or unpaid), and for whom the leave is providing care. Some states also provide mandated school-related parental leave.

"**Paid Family Medical Leave: An Issue Whose Time Has Come**" (https://
www.brookings.edu/wp-content/uploads/2017/06/es_20170606
_paidfamilyleave.pdf) is the 2017 joint publication of a group of scholars
from the free-market-leaning American Enterprise Institute and the
center-left Brookings Institution. The work includes data on family medical leave policies in the United States and countries in the Organization
for Economic Cooperation and Development.

The **Independent Women's Forum** (http://www.iwf.org/) is a libertarian
organization that provides a number of reports and opinion pieces opposing government-mandated paid medical leave.

Chapter 10
Researching Pennsylvania Online

MICHELLE J. ATHERTON
J. WESLEY LECKRONE

Τ he following guide is designed to help researchers find information on Pennsylvania government, politics, and policy through internet resources. The web links focus on providing in-depth sources of information on their respective topics.

Pennsylvania State Government

The official portal of the **Commonwealth of Pennsylvania** is https://www.pa .gov.

The Pennsylvania Manual (http://www.dgs.pa.gov/State%20Government/ Print,%20Design%20and%20Mail%20Services/Pages/The-Pennsylvania -Manual.aspx) is an official publication of the Commonwealth that provides information on the state's history, government organization and public officials, election results, media outlets, and state parks. The manual is an excellent starting point for any research on Pennsylvania.

The **Constitution of the Commonwealth of Pennsylvania** is available at http://www.legis.state.pa.us/WU01/LI/LI/CT/HTM/00/00.HTM. The Duquesne University School of Law also houses a **Pennsylvania Constitution** website (http://www.duq.edu/academics/gumberg-library/pa-constitution)

that contains the texts of all five Pennsylvania constitutions as well as research and commentary on the constitution.

The official site of the **General Assembly** is http://www.legis.state.pa.us, where researchers can find information about both the House of Representatives and the Senate. Individual legislator profiles, links to legislative committees, schedules of legislative business and a database of legislation since 1965 are also found here. Bills can also be tracked according to where they stand in committee and by draft status. Researchers can also sign up for alerts on specific legislation throughout the legislative process, for example, as it moves through committee and each chamber.

The **Pennsylvania House of Representatives Archives** (http://www .house.state.pa.us/BMC/archives/index.cfm) collects, preserves and provides access to the valuable historic records created by representatives, committees, offices and staff in order to promote understanding of the history of the Pennsylvania House of Representatives and its impact on the state's citizens. This site contains links to the listings of the official records of the House of Representatives as well as personal papers and memorabilia of former House Members and staff. There are also historic biographies and transcripts of former Members' oral history interviews.

The official site of the **governor** is http://www.governor.pa.gov. The site contains the governor's agenda, biographies of him and staff, press releases, and executive orders. Links to state government agencies and the elected offices of the lieutenant governor, attorney general, auditor general, and treasurer are available at http://www.pa.gov/#government.

The website of the Pennsylvania **Unified Judicial System** (http://www .pacourts.us) provides a description of the types of courts in the Commonwealth, how they function, judicial history, and a listing of current judges. There are also links to the texts of court decisions.

The **Pennsylvania Code** is available at http://www.pacode.com. The code contains regulations and other documents filed with the Legislative Reference Bureau pursuant to state law. There are a total of fifty-five titles.

The *Pennsylvania Bulletin* (https://www.pabulletin.com/index.asp) contains statewide and local court rules, the governor's proclamations and executive orders, actions by the General Assembly, rulemakings by state agencies, proposed rulemakings by state agencies, and state agency notices.

General Resources on Pennsylvania Government

The **Joint State Government Commission** (http://jsg.legis.state.pa.us) is the legislature's primary source for nonpartisan research on policy issues. The commission's website contains numerous reports requested by the General Assembly, task forces, state agencies, and others. Issues include education, the opioid crisis, health policies, and more.

Commonwealth: A Journal of Pennsylvania Politics and Policy (https://
tupjournals.temple.edu/index.php/commonwealth/index) publishes three
times a year, as well as a year in review with supplemental material for easy
class adoption, including notes on further information, discussion questions,
and pro-con arguments. Special issues by guest editors have included education and environmental policy. Back issues of *Commonwealth: A Journal of
Political Science* are archived at https://sites.temple.edu/commonwealth.

The **Center for Rural Pennsylvania** (http://www.rural.palegislature.us)
is a bipartisan, bicameral legislative agency for the General Assembly, which,
as the name would suggest, serves to research matters related to rural policy.
The center sponsors research related to rural issues for consideration by the
legislature and the executive branch, and it collects data related to rural life
in Pennsylvania. Reports and data are available on its website.

The **Center for Opinion Research** (https://www.fandm.edu/opinion
research) and the **Center for Politics and Public Affairs** (https://www
.fandm.edu/politics) at Franklin and Marshall College produce publications
and news pieces on Pennsylvania politics, as well as detailed reports on statewide and intrastate regional polls.

The **Center on Regional Politics** (http://www.temple.edu/corp) at Temple University publishes issue briefs and memos about state and local politics
and policy. The **Institute for Public Affairs** (http://www.cla.temple.edu/ipa),
in which the center is housed, also lists all these publications and more, including a series on history and development of the Pennsylvania General
Assembly.

The **Institute of Politics** (http://iop.pitt.edu) at the University of Pittsburgh publishes numerous case studies and reports on policy issues affecting
the state and the Pittsburgh region. Recent reports have covered the opioid
epidemic, shale tax policies, and green infrastructure.

The **Pennsylvania Center for Women and Politics** (http://www.chatham
.edu/pcwp) at Chatham University is a nonpartisan organization dedicated
to bringing more women into leadership roles and educating and training
women about politics and public policy.

The **Pennsylvania Policy Database Project** (http://www.temple.edu/
papolicy) is an online resource providing access to more than two hundred
thousand state and news records dating from 1979 to the present, including
bills, Supreme Court decisions, polls, budget addresses, a sample of news
media, and more. The media records are abstracts of an extensive random
sample of articles and news alerts that are drawn from the news digests of
governors. Users can trace the public policy history of the state with a user-
friendly data interface. The coding system is aligned with the Comparative
Agendas Project website (http://www.comparativeagendas.net), allowing for
comparative studies with the United States, twenty other countries, the European Union, and Florida.

Budgets and Revenue

"**The Budget Process in Pennsylvania**" (http://www.budget.pa.gov/Pub
licationsAndReports/Documents/OtherPublications/Budget%20Process
%20In%20PA%20-%20Web.pdf) is a publication from the Pennsylvania Office of the Budget that covers the budget process from beginning to end,
through preparation, approval, and execution. It also covers the funding of
programs, the capital budget, and revenue estimating. It has a useful appen-
dix of common terms used in state fiscal affairs.

The website of the **Legislative Budget and Finance Committee** (http://
lbfc.legis.state.pa.us) contains reports and presentations related to the budget
process of the Commonwealth. The committee is a bipartisan, bicameral
legislative service agency consisting of twelve members of the General Assembly. It conducts studies, promotes economy in government, and assures
state funds are being spent in accordance with law and legislative intent.

The **Independent Fiscal Office (IFO)** (http://www.ifo.state.pa.us), created in 2010, provides revenue projections for use in the budget process
and analysis of fiscal, economic, and budgetary issues to assist the General
Assembly and the public in the analysis of public policy proposals. The
IFO makes no declarations in support or opposition to a policy. Their website has a wealth of valuable reports on various legislative and budgetary
proposals.

The **National Association of State Budget Officers** publishes the "**Fiscal
Survey of the States**" twice annually (https://www.nasbo.org/reports-data/
fiscal-survey-of-states). The report includes data from all fifty states on
spending and revenue. The U.S. Census Bureau also conducts an "**Annual
Survey of State and Local Government Finance**" (https://www.census.gov/
govs/local). These data sets are excellent sources for comparing Pennsylvania
to other states.

The Department of Revenue produces "**The Tax Compendium**," which
explains the types of taxes and fees collected in the Commonwealth as well
as the purpose of special funds. It is especially useful when researching the
evolution of state taxes and the laws under which they were enacted. The
compendium is available at http://www.revenue.pa.gov/GeneralTaxInforma
tion/News%20and%20Statistics/Pages/Reports%20and%20Statistics/Tax
-Compendium.aspx#.WY3wVOn1g2x.

Demographic Information

American FactFinder is the federal government's quick search mechanism
for multiple national data sets, including the Census and American Community Survey (https://factfinder.census.gov). Information can be searched

based on state, county, metropolitan statistical area, municipality, census tract, or zip code.

The **Pennsylvania State Data Center** (https://pasdc.hbg.psu.edu) at Penn State Harrisburg has parsed census data to create a database of useful information about the Commonwealth. Of particular interest are its interactive "dashboards" that provide colorful charts of a variety of data by county.

Pennsylvania Spatial Data Access (PASDA) (http://www.pasda.psu .edu) is the clearinghouse for public access geospatial data for the Commonwealth of Pennsylvania. Geographic information system (GIS) files for transportation, recreation, topography, government boundaries, and more are found here for downloading.

Voting and Elections

Information on who can register to vote, how to vote, and a "Voter Toolkit" can be found at the Pennsylvania Department of State's **Votes PA** page (http://www.votespa.com/en-us). The department also has current and historical state and county voter registration statistics dating back to 1998. The information is broken out by major and minor party of voters as well as unaffiliated voters (see http://www.dos.pa.gov/VotingElections/Other ServicesEvents/VotingElectionStatistics/Pages/VotingElectionStatistics .aspx#.VBMH5_ldUQ0).

The **Pennsylvania Department of State** provides election returns since 2000 for federal, state, and municipal elections by county in graphic form, at http://www.electionreturns.pa.gov/Home/SummaryResults.

The **Wilkes University Election Statistics Project** (http://staffweb .wilkes.edu/harold.cox) has election information from Pennsylvania federal and state elections dating back to 1682. Votes for president, U.S. Senate, and governor are available in both charts and maps with data by county. U.S. House and state legislative election data are available by chart but not map. The final year in the data set is 2006.

The **Pennsylvania Department of State** provides an online database of spending in the Commonwealth's elections (https://www.campaign financeonline.pa.gov/Pages/CampaignFinanceHome.aspx). The database of campaign finance reports allows searches by candidate, political action committee (PAC), and individual. It also includes information about independent expenditures and registered PACs in Pennsylvania.

The **Pennsylvania Legislative Data Processing Center** hosts the **Pennsylvania Redistricting** website (http://www.redistricting.state.pa.us). This interactive site allows viewers to see the boundaries of state legislative and U.S. House districts, including shape files for GIS, and explains the process of the decennial redistricting process.

Polling

Several nonpartisan polling organizations regularly survey Pennsylvanians on policy issues, approval ratings of politicians, and election preferences. The three most prominent are the **Franklin and Marshall College Poll** (https://www.fandm.edu/opinionresearch/projectsandpublications/franklin -marshall-college-poll), the **Muhlenburg College Polling Institute** (https://www.muhlenberg.edu/main/aboutus/polling), and the **Quinnipiac University Poll** (https://poll.qu.edu). Common questions include the most important problem facing Pennsylvania, whether the state is on the right or wrong track, and questions about budgetary issues.

Media

Reporters covering Pennsylvania legislative politics can be found on the website of the **Pennsylvania Legislative Correspondents' Association**, at http://www.pacapitolreporters.org/pacapitolreporters-membership.html.

Several sources provide daily digests of media sources from around the state that are delivered for free via e-mail. The *PLS Reporter* offers the *PLS Eye Opener* (http://www.plsreporter.com), *City and State Pennsylvania* has *First Read* (http://cityandstatepa.com/first-read), Greenlee Partners sends out a daily *Harrisburg Online* (http://www.greenleepartners.com), and Crisci Associates provides the PA Capitol Digest (http://pacapitoldigestcrisci .blogspot.com/). In addition, *City and State Pennsylvania* publishes articles nearly daily related to state and local government and politics and has a monthly print issue available in hard copy or online.

Pennsylvania Cable Network (PCN) (https://pcntv.com) provides citizens with access to the processes of state government and does programming on the state's history, culture, and public affairs. It is, according to its website, "the largest statewide privately funded public affairs network in the country."

Politics PA (http://www.politicspa.com) is meant to be a comprehensive news source for all things politics in Pennsylvania. The site is updated throughout the day with trending stories, press releases, and original reporting. It has articles and op-eds from a variety of political perspectives.

StateImpact Pennsylvania (https://stateimpact.npr.org/pennsylvania) is a product of member National Public Radio stations WITF and WHYY covering the topics of energy, the environment, and the economy. It was developed in response to the last decade's growing energy economy in the state.

Keystone Crossroads (https://whyy.org/programs/keystone-crossroads) is a collaboration among four public newsrooms around the state and focuses on urban issues. It includes comprehensive reports on education finance, pensions, and energy issues around the state.

Advocacy Groups, Political Parties, and Think Tanks

The **Commonwealth Foundation** (https://www.commonwealthfoundation .org), backed by the Pennsylvania Manufacturers Association and business, is more or less the state equivalent of the American Enterprise Institute or the Heritage Foundation.

The **Keystone Research Center** (https://keystoneresearch.org) is backed by labor and more or less the state equivalent of the Center for American Progress.

The **Pennsylvania Chamber of Business and Industry** (https://www .pachamber.org) is headquartered in Harrisburg, with offices in Philadelphia and Pittsburgh. Its goal is to be the statewide voice of business and advocate for those issues. Its website has useful reports and surveys on the economy and workforce development.

The **Pennsylvania Economy League (PEL)** has three regional branches that focus on public policy issues for their area and the state as a whole. Reports and information are available at PEL Central (http://pelcentral.org), PEL Greater Philadelphia (http://economyleague.org), and PEL Greater Pittsburgh (https://www.pelgp.org).

Information on the issues and candidates related to the state's two major parties can be found at the website of the **Pennsylvania Democratic Party** (http://www.padems.com) and the website of the **Republican Party of Pennsylvania** (http://www.pagop.org).

General State Government Resources

The **National Governors Association (NGA)** (https://www.nga.org) represents the interests of the nation's fifty-five governors of states, commonwealths, and territories. Through the NGA, governors share best practices, learn from each other, and develop policy solutions. The site has numerous news items and reports as they relate to the role of the state executive.

The **National Conference of State Legislatures** (http://www.ncsl.org) monitors policy issues at the state level. It also tracks institutional structures, election results, fiscal matters, and more across each state on a comparative basis.

The **Council of State Governments (CSG)** (http://www.csg.org) is the country's only organization dedicated to all three branches of state government. It is nonpartisan and engages leaders to solve problems across states based on a regional model. There is a CSG in the east, midwest, south, and west. The council's website has reports and commentary on a multitude of policy issues.

Governing magazine (http://www.governing.com) is available in print or free online. The magazine delivers daily updates of state and local news around the country and, depending on subscription preferences, weekly updates on particular areas, such as finance and management. Readers can subscribe to updates at http://www.governing.com/subscribe.

Stateline, a journalistic project of the Pew Charitable Trusts, provides in-depth articles on state policy (http://www.pewtrusts.org/en/research-and -analysis/blogs/stateline).

The **Center for the Study of Federalism** (http://federalism.org) provides news and linked bibliographies of research about states and American federalism. It also has an extensive list of state and local firsts in law and public policy.

Local Government in Pennsylvania

The *Citizen's Guide to Pennsylvania Local Government* (https://dced.pa .gov/download/citizens-guide-to-pennsylvania-local-government-pdf) and the *Pennsylvania Legislator's Municipal Deskbook* (http://www.lgc.state.pa .us/deskBook.cfm) provide a comprehensive overview of the design, operation, and policy responsibilities of local governments in Pennsylvania.

The **Department of Community and Economic Development (DCED)** and the **Local Government Commission (LGC)** websites house data and reports about local government in Pennsylvania. Of particular interest to researchers are the DCED's section on municipal statistics (https://dced.pa .gov/local-government/municipal-statistics) and the LGC's list of frequently cited municipal laws of Pennsylvania (http://www.lgc.state.pa.us/fre quentlyCitedLaws.cfm).

Several organizations represent local governments in Pennsylvania. The **County Commissioners Association of Pennsylvania** (http://www .pacounties.org) provides news and reports on policy issues and legislation relevant to county government. It also provides links to the official websites of all counties in Pennsylvania. The **Pennsylvania State Association of Boroughs** (http://boroughs.org) provides similar resources for topics related to borough government. The **Pennsylvania State Association of Township Supervisors** (https://connect.psats.org/home) and the **Pennsylvania Municipal League** (http://www.pamunicipalleague.org) advocate for local governments but do not provide as much information to the general public.

The **Philadelphia Research Initiative** (http://www.pewtrusts.org/en/ projects/philadelphia-research-initiative) of the Pew Charitable Trusts archives studies of Philadelphia policy issues and problems. It also publishes yearly reports on the state of the city, with comprehensive overviews of demographic information, the economy, and trends.

The *Philadelphia Citizen* (http://thephiladelphiacitizen.org) is an online publication edited by Larry Platt that provides thoughtful articles and commentary on Philadelphia politics and policy. It sends out new stories once a week.

BeHeardPhilly is a new poll of Philadelphians on various public policy issues conducted by Temple University's Institute for Survey Research. It is available at http://www.beheardphilly.com. Recent polls have included questions on attitudes about poverty, the major issues city government should tackle, and the allocation of government resources.

The **Center for Metropolitan Studies** (http://www.metrostudies.pitt .edu) at the University of Pittsburgh is the premier U.S. resource for the study of regional intergovernmental organizations. Additionally, it publishes quarterly policy briefs on significant issues facing western Pennsylvania to provide evidence to policy makers and researchers looking for solutions.

Contributors

David G. Argall is a member of the Pennsylvania Senate leadership, serving as the chair of the Majority Policy Committee. He earned his Ph.D. in public administration from Pennsylvania State University and has taught a variety of public policy classes as a part-time public policy instructor at Penn State and Lehigh Carbon Community College.

Michelle J. Atherton is associate director of the Institute for Public Affairs at Temple University. She is also a senior adviser to the Pennsylvania Policy Database Project and senior policy writer and editor for Temple's Center on Regional Politics. Her publications include articles in *State and Local Government Review* and *State Politics and Policy Quarterly* and white papers on subjects including institutional reform in legislatures, municipal services, public pension, and education finance.

Thomas J. Baldino is a professor of political science at Wilkes University. He and Kyle L. Kreider of Wilkes University have published three books on voting and elections, the most recent of which is an edited volume, *Minority Voting in the United States* (2015). His current book project, with Paula Holoviak, concerns Pennsylvania government and politics.

Michele Moser Deegan is professor of political science at Muhlenberg College. She is also the founding director of the Lehigh Valley Research Consortium. Her research and publications focus on issues of inequality at the local level, particularly in the areas of education and health policy. Her publications include articles in the *Journal of Urban Affairs, Public Administration Review,* and *Educational Evaluation and Policy Analysis* and multiple research studies of the Lehigh Valley region of Pennsylvania.

Michael R. Dimino, Sr., is professor of law at Widener Law Commonwealth. He served as chief clerk to Associate Judge Albert M. Rosenblatt of the New York State Court of Appeals and then clerked for Senior Circuit Judge Laurence H. Silberman of the U.S. Court of Appeals for the District of Columbia Circuit and Judge Paul L. Friedman of the U.S. District Court for the District of Columbia. He is a graduate of Harvard Law School (2001), where he was articles editor of the *Harvard Journal of Law and Public Policy.* Professor Dimino has written extensively on constitutional law, particularly with regard to judicial elections, and has coauthored *Voting Rights and Election Law* (2015) and *Understanding Election Law and Voting Rights* (2016).

William A. Fischel has taught economics at Dartmouth College since 1973. He received his Ph.D. from Princeton University and his B.A. from Amherst College. His research focuses on local government, and his most recent book is *Zoning Rules! The Economics of Land Use Regulation* (2015).

George E. Hale is an associate professor of political science at Kutztown University of Pennsylvania. He received his doctoral degree from Syracuse University. For three decades, he served in federal, state, and local government, including eight years as Delaware's secretary of administrative services. His research focuses on state budgets, governors, and organizational change in public agencies.

Rachel L. Hampton is a third-year law student at the University of Michigan Law School. She is also a current policy analyst at the Center for Local, State, and Urban Policy (CLOSEUP), housed in the Gerald R. Ford School of Public Policy at the University of Michigan. Her research focuses on state oil and gas severance taxes, as well as state trust funds tied to energy taxes.

Paula A. Duda Holoviak is a professor in the Department of Political Science and Public Administration at Kutztown University and the program coordinator for the master of public administration degree. Her research interests include state and local government with an emphasis on issues in rural Pennsylvania. She is currently completing a book on Pennsylvania politics with Thomas J. Baldino.

Jon Hopcraft is the executive director of the Senate Republican Policy Committee.

Vera Krekanova is chief strategy officer at Partner4Work, a Pittsburgh-based entity that directs the public workforce development system for the city of Pittsburgh and Allegheny County. In addition, she teaches as an adjunct faculty member at the University of Pittsburgh's Graduate School of Public and International Affairs. She holds a B.A. from Charles University in Prague, an M.S. in nonprofit management from Robert Morris University, and a Ph.D. in social and comparative analysis in public policy from the University of Pittsburgh.

J. Wesley Leckrone is an associate professor and department chair of political science at Widener University. He is the editor of *Commonwealth: A Journal of Pennsylvania Politics and Policy*. His publications include articles in *Publius: The Journal of Federalism*, *State and Local Government Review*, *State Politics and Policy Quarterly*, and the *Journal of Urban Affairs*.

A. Lanethea Mathews-Schultz is professor and department chair of political science at Muhlenberg College, where she teaches classes on American politics, gender and public policy, citizenship, and political institutions. As an independent researcher affiliated with the Lehigh Valley Research Consortium, she has conducted several regional studies of community health, focusing on access and equity issues in health and well-being. Her recent work has been published in *Political Research Quarterly* and *Progress in Community Health Partnerships: Research, Education, and Action*.

Maureen W. McClure is an associate professor of administrative and policy studies and senior research associate at the International Institute for Studies in Education in the School of Education at the University of Pittsburgh.

Barry G. Rabe, Ph.D., is the J. Ira and Nicki Harris Family Professor of Public Policy at the Gerald R. Ford School of Public Policy at the University of Michigan. He is also a fellow of the National Academy of Public Administration and a nonresident senior fellow at the Brookings Institution. Rabe examines policy at the intersection of energy development and environmental protection in federal systems and has done extensive work on federal and state climate policy implementation. He is currently completing a book on the politics of carbon pricing and is a member of the American Academy of Arts and Sciences project on energy policy durability, focused particularly on the Clean Air Act.

Marguerite Roza is the director of the Edunomics Lab at Georgetown University and a senior research affiliate at the Center on Reinventing Public Education.

Jennie Sweet-Cushman is an assistant professor of political science and assistant director of the Pennsylvania Center for Women and Politics at Chatham University. She earned her doctoral degree at Wayne State University. Her research focuses on women, politics, and public policy, with particular emphasis on political ambition and candidate emergence.

Amanda Warco is director of data and assessment at Coney Island Prep charter schools in Brooklyn, New York. From 2014 to 2016 she served as research associate at Edunomics Lab at Georgetown University. Her previous roles include special projects coordinator for Uncommon Schools in Brooklyn, New York, where she focused on data and operations support and helped manage a strategic redesign of the student recruitment process, and education pioneers fellow and research intern with the Research and Policy Support Group at the New York City Department of Education. She holds a B.A. in English and a B.A. in French from Wake Forest University and a master's of public administration from the Robert F. Wagner School of Public Service at New York University.